Dedicated
to
another 'chosen lady and her children,
whom I love in the truth',
the congregation of
All Souls Church, Langham Place,
London

THE LETTERS OF JOHN

AN INTRODUCTION AND COMMENTARY

by

JOHN R. W. STOTT, M.A., D.D.
*Rector Emeritus of All Souls Church,
Langham Place, London,
and President of the London Institute
for Contemporary Christianity*

Inter-Varsity Press
Leicester, England

William B. Eerdmans Publishing Company
Grand Rapids, Michigan

Inter-Varsity Press
38 De Montfort Street, Leicester LE1 7GP, England

Wm. B. Eerdmans Publishing Company
255 Jefferson S.E., Grand Rapids, MI 49503

Published and sold only in the USA and Canada by Wm. B. Eerdmans Publishing Co.

Unless otherwise stated, quotations from the Bible are taken from the HOLY BIBLE: NEW INTERNATIONAL VERSION. Copyright © 1973, 1978, 1984 by the International Bible Society, New York. Published in Great Britain by Hodder and Stoughton Ltd, and used in North America by permission of Zondervan Bible Publishers, Grand Rapids, Michigan.

British Library Cataloguing in Publication Data

Stott, John R. W. (John Robert Walmsley), 1921–
The letters of John — 2nd ed.
1. Bible. N.T. Epistles of John – Commentaries
I. Title. II. Stott, John R. W. (John Robert Walmsley), 1921– Epistles of John
227′. 9407
III. Series

ISBN 0-85111-888-7

Library of Congress Cataloging-in-Publication Data

Stott, John R. W.
  The Letters of John.
  (The Tyndale New Testament commentaries)
  Rev. ed. of: The Epistles of John. 1964.
  1. Bible. N.T. Epistles of John — Commentaries.
  I. Stott, John R. W. Epistles of John. II. Title.
  III. Series.
  BS2805.3 1988   227′.9407   88-772
  ISBN 0-8028-0368-7 (Eerdmans)

Set in Palatino
Typeset in Great Britain by Parker Typesetting Service, Leicester
Printed in USA by Eerdmans Printing Company, Grand Rapids, Michigan

Inter-Varsity Press is the publishing division of the Universities and Colleges Christian Fellowship (formerly the Inter-Varsity Fellowship), a student movement linking Christian Unions in universities and colleges throughout the United Kingdom and the Republic of Ireland, and a member movement of the International Fellowship of Evangelical Students. For information about local and national activities write to UCCF, 38 De Montfort Street, Leicester LE1 7GP.

GENERAL PREFACE

The original *Tyndale Commentaries* aimed at providing help for the general reader of the Bible. They concentrated on the meaning of the text without going into scholarly technicalities. They sought to avoid 'the extremes of being unduly technical or unhelpfully brief'. Most who have used the books agree that there has been a fair measure of success in reaching that aim.

Times, however, change. A series that has served so well for so long is perhaps not quite as relevant as when it was first launched. New knowledge has come to light. The discussion of critical questions has moved on. Bible-reading habits have changed. When the original series was commenced it could be presumed that most readers used the Authorized Version and one could make one's comments accordingly, but this situation no longer obtains.

The decision to revise and up-date the whole series was not reached lightly, but in the end it was thought that this is what is required in the present situation. There are new needs, and they will be better served by new books or by a thorough up-dating of the old books. The aims of the original series remain. The new commentaries are neither minuscule nor unduly long. They are exegetical rather than homiletic. They do not discuss all the critical questions, but none is written without an awareness of the problems that engage the attention of New Testament scholars. Where it is felt that formal consideration should be given to such questions, they are discussed in the Introduction and sometimes in Additional Notes.

But the main thrust of these commentaries is not critical. These books are written to help the non-technical reader to understand the Bible better. They do not presume a knowledge of Greek, and all Greek words discussed are transliterated; but the authors have the Greek text before them and their comments are made on the basis of the originals. The authors are free to choose their own modern translation, but are asked to bear in mind the variety of translations in current use.

The new series of *Tyndale Commentaries* goes forth, as the former series did, in the hope that God will graciously use these books to help the general reader to understand as fully and clearly as possible the meaning of the New Testament.

LEON MORRIS

CONTENTS

AUTHOR'S PREFACE TO THE FIRST EDITION

If it be said (as it quite reasonably may) that one who is in no sense a New Testament scholar should not presume to write a commentary on New Testament Epistles, I would reply in respectful self-defence that I have written as a pastor and not as a theologian. Nor is this entirely a disadvantage, since insight into the New Testament literature demands some acquaintance, not only with Greek usage, but also with a local church situation such as lies behind the Johannine Epistles. Certainly John writes as a pastor to his people in language which every modern pastor will understand. He loves them. He is deeply concerned to protect them from the enticements of the world and the errors of false teachers, and to see them established in faith, love and holiness. So he appeals to what they are and what they know. He warns them, exhorts them, argues with them, instructs them. All this will find an echo in the experience of every pastor who has been entrusted by the Chief Shepherd with the care of a flock. I am hopeful that the readers of this commentary, though not neglecting academic questions raised by the Epistles, will not forget the practical purposes for which they were written.

A fuller consideration of some of the chief exegetical problems of the First Epistle has been reserved for the Additional Notes. Even so the commentary is longer than it should have been, and I am grateful to the publishers for their indulgent acceptance of it as it now stands. My indebtedness to other commentators will be apparent in the exposition of the text, although I have tried to resist the temptation to be a merely slavish copyist of abler and better men.

I pray that we may be given grace to do more than study these Epistles, namely submit to them in mind and life. The Church needs their message. To borrow John's own phraseology, we must abide in it, and let it abide in us (2 Jn. 9; 1 Jn. 2:24, AV).

JRWS

AUTHOR'S PREFACE TO
THE SECOND EDITION

Nearly twenty-five years have passed since the publication of
the first edition of this commentary. They have been eventful
years of social and theological upheaval. Yet, as I have
meditated afresh on John's three letters, they have struck me as
being still extraordinarily relevent to the current scene in the
world and the church. Moreover, as I have re-read the commentary I wrote in 1964, I have wanted to leave its substance
and emphases unchanged. Nevertheless, this second edition
incorporates a thorough revision. The English text on which I
now comment is no longer the Authorized Version but the New
International Version. I have also tried to clarify the obscurities,
modernize the phraseology, eliminate what seemed repetitious,
expand what was too compressed, and add more contemporary
application.

I have also consulted several more commentaries which have
appeared since 1964, in particular those by F. F. Bruce (1970),
James L. Houlden in Black's New Testament Commentary series
(1973), I. Howard Marshall in the New International Commentary series (1978), the monumental tome by Raymond E.
Brown in the Anchor Bible series (1982), following his *The Community of the Beloved Disciple* (1979), and the commentaries by
Kenneth Grayston in the New Century Bible Commentary series
and by Stephen S. Smalley in the Word Biblical Commentary
series (both 1984). I have quoted from them, as from their
predecessors, while endeavouring to preserve a measure of
independence. As with the former edition, so with this one, the
chief exegetical problems raised by John's first letter have been
discussed in eleven Additional Notes.

Those students of John's letters who are likely to profit from them most, are those who share with the author his own combination of theological and ethical concerns. For John is above all else a pastor, entrusted with the care of a group of local churches, and anxious to help their members to learn how to think and live Christianly. At the foundation of their Christian thinking must be a right grasp of the unique divine-human person of Jesus, and at the foundation of their Christian living a transparent integrity of righteousness and love. The false teachers have disturbed them. But John shows them how to develop a healthy assurance about Christ and about their relationship to him.

John evidently loves the people committed to his care. They are his 'dear children', his 'dear friends' (1 Jn. 2:1, 7). He longs to protect them from both error and evil, and to see them firmly established in faith, love and holiness. He has no new doctrine for them. On the contrary, he appeals to them to remember what they already know, have and are. He warns them against deviating from this and urges them to remain loyal to it. Whenever innovators trouble the church, and ridicule whatever is old or traditional, we need to hear and heed John's exhortation, to continue in what we have learnt and received, and to let it continue in us (*e.g.* 1 Jn. 2:24, 27; 2 Jn. 9).

I am very grateful to Steve Andrews, who undertook, with his customary meticulousness, the laborious task of converting the biblical text from the AV to the NIV; to Frances Whitehead, who then reduced many pages which looked like a game of 'Snakes and Ladders' into beautiful typescript; to Toby Howarth, who checked the script, in addition to compiling the bibliography; and to Leon Morris, friend and editor, for his very helpful suggestions.

JOHN R. W. STOTT

CHIEF ABBREVIATIONS

Alexander	Neil Alexander, *The Epistles of John*, Torch Bible Commentaries (SCM Press, 1962).
Alford	Henry Alford, *Commentary on the Epistles of John* in Alford's Greek Testament (Rivingtons & Deighton & Bell, ³1866).
AV	Authorized (King James') Version, 1611.
BAGD	*A Greek-English Lexicon of the New Testament and Other Early Christian Literature*, translated and adapted by W. F. Arndt and F. W. Gingrich; second edition revised and augmented by F. W. Gingrich and F. W. Danker (University of Chicago Press, 1979).
Barclay	William Barclay, *The Letters of John and Jude*, The Daily Study Bible (St Andrew Press, 1976).
Blaiklock	E. M. Blaiklock, *Faith is the Victory: Devotional Studies in the First Epistle of John* (The Paternoster Press, 1959).
Brooke	A. E. Brooke, *Commentary on the Johannine Epistles*, The International Critical Commentary (T. & T. Clark, 1912).
Brown (*Epistles*)	Raymond E. Brown, *The Epistles of John*, The Anchor Bible (Doubleday, 1982; Geoffrey Chapman, 1983).
Brown (*Community*)	Raymond E. Brown, *The Community of the Beloved Disciple* (Geoffrey Chapman, 1979).
Bruce	F. F. Bruce, *The Epistles of John* (1970; Pickering & Inglis, ²1978).

Calvin — John Calvin, *Commentary on the First Epistle of John*, Calvin's Commentaries, ET by T. H. L. Parker (Oliver & Boyd, 1961).

Candlish — Robert S. Candlish, *The First Epistle of St John Expounded in a Series of Lectures* (1877; Banner of Truth, 1973).

Dodd — C. H. Dodd, *Commentary on the Johannine Epistles*, Moffatt New Testament Commentary (Hodder & Stoughton, 1946).

Ebrard — John H. A. Ebrard, *Commentary on St John's Epistles* (T. & T. Clark, 1860).

Ellis — E. Earle Ellis, *The World of St John* (Eerdmans, 1984).

Eusebius — Eusebius of Caesarea, *Ecclesiastical History*, *circa* 260–340, ET, with introduction and notes, by H. J. Lawler and J. E. L. Oulton (SPCK, 1927–28; two vols.).

Findlay — George G. Findlay, *Fellowship in the Life Eternal: An Exposition of the Epistles of John* (Hodder & Stoughton, 1909).

Grayston — Kenneth Grayston, *The Johannine Epistles*, New Century Bible Commentary (Eerdmans/ Marshall, Morgan & Scott, 1984).

Grimm-Thayer — C. L. W. Grimm, *Greek Lexicon of the New Testament*, translated, revised and enlarged by J. H. Thayer (T. & T. Clark, ⁴1901).

Houlden — James L. Houlden, *A Commentary on the Johannine Epistles*, Black's New Testament Commentary (A. & C. Black, 1973).

Law — Robert Law, *The Tests of Life: A Study of the First Epistle of St John* (1909; Baker, 1968).

Lewis — G. P. Lewis, *The Johannine Epistles*, Epworth Preacher's Commentaries (Epworth Press, 1961).

Lightfoot — J. B. Lightfoot, *Biblical Essays* (Macmillan, 1893).

LSJ — *A Greek-English Lexicon*, compiled by H. G. Liddell and R. Scott, new edition revised by H. S. Jones and R. Mackenzie (Oxford University Press, ⁹1940).

Marshall	I. Howard Marshall, *The Epistles of John*, The New International Commentary on the New Testament (Eerdmans, 1978).
Metzger	Bruce M. Metzger, *A Textual Commentary on the Greek New Testament* (United Bible Societies, ³1975).
mg.	margin.
Moffatt	James Moffatt, *The Moffatt Translation of the Bible* (Hodder & Stoughton, ²1935).
MS(S)	manuscript(s).
NEB	The New English Bible: Old Testament, 1970; New Testament, ²1970.
NIV	New International Version: Old Testament, 1978; New Testament, ²1978.
Plummer	Alfred Plummer, *Commentary on the Epistles of St John*, Cambridge Greek Testament for Schools and Colleges (Cambridge University Press, 1894).
RSV	Revised Standard Version: Old Testament, 1952; New Testament, ²1971.
RV	Revised Version, 1884.
Smalley	Stephen S. Smalley, *1, 2, 3 John*, Word Biblical Commentary, vol. 51 (Word Books, 1984).
Smith	David Smith, *Commentary on the Epistles of John*, The Expositor's Greek Testament (Hodder & Stoughton, 1910).
Tyndale	William Tyndale, *The Exposition of the Fyrst Epistle of Seynt Jhon* (1531), reprinted in *English Reformers*, vol. 26 of the Library of Christian Classics, edited by T. H. L. Parker (SCM/Westminster, 1966).
Westcott	B. F. Westcott, *Commentary on the Epistles of St John* (1883; Eerdmans, 1966).

INTRODUCTION

I. AUTHORSHIP

The natural place in which to look for information about the authorship of any ancient letter is in the letter itself. It was customary in antiquity for a correspondent to begin by announcing his identity. This was Paul's invariable rule, and the same holds good of the letters of Peter, James and Jude. The author of 2 and 3 John styles himself 'the elder' without disclosing his name. Only the letter to the Hebrews and the first letter of John begin without any announcement of the author's name or title, and indeed without any introductory greeting. The anonymity of 1 John is not to be explained by the suggestion that the author is writing a theological treatise, or even a general or 'catholic' letter, as Origen first called it. Although it has a considerable theological content, it contains a genuinely personal message addressed to a particular congregation, or group of them, in a particular situation (*cf.* 2:19). The 'I – you – we' form of address is maintained throughout; the recipients of the letter are the author's 'dear children' or 'dear friends', whose spiritual history and present circumstances he knows. Moreover, 'the writing is . . . instinct from first to last with intense personal feeling' (Westcott). It is a truly pastoral letter, sent by a pastor to his flock, or a part of it, as are also (and even more clearly) the two shorter letters.

Who, then, was the author of these letters? Since they are anonymous, there is no *a priori* need to ascribe them to the apostle John or to any other John. Nevertheless, the external evidence is strongly in favour of this ascription, particularly in the case of the first letter.

A. EXTERNAL EVIDENCE FOR THE FIRST LETTER

All three letters are found in the oldest Greek codices. The first letter is also included in the most ancient versions of the church of the East and the West, namely the Syriac and Latin, although the second and third letters are not found in the Syriac.

Commentators have found possible allusions to the letters of John in a number of early patristic writings. Thus, Clement of Rome twice described God's elect people as being 'perfected in love', and there is a similar expression in the *Didache*. *The Epistle to Diognetus* includes such phrases as 'from the beginning', 'God loved men' and 'sent his only begotten Son', so that we love 'him who thus first loved' us. But none of these is more than an echo of Johannine language, derived as well from the Gospel or current Johannine theology as from the first letter. There is no formal or exact quotation, nor any mention of John or the letters by name.

The earliest definite reference to these letters in the Fathers comes from Polycarp of Smyrna (d. *c*. AD 155), who in the seventh chapter of his letter to the Philippians, written perhaps thirty or forty years before his martyrdom, asserts that whoever does not confess that Jesus Christ has come in the flesh is antichrist. He goes on to urge a return to the message handed down from the beginning. Here are quotations from 1 John 4:2–3 (with a possible reminiscence of 1 Jn. 2:22 and 2 Jn. 7) and 1 John 2:24. Polycarp does not, however, attribute his quotations to John.

The first to refer specifically to a Johannine letter was Papias of Hierapolis in the middle of the second century, who, according to Eusebius (3.39. 17), 'used testimonies drawn from the former Epistle of John'.

It is not until we reach Irenaeus of Lyons (*c*. 130–200) that at least the first and second letters are clearly attributed to the John who was both the 'disciple of the Lord' and the author of the Fourth Gospel. In his *Adversus Haereses* (3. 16. 18) he quotes fully from 1 John 2:18–22; 4:1–3; 5:1, and 2 John 7, 8.

Clement of Alexandria, who survived Irenaeus by a few years, evidently knew more than one Johannine letter, since he uses the expression 'the greater Epistle', which he ascribes to 'the apostle John'. His quotations are even more numerous than those of Irenaeus. In chapters 2–5 of *Stromateis* he quotes 1:6–7; 2:4, 18–19; 3:3, 18–19; 4:16, 18 and 5:3, 16–17, while in *Quis Dives Salvetur?* chapters 37 and 38, he quotes 3:15 and again 4:18.

Tertullian, his Latin contemporary (d. *c*. 220), made considerable use of the first letter, quoting it about fifty times (especially 1:1, 3; 2:22; 4:1–2; 5:1) in his polemical writings against Marcion, Praxeas and the Gnostics. Origen of Alexandria, a little later (d. *c*. 255), also relied much on the first letter, ascribing it to John, although like Tertullian he does not quote from the two shorter letters.

The Muratorian Canon, which was probably compiled in Rome between AD 170 and 215, perhaps by Hippolytus, contains two relevant passages, though of somewhat uncertain meaning. In one the author describes how he believed John had come to write his Gospel, and immediately adds a reference to 'his Epistles' in which he claimed to write 'what we have seen with our eyes, heard with our ears and touched with our hands' (quoting 1 Jn. 1: 1, 4). In the other, 'two' letters of John are mentioned (it is not clear which are meant); they are then described by the phrase *in catholica habentur*, which has been understood by scholars as meaning that they were recognized either 'in the Catholic Church' or 'among the Catholic Epistles'.

Cyprian, Bishop of Carthage in the middle of the third century, quoted from 1: 8 and 2: 3–4, 6, 15–17, and it is interesting to note that the passages he used are concerned rather with ethical conduct than with theological controversy.

When we reach Eusebius (*c*. AD 325), we find that he numbers the first letter among the *homologoumena* or 'acknowledged books', while he puts the second and third letters among the *antilegomena* or 'disputed books' (3.25. 2–3).

B. EXTERNAL EVIDENCE FOR THE SECOND AND THIRD LETTERS

The external evidence for the second and third letters is not so clear or strong as that for the first. The first definite quotation occurs in Irenaeus (*Adversus Haereses* 3. 16. 3, 8), who mentions two letters, ascribing them to 'John the disciple of the Lord', and quotes 2 John 7–8, 10 and 11. Clement of Alexandria implies by his reference to John's 'greater letter' (*Stromateis* 2. 15. 66) that he also wrote one or more lesser works, and elsewhere, according to Eusebius, he mentions 'the second Epistle of John', which he said was written to a certain lady who signifies 'the holy church'. It is in Origen that we come across the first explicit mention of any doubt about the authorship of these two letters. He knew of both, but no quotation of either has survived from his pen, and according to Eusebius he knew that they were not universally acknowledged as 'genuine' (6. 25. 10).

Eusebius himself, as has already been mentioned, placed the second and third letters among the *antilegomena* (3. 25. 3), although 'well known and acknowledged by most'. He adds the interesting explanation of the uncertainty surrounding them, namely 'whether they belong to the Evangelist, or to another of the same name'. In another place he states his own conviction that they were written by the apostle John (6. 25. 10). The reference in the Muratorian Canon to 'two Epistles' of John might as easily be an allusion to the first and second as to the second and third. Jerome said that the two shorter letters were ascribed to John the presbyter, and, although throughout the Middle Ages the letters seem to have been accepted as the work of John the apostle, Erasmus reverted to the theory mentioned by Jerome. It is not surprising that this attestation of the second and third letters is scantier than in the case of the first, for they are both slight and contain little distinctive matter which would be suitable for quotation.

C. COMMON AUTHORSHIP OF THE GOSPEL AND THE FIRST LETTER

Such evidence for the authorship of the letters as can be gathered from the letters themselves is indirect rather than direct. It is a complex problem, concerning the mutual relations between the Gospel and each of the three letters. If it can be shown that any or all of the letters were written by the author of the Fourth Gospel, then clearly arguments for the authorship of the Gospel will be equally applicable to the letters. More simply, if the Gospel is the apostle John's, then the letters will be also. This is not the place to attempt even an introduction to the complicated question of the authorship of the Fourth Gospel. The reader must be referred to competent commentaries on that Gospel for this subject. What must be done here, however, is an examination of the relation between the Gospel and the letters. The best way to proceed is to consider the evidence of common authorship first between Gospel and first letter, then between the second and third letters themselves, and finally between them and the first letter.

Even a superficial reading of the Gospel and the first letter reveals a striking similarity between the two in both subject-matter and syntax. The general subjects treated are much the same. It has often been pointed out that the author of each has the same love of opposites set in stark contrast to one another – light and darkness, life and death, love and hate, truth and falsehood – while people are said to belong to one or other of two categories, with no third alternative. They are children of God or children of the devil; they belong to the world or do not belong to the world. They have life or do not have life. They know God or do not know him. In style one is aware of what Westcott called 'the same monotonous simplicity of construction', and the same Hebriac love of parallelism. The author uses few particles, and does not like subordinate clauses introduced by the relative pronoun. On the other hand, he has a great fondness for sentences beginning with certain emphatic formulae like 'This is . . . that . . .', 'By this . . . that . . .', 'For this . . . that' and 'Everyone who . . .'[1]

When we compare the occurrence of precise phrases in both Gospel and first letter, we find that in fact the same divine purpose or scheme of salvation is set forth in almost identical terms. It might be summarized as follows, the reference in the letter being printed first in each parenthesis: In our natural and unredeemed state we are both 'of the devil', who has sinned and lied and murdered 'from the beginning' (3:8/8:44), and 'of the world' (2:16; 4:5/8:23; 15:19). We therefore 'sin' (3:4/8:34) and 'have' it (1:8/9:41), 'walk in the darkness' (1:6; 2:11/8:12; 12:35)

---

[1] For a detailed examination of linguistic similarities and dissimilarities, see Brooke, pp. i-xix, 235–242, and Law, pp. 341–363.

and are spiritually 'blinded' (2:11/12:40) and 'dead' (3:14/5:25). But God loved us and sent his Son to be 'the Saviour of the world' (4:14/4:42) and that 'we might live' (4:9/3:16). This was his 'one and only' (*monogenēs*, 4:9/1:14, 18; 3:16, 18), who, though in or from 'the beginning' (1:1/1:1), yet became, or came in, 'flesh' (4:2/1:14) and then 'laid down his life' for us (3:16/10:11–18), in order to 'take away' sin (3:5/1:29). To him 'testimony' has been borne, partly by those who have seen' and therefore 'pro-claimed' (1:2–3; 4:14/1:34; 19:35), but especially by God himself (5:9/3:33; 5:32, 34, 36, 37) and by the Spirit (5:6/15:26). We should 'accept' this divine testimony (5:9/3:11, 32, 33; 5:34), 'believe' in the One thus adequately attested (5:10/5:37–40) and 'acknow-ledge' him (4:2, 3/9:22). Believing in him or his 'name' (5:13/1:12, *etc.*), we pass from death to life (3:14/5:24). We 'have life' (5:11, 12/3:15, 36; 20:31), for life is in the Son of God (5:11, 12/1:4; 14:6). This is to be 'born of God' (2:29; 3:9; 5:4, 18/1:13).

Those who have been born of God, God's 'children' (3:1, 2, 10; 5:2/1:12; 11:52), are variously described, in relation to God, to Christ, to the truth, to each other, and to the world. They are 'of God' (3:10/8:47) and have come to 'know' God, the true God, through Jesus Christ (5:20/17:3). It may even be said that they have 'seen' God (3:6; *cf.* 3 Jn. 11/14:9), although in the literal sense no-one has ever seen God (4:12, 20/1:18; 6:46). Christians are not only of God but of the truth as well (2:21; 3:19/18:37). The truth is also 'in' them (1:18; 2:4/8:44) and they 'do' it (AV) or 'live by' it (NIV; 1:6/3:21), for the Spirit given to them is 'the Spirit of truth' (4:6; 5:6/14:17; 15:26; 16:13). The relation of Christians to God and to the truth is through Jesus Christ, in whom and in whose love they 'abide' (AV), which the NIV a little unfortunately renders either 'live' or 'remain' (2:6, 27, 28; 3:6, 24; 4:13, 15, 16/15:4-10), and who himself lives in them (2:24; 3:24; 4:12–16/6:56; 15:4, 5). His word lives in them too (1:10; 2:14, 24/5:38; 15:7) and they in it (2:27/8:31). Thus they 'obey his word' (2:5/8:51–55; 14:23, 15:20; 17:6) or 'his commands' (2:3, 4; 3:22, 24; 5:2, 3/14:15, 21; 15:10), his 'new command' being that they love one another (2:8–10; 3:11, 23; *cf.* 2 Jn. 5, 6/13:34). 'The world', however, will 'hate' them (3:13/15:18). They must not be surprised by this. The reason for it is that they no longer belong to the world (4:5, 6/15:19; 17:16), and while remaining in it must not love the things that are in it (2:15,16/17:15). Christ has 'overcome the world', and so also through faith in him have they (5:4,5/16:33). The end result of all that Christ has done for, and given to, his people is fullness of joy (1:4/15:11; 16:24; 7:13).

In view of these remarkably close parallels, Alford does not seem to be expressing himself too strongly when he attributes an obstinate 'perverseness' to those who maintain a different authorship. Yet during the last hundred or so years a small but persistent minority of scholars have held that the evident similarity between letter and Gospel is due rather to conscious or unconscious imitation than to identity of authorship. Thus, Dodd, who argues that the three letters (but not the Gospel) were written by the same author, supposes that he was 'not a mere imitator' of the evangelist but his 'disciple' or 'student', who reflected and yet modified his master's thought, much as modern Barthians accept and yet adapt the theology of Karl Barth. These scholars point mainly to three phenomena: first to words and concepts in the letter which do not appear in the Gospel, secondly to peculiarities in the Gospel without parallel in the letter, and thirdly to subtle but significant differences in doctrines which are common to both Gospel and letter.

Brooke analyses the fifty peculiarities of the letter which Holtzmann listed, and they do not amount to much in the end. The most important words of the letter which do not occur in the Gospel are *angelia* (message), *koinōnia* (fellowship), *hilasmos* (propitiation), *chrisma* (unction, or anointing), *antichristos*, *anomia* (lawlessness) and *sperma* (seed). But, even though these words are missing from the Gospel, it would be rash to assert that the ideas about human sin or Christ's death or the Holy Spirit's work which are conveyed by them are absent also. To Dodd these linguistic differences are largely due to the fact that the Gospel reflects the language, thought and customs of Palestinian Judaism, whereas the letter is coloured by Hellenistic mysticism with its characteristic vocabulary of 'light', 'seed', 'chrism' and its abstract ideas (*e.g.* 'God is love'). But apart from the fact that one would naturally expect the Gospel with its Palestinian setting to be more Aramaic than Hellenistic, Alexander is surely right that in the letter 'these Hellenistic terms often carry invisible quotation marks'. John is deliberately borrowing from the vocabulary of the false teachers he is opposing.

Peculiarities of the Gospel are fully listed in eight pages by Brooke. He gives a catalogue of 813 words which occur in the Gospel but not in the letter. This may seem impressive, but not when it is examined. The great majority of these words are unimportant and are used only once or twice. More notable words are cross and crucify (fourteen times between them), disciple (seventy-eight times), glory and glorify (thirty-nine times between them), heaven (twenty times), law (thirteen times), Lord (fifty-two times), seek (thirty-four times) and sign (seventeen times). But of these only 'glory' and 'glorify' can be said to have any distinctive doctrinal meaning, for the *ideas* of the cross, discipleship, heaven, *etc.* are present in the letter even if the words are absent.

Turning from the words which are peculiar to either Gospel or letter, we must now consider those words and themes which are handled in both but with a difference, indeed, according to Dodd, 'a formidable difference'. There are seven major ones, which have been advanced as reasons for accepting a diversity of authorship.

1. In the Prologue to the Fourth Gospel the *Logos* is personal, referring to the 'one and only' Son, whereas the preface to the letter 'the *logos* of life' is impersonal and refers to the life-bringing gospel. This is probably true, as is accepted in the notes *ad loc.* (although it is still maintained by some that the 'Logos of life' is personal), but the similarities between Prologue and preface far outweigh this difference and are summarized in the Additional Note, 'The Word of life', on pp. 72–75.

2. The Paraclete in the Gospel is the Holy Spirit, 'the Comforter', whereas in the letter this title, which is found nowhere else in the New Testament, is applied to Jesus Christ the righteous, who is our advocate in heaven, not on earth. But neither concept contradicts or excludes the other. Why should it be thought impossible that both the second and the third persons of the Trinity should exercise a ministry of aid and advocacy, the Spirit on earth and the Son in heaven? Besides, if Jesus called the Spirit *'another* Paraclete' (Jn. 14:16), who is the first?

3. In the Fourth Gospel it is Jesus Christ who is 'the true

light', 'the light of men' and 'the light of the world' (1:9, 4 and 8:12), whereas the message of the letter is that 'God is light' (1:5). Again, both are true; they cannot be said in any way to be irreconcilable in the mind of the same author who has such a high view of the relation between Father and Son. Nor is it altogether correct to say that 'the Gospel is Christocentric, the Epistle Theocentric',[1] since in the latter the author many times uses the pronoun 'he' (*autos, ekeinos*), without specifiying to whom he is referring. His allusion is normally to the Son, but he does not always consider it necessary to say so.

4. The Gospel contains the affirmation that 'God is spirit' (4:24), while the letter declares once that 'God is light' (1:5) and twice that 'God is love' (4:8, 16). It is extraordinary that anybody could seriously consider these statements as being in any way inconsistent in the same author.

5. The death of Christ, it is rightly said, is presented in the Gospel as his 'uplifting' and his 'glorification'. Neither word occurs in the letter, where the purpose of his death is propitiatory (2:2; 4:10) and brings cleansing and life (1:7; 4:9). But the references to the death of Christ in the letter are in largely polemical passages, where the author's purpose is to emphasize its benefits for us in salvation rather than its significance for him in glorification. Moreover, teaching about the achievement of the Saviour's death cannot be said to be absent from a Gospel which declares that the wrath of God remains on the unbeliever (3:36) and includes verses like 1:29; 3:14–16; 6:51; 10:11, 15; 11:49–52; 12:24, *etc.*

6. The word *parrēsia*, bold outspokenness, occurs in both Gospel and letter; but in the former it denotes plainness of speech to human beings (*e.g.* 10:24; 11:14; 16:29; 18:20), and in the latter confidence before God in prayer and on the day of judgment (2:28; 3:21; 4:17; 5:14). All that needs to be said here is that boldness should characterize Christians in their approach to both God and others, and that there is no reason why the same author should not believe in both and write about both.

7. Lastly, the eschatological teaching is said to be different. In the Gospel, we are told, the eschatology is 'realized'. Eternal life

---

[1]Law, who himself very much modifies his own aphorism.

25

and judgment are both experienced now, since lifegiving and judging are the present activities of God through Christ (3:14–19; 5:19–27), and Jesus Christ promises to come again not in glory on the clouds of heaven but spiritually through the Holy Spirit (14:15–24, *etc.*). In the letter, on the other hand, the older and more popular expectations are preserved, namely Christ's personal 'coming' (*parousia*, 2:28) and visible 'appearing' (*phanerōsis*, 2:28; 3:2), and a final 'day of judgment' (4:17). This, we are told, takes no account of the profound reinterpretation of eschatology which is given in the Fourth Gospel; it is rather the 'naïve thinking of the primitive Church' (Dodd). But this reconstruction is much too categorical, as if there were no 'popular' eschatology in the Gospel and no 'realized' eschatology in the letter. The truth is that the Gospel includes sayings of Jesus about his coming to take his people to himself and about 'the last day' of resurrection and judgment (*e.g.* 14:3; 5:28–29; 6:39–40, 44, 54; 11:24–26; 12:48), while eternal life is clearly regarded in the letter as a present possession, received and enjoyed in Christ now (5:11–13). The present, personal activity of the Holy Spirit in witnessing is also taught in the letter; it is just not accurate to say that it contains 'no trace of the high "Johannine" doctrine which is found in the Gospel' (Dodd).

These differences of emphasis constitute no solid ground on which to base a theory of different authorship. They are sufficiently accounted for by the different purpose which the author had in writing each (which many commentators do not seem adequately to have noted) and by the interval of time which may have elapsed between the composition of each. The author's purpose in writing is known from his own definition of it. He wrote the Gospel for unbelievers in order to arouse their faith (20:30–31), and the letter for believers in order to deepen their assurance (5:13). His desire for the readers of the Gospel was that through faith they might receive life; for the readers of the letter that they might know they already had it. Consequently, the Gospel contains 'signs' to evoke faith (20:30–31), and the letter tests by which to judge it. Further, the enemies of the truth in the Gospel are unbelieving Jews, who doubt, not the historicity of Jesus (whom they could see and hear), but whether he is the Christ, the Son of God. The enemies of the truth in the letter, however, are professing Christians (although John's tests show that their profession is a lie), and their problem concerns not the divinity of the Christ but his relation to the historical Jesus. Westcott provides a neat summary of this distinction: 'the theme of the Epistle is "the Christ is Jesus"; the theme of the Gospel is "Jesus is the Christ" '.

This double difference of purpose implies a difference of time and would seem also to establish, not that the letter was written to accompany the Gospel (Ebrard, Lightfoot), still less that it preceded the Gospel, but that it was 'a kind of sequel to the gospel' (Ellis, p. 84). For John's readers must be brought to faith through testimony and to life through faith before they could be brought to an assurance of life. Those commentators who think that the letter was prior to the Gospel, have argued that they detect in it embryonic ideas (about the Logos, the atonement and the last things) which only come to birth in the Gospel. Kenneth Grayston goes further. He considers the theology of the first letter to be 'well below the level of the Gospel' (p. 9), especially in its doctrines of Christ and of the Spirit, so that these look like 'first attempts at material which later appears in the Gospel' (p. 14) and so 'contributed to its composition' (p. 16). But this is surely topsy-turvy. The letter is written to people who already know the truth and do not need anyone to teach them (2:20–21, 27), provided that they allow what they have heard from the beginning to remain in them (2:24). The NEB rightly entitles the letter a 'Recall to Fundamentals'. John is not teaching new truths or issuing new commands; it is the heretics who are the innovators. John's task is to recall them to what they already know and have. All this seems to presuppose on the part of the readers a knowledge of the Gospel, or at the very least of the body of doctrine contained in the Gospel. We may then agree that the letter is 'a comment on the Gospel, "a sermon with the Gospel for its text" ' (Plummer).

So far, then, we have suggested that the similarities of subject-matter, style and vocabulary in the Gospel and the first letter supply very strong evidence for identity of authorship, which is not materially weakened by the peculiarities of each or the differences of emphasis in the treatment of common themes. These are explained by the distinctive purpose behind each writing and by the lapse of time which can therefore be assumed between them. The similarity between Gospel and letter is considerably greater than that between the third Gospel and the Acts, which are known to have come from the same pen; between the Pastoral Epistles to Timothy and Titus; and even, it could be argued, between the two Thessalonian letters written during the apostle's second missionary journey, and between the letters to the Ephesians and the Colossians written during his first Roman imprisonment. 'The usage suggests a writer who varies his own phrases, rather than a mere copyist' (Brooke). 'The same mind deals with the same ideas in different connections . . . The Epistles give later growths of common and characteristic ideas. No imitator of the Gospel could have combined elements of likeness and unlikeness in such a manner . . .' (Westcott).

D. THE RELATION OF THE SECOND AND THIRD LETTERS TO EACH OTHER AND TO THE FIRST LETTER

It is not necessary to marshal lengthy arguments for the common authorship of 2 and 3 John; it is almost self-evident. It is true that the third letter has one or two words peculiar to itself (*e.g. philoprōteuein* in v. 9 and *phlyarein* in v. 10). Nevertheless, in spite of the different circumstances which evoked them and the fact that the male recipient of the third letter was a person and the female recipient of the second letter probably a personification, there is a striking similarity of address (from 'the elder' to one 'whom I love in the truth'), the same background situation of itinerant missionaries, the same length, pattern, style, language and conclusion. They are 'like twin sisters' (Alford). 'The similarity between them is too close to admit of any explanation except common authorship or conscious imitation' (Brooke); and the latter is hardly credible in view of the brevity and comparatively unimportant content of the letters.

If we consider the relation between the two shorter letters and what Clement of Alexandria called 'the greater', the divergences are seen to be insignificant. When it has been pointed out that the author of the first letter nowhere identifies himself, while the author of the second and third letters announces himself as 'the elder', that the tense of the verb in the expression 'Jesus Christ . . . come in the flesh' is perfect in the first (4:2) but present in the second (v. 7), and that 'antichrists' are plural in the first (2:18), while only singular in the second (v. 7, though he is there plainly representative of the class called 'many deceivers'), this seems to be the sum total of differences which can be discovered.

In contrast to these trivial points, the similarities between the greater and the two lesser letters are striking. There is the same emphasis on 'truth' (eleven times in the second and third letters, nine times in the first), which consists pre-eminently of the doctrine that 'Jesus Christ has come in the flesh' (2 Jn. 7/4:2). Loyalty to this truth is to have 'both the Father and the Son' (2 Jn. 9/2:23); disloyalty to it is to be a 'deceiver' and 'antichrist' (2 Jn. 7/2:22, 26). This doctrine is not new, but old. They must 'continue' in it (2 Jn. 9/2:27) and let it 'live' or 'remain' in them (2 Jn. 2/2:14, 24). Christian ethics like Christian doctrine are not new; John is writing to them not 'a new command' but 'one we have had from the beginning', namely that we 'love one another' (2 Jn. 5–6/2:7; 3:11). It is in such fellowship that fullness of joy may be found (2 Jn. 12; *cf.* 3 Jn. 4/1:4). Those who love and who do good give evidence that they are 'from God' (3 Jn. 11/3:10; 4:4, 7); those who sin and do evil show that they have 'not seen God' (3 Jn. 11/3:6).

We conclude that both shorter letters were written by the same person, and that this person was also the author of the first letter, who, we have already argued, had previously composed the Fourth Gospel. If this reasoning is sound, it means that whatever may be learnt of the author of the Fourth Gospel from internal evidence will apply to the author of the letters, and vice versa; it is impossible to study the Johannine problem if any one of these four writings is isolated, not to mention also the Apocalypse. What concerns us now, however, is to enquire if any further evidence can be discovered from within the three letters themselves, which may throw light on their authorship. Such additional internal evidence is both the writer's apparent claim to have been an eyewitness of the historical Jesus, and the authoritative tone with which he addresses his readers, calling himself 'the elder'. If it can be shown that he wrote as a personal eyewitness and with self-conscious authority, we have gone a considerable way towards asserting that the author was an apostle, since one of the qualifications of the apostolate was to have been an eyewitness (*e.g.* Mk. 3:14; Lk. 24:48; Jn. 15:27; Acts 1:21–26; 22:12–15; 26:16; 1 Cor. 9:1; 15:8–9), while the uniqueness of the apostolate was the special authority with which they were invested by Jesus Christ himself (*e.g.* Mk. 3:14–15; 6:7; Lk. 6:13; Gal. 1:1).

E. THE AUTHOR AS AN EYEWITNESS

The clearest and most definite claim of the author of the first letter to be an eyewitness is found in its opening words (1:1, 3). He is announcing his particular emphasis. What he proclaims concerning the word of life, the gospel, he says is 'that which was from the beginning, which we have heard . . . seen . . . touched . . .' His message is supremely concerned with the historical, audible, visible, tangible manifestation of the eternal. He could hardly have conveyed his meaning more forcefully. He is vouching for his message from his own personal experience. It consists not of 'cleverly invented stories' (2 Pet. 1:16), but of a historical revelation verified by the three highest of the five human senses: hearing, sight and touch.

This claim to empirical experience he repeats, in the parenthesis of verse 2 ('we have seen it and testify to it . . .'), and again when he resumes his theme after the parenthesis: 'We proclaim to you what we have seen and heard' (v. 3). His declaration is a testimony, and his testimony depends on the personal experience granted to his ears, eyes and hands. A similar claim seems to be made in 4:14, 'we have seen and testify that the Father has sent his Son to be the Saviour of the world'. He is able to testify in the present because of what he has seen in the past. It is this objective testimony which the Spirit's inward and subjective witness confirms (4:13). Perhaps a third, though indirect, allusion to the author's eyewitness experience may be found in the reference to the water and the blood in 5:6–7 (*cf.* Jn. 19:34–35).

Some commentators, however, regard this claim to have 'seen' as relating only to a vicarious eyewitness experience. Brown and Grayston, who both relate John's letters to the development of a 'Johannine Community', think the 'we' was a particular group of leaders in that community who were 'the tradition-bearers and interpreters' (Brown).[1]

Certainly in 1:1–3 and 4:14 the claim to have been an eyewitness is couched in the first person plural. It is in each case 'we' who 'have seen' and 'testify'. The question is: Whom does the author include in his 'we'? Is it merely an editorial or epistolary 'we' by which (like the royal 'we') he is in reality referring to himself alone? So Ebrard: 'St John is speaking of *himself* and *his* announcement and writing.' His 'we' is 'full of dignity and prerogative'. That this is John's meaning at least sometimes is clear from 3 John 9, where he slips from the singular, 'I wrote to the church' into the plural, 'but Diotrephes . . . will have nothing to do with us', which the RSV significantly expresses in the singular: 'Diotrephes . . . does not acknowledge my authority'. Similarly, in verse 12 the NIV literal rendering, 'We also speak well of him, and you know that our testimony is true,' becomes in the RSV the singular, 'I testify to him too, and you know my testimony is true.' Alternatively, is John, as Dodd believes, identifying himself with the whole church? Or again, is he, as has been traditionally accepted, distinguishing himself from the church at large and associating himself with the other apostles, as if to say that, although they were dead and he alone survived, yet he was declaring the one, common apostolic message based upon the one, common apostolic eyewitness experience? 'St John . . . uses the plural . . . as speaking in the name of the apostolic body of which he was the last surviving representative' (Westcott). True, he sometimes abandons the 'we' and uses the more direct first person singular, but there does not seem to be any change of subject between the 'We write this . . .' of 1:4 and the 'I write this . . .' of 2:1.

Certainly the use of the first person plural as an indication that his message was not his alone but the apostolic faith has parallels in Paul's letters (*e.g.* 1 Cor. 15:11 and Gal. 2:14–16).

[1]Brown, *Epistles*, p. 95; *cf.* pp. 158–161, 175 and Grayston, p. 3.

Dodd, however, after a lengthy excursus on the identity of the 'we' in 1:1–4 (pp. 9–16), concludes that the author speaks 'not exclusively for himself or for a restricted group, but for the whole Church, to which the apostolic witness belongs by virtue of its *koinōnia* . . .' The corollary is that 'this kind of language . . . is not in itself sufficient to prove authorship by an eyewitness'. His argument is persuasive and deserves careful consideration. He points out that elsewhere in the letter 'the first person plural . . . is very frequently used in a way which includes author and readers in one class. It is what we might call the preacher's "we".' But, he continues, its use is occasioned by more than tact and humility. 'It belongs to the language of the Church as a fellowship.' So far we must agree. The author does clearly identify himself with his readers in many parts of the letter, much as the preacher does with his congregation in a sermon, whether in confession (*e.g.* 1:6 – 2:2), in affirmation (*e.g.* 2:3; 3:2, 14, 19–24; 4:19 and 5:18–20) or in exhortation (*e.g.* 3:11; 4:7, 11). In these (and other) 'we' sentences the author is neither speaking editorially nor associating himself with the other apostles but identifying himself with the whole Christian community, or at least with his readers. In each case 'we' introduces a general statement of appeal applicable to all Christian people alike. In such passages the antithesis to 'we' is not 'you' but 'they', meaning 'the world' of non-Christians, to which group the heretics properly belong, *e.g.* 2:19 ('They went out from us, but they did not really belong to us') and 5:19 ('We know that we are children of God, and that the whole world is under the control of the evil one').

The problem is more difficult, however, in three passages which Dodd goes on to discuss, and in which the antithesis is not between 'we' and 'they' but between 'we' and 'you': 4:4–6, 14 and 1:1–5. In the first passage the crucial question is whether there is any difference of subject in the expressions 'You . . . are from God' (v. 4) and 'We are from God' (v. 6). Dodd says there is not and concludes that the test of knowing God or being of God, *viz.*, whether people listen to 'us', means whether they listen to 'the Church . . . proclaiming the Gospel'. Certainly the sequence of thought in these verses is complicated, since at least five persons or groups are mentioned, and possibly six, namely 'you' (the church), God, 'they' (the false teachers), 'the one who is in the world' (the devil), 'the world', and the controversial 'we'. As the argument unfolds, it seems more natural that the statements 'You . . . are from God' (v. 4) and 'We are from God' (v. 6) refer to different groups ('you' to the Christian community, 'we' to the apostolic body), since they lead to different conclusions. 'You . . . are from God and have overcome them' (v. 4). That is, your divine birth has enabled you to resist the false teaching. 'We are from God, and whoever knows God listens to us' (v. 6). That is, just as the world listens to the message of the false teachers who themselves belong to the world (v. 5), so those who know God and belong to God will listen to the apostolic faith because the apostles' message and commission were themselves from God. The contrast in verse 4 is between the false teacher and the Christian *hearer*; in verse 6 between the false teacher and the Christian *teacher*. 'The hearer discerns the true message. The teacher discovers the true disciple' (Westcott on v. 6). This is an application of Christ's word to the twelve apostles, 'He who receives you receives me, and he who receives me receives the one who sent me' (Mt. 10:40).

The next verse Dodd examines is 4:14: 'we have seen and testify that the Father has sent his Son to be the Saviour of the world'. He again refers the 'we' to the Christian community, particularly because the verse is embedded in a paragraph (vv. 7–19) in which 'we' does plainly refer to Christians in general. He claims this as 'an example of a type of argument which recurs all through the Epistle, in which the validity of certain propositions is tested by reference to the common Christian faith and experience'. He continues, 'it is difficult to accept a sudden shift of meaning so radical that whereas all through the passage "we" has meant Christians in general, it now means a group of eyewitnesses sharply distinguished from Christians in general'. The solution he proposes is derived from the New Testament, and not least Johannine, view of *koinōnia*, 'which connotes a sharing of life and experience so deep and thoroughgoing that what is predicated of the whole community can in some real sense be predicated of each member, and vice versa'. He cites as Old Testament parallels the 'I' of the Psalms, which sometimes 'expresses the solidarity of the Psalmist with the Israel of God' – a solidarity extending to 'the successive generations of Israel' as is plain from Amos 2:10 and Joshua 24:7, where the redemption from Egypt is said to have been experienced and seen by a generation who had themselves personally neither seen nor experienced it. Similarly, Dodd suggests, the author of the first letter could write of the whole Christian community 'seeing' and therefore testifying to 'the mighty acts of the Lord' by which they had been redeemed, even if they had not individually been eyewitnesses of them.

This is an impressive argument, containing undoubtedly much truth, and comment on it will be reserved until we have considered the conclusion which Dodd reaches as he now returns to the preface (1:1–4). He agrees that 'here certainly a distinction is made . . . between the author and his readers', which is expressed by 'we – you' at least in verses 3 and 4, although even here he refers the 'our' of 'our fellowship' (v. 3) and 'our joy' (v. 4, RSV) to the whole church. As for the 'we' of verses 1 and 2, although conceding that 'this kind of language would be very natural from the Apostle John or the Presbyter John . . . or some other eyewitness . . . it is not in itself sufficient to prove authorship by an eyewitness'. The emphasis, he argues, is on the literal hearing, seeing and touching, and not on the identity of those who heard, saw and touched, nor on 'the direct knowledge of some Christians over against the secondhand knowledge of others'.

All this is plausibly argued, but leaves the critical reader of Dodd's commentary uneasy, particularly with regard to the letter's preface. Approaching this paragraph *de novo*, there are some points to which insufficient weight has been given. First, the author more clearly distinguishes himself from those he is addressing than Dodd allows, not only as writer to readers, but as eyewitness and authoritative teacher to taught. The preface contains seven verbs in the first person plural, describing both the empirical experience and the announcement, before the writer adds the 'you' to whom the announcement is made. Who is this 'you' to whom 'we proclaim' the gospel, if the 'we' who proclaim it includes the whole Christian community? It is certainly not 'the world'. But how can it be the church? Alexander's note hardly makes sense: 'the *you* in verses 2, 3 and 4 (John's readers) are not over against, but included in the *we*. *You* and *we* alike are the church.' Are we then to understand that preaching the gospel is a kind of self-proclamation, the church talking to itself? No. The sequence of thought in the parenthesis of verse 2 is that the life which was with *the Father* was made manifest to *us*, that *we* might proclaim it to *you*. And the purpose of the proclamation is that *you* (of a subsequent generation) may have fellowship with *us* (the original eyewitnesses of the Word made flesh). We desire this for *you* because *our* fellowship is so privileged and precious; it is with *the Father* and with *his Son Jesus Christ* (v. 3).

Nor does it seem fair to say that the emphasis of the first verse is on the empirical experience itself as a fact rather than on the identity of those who had it. On the contrary, the author seems to stress not only the material reality of what was heard, seen and felt, but the persons who had the experience also, because he mentions that it was 'our eyes' which saw and 'our hands' which handled. Moreover, the first person plural is used not only of the verbs describing the historical experience, but also of the verbs denoting the proclamation of it. The persons who make the announcement are the persons who had the experience. The natural interpretation of these verses is, therefore, not merely of an empirical experience in general, nor of the original eyewitnesses with whom the Christian community is identified in the *koinōnia*, but of the personal experience of the very ones who are now making the proclamation. It is they whose eyes have seen, ears heard and hands handled, whose mouths are opened to speak.

This is particularly clear from the author's use, in addition to 'we proclaim' (*apangellomen*), of the verb 'we bear witness' or 'testify' (*martyroumen*) preceded by 'we have seen' (*heōrakamen*). Although it is true that *martyreisthai* is commonly employed in the Acts for preaching, which is a public testimony to the facts of the gospel, yet the compound expression 'see and testify' is used exclusively of eyewitnesses, especially by John. The two form 'a compacted pair of ideas' (Ebrard). Thus John the Baptist 'bore witness', saying, 'I saw the Spirit come down . . . on him . . . I have seen and I testify that this is the Son of God' (Jn. 1:32,

35

34). The same combination is used of the teaching of Jesus himself (Jn. 3:11, 32), and of the evangelist's own testimony in the Gospel, in connection with the spear thrust, 'The man who saw it has given testimony' (19:35). *Cf.* Acts 22:14–16. In all these occurrences of the linked 'see and bear testimony', it is plain that the seeing qualified the witness. He could testify only to what, and because of what, he had seen.

In view of this consistent New Testament (and especially Johannine) usage, we must respectfully dissent from Dodd's interpretation of the 'we' both in the preface and, with a little less conviction, in 4:14. To interpret these words of 'a spiritual vision', writes Brooke, would be 'forced and unnatural in the extreme'. A kind of second-hand vision by the Christian community is unconvincing also. Alford is nearer the truth when he writes of the emphatic 'we' of 4:14, 'this *hēmeis* brings up in sharp relief the apostolic body whom Christ appointed His witnesses, Jn. xv. 27, Acts i. 8. The assertion is of the same kind as that in chapter i. 1.' The whole difficulty arises because the writer (if an apostle) was a man holding two positions. In one sense, associated with his fellow-apostles, he was unique; in another sense, associated with his readers, he was just a common Christian. We see this same tension in the apostle Paul, who could style himself at the beginning of a letter both 'a servant of Christ Jesus', a title shared by all Christians, and 'called to be an apostle' or 'an apostle of Jesus Christ', which set him apart from his readers (Rom. 1:1; Tit. 1:1). So too can John call those to whom he writes both his *teknia*, 'little children' (AV, RSV) or 'dear children' (NIV), which indicates his authority as well as his affection and age, and his 'brothers and sisters', on an equal footing with them. He can begin by writing, 'we have seen . . . and testify . . . and proclaim to you' (1:1–5), distinguishing himself from them, and immediately continue, 'If we claim to have fellowship with him' (v. 6), including himself with them. Similarly, 'My dear children, I write this to you so that you will not sin' (which is an 'I – you' situation), is followed at once by, 'if anybody does sin, we have one who speaks to the Father in our defence' (2:1).

Only the context can guide us as to whether his 'we' is uniquely apostolic or commonly Christian. It appears that when doctrine is at stake, he retains the 'we – you' mode of address. This is so in 4:1–6. The change comes abruptly with verse 7, 'Dear friends, let us love one another . . .' Although he and they were distinct in the teaching-learning relationship, they were one in ethical responsibility. Certainly when he is teaching them, or referring to the apostolic faith which they have received from him 'from the beginning', he slips into direct 'I (or we) – you' speech (*e.g.* 2:7, 18, 21, 24). 3:11 is a particularly interesting example, because it begins, 'This is the message you heard from the beginning' and continues, 'We should love one another.' It is 'I – you' in the issuing of the message, but 'we' in the receiving and obeying of it. It is for this reason, no doubt, that the only exception to the rule mentioned above is 2 John 5, where he at first describes the command as one 'we have had from the beginning . . . that *we* love one another', since the command applies to him as much as to them and he does not exempt himself from it. But in the next verse he is back to direct speech, 'As *you* have heard from the beginning, his command is that *you* walk in love.' All these examples of the author's use of 'we' may enable us to agree with Calvin: 'As the words are in the plural and the matter applies equally to all the apostles, I interpret it of them; especially as it deals with the authority of witness.'

F. THE AUTHOR'S SELF-CONSCIOUS AUTHORITY

The author's authoritative tone is particularly evident in the 'I – you' passages and appears the more striking when viewed in contrast to the humble way in which he associates himself with his readers in some 'we' passages. There is nothing tentative or apologetic about what he writes. He does not hesitate to call certain classes of people 'liars', 'deceivers' or 'antichrists'. He supplies tests by which everybody can be sorted into one or other of two categories. According to their relation to his tests, they either have God or have not, know God or do not, have been born of God or have not, have life or abide in death, walk in the darkness or in the light, are children of God or children of the devil. This dogmatic authority of the writer is seen particularly in his statements and in his commands. For some of his pronouncements, see 1:5; 2:1–2, 8, 17, 23; 3:6, 9; 4:8, 16, 18; 5:12. For positive commands see 2:15, 28; 4:1; 5:21. More striking than the general ethical commands of the first letter are the personal and particular directions of the second and third: 'If anyone comes to you and does not bring this teaching, do not take him into your house or welcome him' (2 Jn. 10); and in the third letter the instruction to entertain itinerant Christian missionaries, an instruction which Diotrephes had disobeyed in defiance of the elder's authority (3 Jn. 5–10).

But who is this who presumes to make such dogmatic affirmations and to issue commands which are reminiscent of what James Denney called the 'sovereign legislative authority' of Jesus himself? True, in statement and command, the author is sometimes quoting or echoing the teaching of Jesus, which he has himself recorded in the Gospel (*e.g.* 1 Jn. 2:25; 3:13), but he goes much further than this. He dares to instruct and to direct in matters beyond the boundaries of the Lord's teaching. Moreover, in doing so he gives no hint that he regards one kind of teaching as less authoritative than the other. Some of the commands of which he writes are God's (*e.g.* 3:23–24; 5:3), some are Christ's (*e.g.* 2:7; 2 Jn. 5), and some are his own (*e.g.* 2 Jn. 10–11; 3 Jn. 9). But he does not distinguish between them; he expects them all to be obeyed. Compare Paul's commands and requirements of obedience in 2 Thessalonians 3:4, 6, 10, 12, 14.

All this 'would have been impossible for any lesser personage than an Apostle' (Smith). It is entirely consistent with the unique position occupied by the apostles of Jesus in view of the promises and commission which he gave them. They were to teach others to observe whatever he had commanded them (Mt. 28:20), but he would by his Spirit continue to teach and command through them (Jn. 14:26; 16:12–13; *cf.* Acts 1:1). It is the bestowal of this authoritative commission and message, together with their eyewitness experience, which constituted the uniqueness of the apostles; and John lays claim to both in the first chapter of his first letter. It was what he had 'seen' of Christ which qualified him to 'testify', and what he had 'heard' from Christ which qualified him to 'proclaim' an authoritative message to others. If John's claim to this twofold qualification is a true claim, then his identity is John the apostle.

G. THE TITLE 'ELDER'

But in his second and third letters the title which the writer gives himself is not 'apostle' but 'elder'. Why is this? Many recent commentators have answered this question by arguing that there were in fact two Johns (who may or may not both have lived in Ephesus), John the apostle and John the presbyter (or 'elder'), and that it is the latter who wrote the three letters. Some add that he wrote the Fourth Gospel also. What is the evidence that such a person existed? It is to be found in Eusebius' *Ecclesiastical History*, at the end of Book 3, in which he has been describing some of the outstanding personalities of the sub-apostolic period. His last chapter (39) is concerned with Papias, Bishop of Hierapolis, whom he quotes as saying that 'if anyone chanced to come who had actually been a follower of the elders', he (Papias) would enquire about (or into) 'the discourses of the elders, what Andrew or what Peter said, or what Philip, or what Thomas or James, or what John or Matthew or any other of the Lord's disciples; and the things which Aristion and John the elder, disciples of the Lord, say' (3.39.4). Eusebius goes on immediately to draw attention to the double mention of John, once with the apostles and once with Aristion. He concludes that Papias was referring to two separate Johns, the apostle and the presbyter. On the strength of this, and in spite of his quotation from Irenaeus that Papias was 'a hearer of John and a companion of Polycarp, a man of primitive times' (3.39.1), he goes on to assert categorically that Papias 'was in no sense a hearer and eyewitness of the holy Apostles', but only learnt from 'their pupils' (3.39.2).

But was Eusebius right in his interpretation? He was writing a century later, and he had a poor opinion of Papias, who, he said, judging from his writings, 'was a man of exceedingly small intelligence' (3.39.13). Papias was not only unintelligent, but 'an uncommonly clumsy writer' (Dodd). Certainly his statement about 'John the elder' is ambiguous. Brooke refers to 'the Elder

John whom Papias so carefully distinguishes from the Apostle',
while other commentators have doubted whether it was Papias'
intention to distinguish between two Johns at all. They rightly
point out that the seven apostles who are named in the quotation are themselves called 'elders' just like 'John the elder'
(3.39.4; *cf.* 3.39.7), and maintain 'it is impossible that the term
should bear different meanings within the compass of a single
sentence' (Smith). Not only are the seven apostles and 'John the
elder' alike 'elders', but they are both termed 'disciples of the
Lord' as well. In this case, it may be asked, if the two Johns are
the same person, why is he mentioned twice?

The ambiguity seems to be due to the fact that Papias has
three categories in mind, according to whether they were
'disciples' in general or 'apostles' ('elders') in particular, and
whether they were dead or still alive. What was common to the
three categories is that they were all 'disciples of the Lord', who
had known him in the days of his flesh. The seven were apostles
or 'elders' as well as disciples, but were mostly dead. Aristion
was alive as well as a disciple, but not an apostle. John was in a
category of his own because only he possessed the three qualifications, being a disciple and an apostle/elder and alive. This is
why he is mentioned twice: first with Andrew, Peter, Philip and
the others who, though not alive, were like him apostles or
elders, and secondly with Aristion who, though not an apostle/
elder, was like him still alive.

This interpretation is suggested by the change of tense, to
which Plummer, Smith and others have drawn attention, from
what the apostles/elders 'said' (*eipen*) to what Aristion and the
elder John 'say' (*legousin*). They argue cogently that Papias was
claiming to draw his materials from two sources; one was
second-hand, namely the 'followers' of the apostles/elders who
had heard them during their lifetime, and the other first-hand,
namely living eyewitnesses, whether disciples like Aristion or
the only surviving apostle/elder, John. Since Papias had heard
the teaching of John in both ways, from others by report and
from his own lips, he mentions him twice. If it cannot be proved
that this, and not Eusebius' interpretation, is the correct one, it
must at least be conceded with Dodd (who believes that the
author of the three letters was a 'presbyter John' distinct from

the apostle) that Papias 'expresses himself so loosely in the crucial passage that it would be possible to hold that he intended to include apostles in the wider class of presbyters'.

Irenaeus, Bishop of Lyons, is also quoted in support of the theory of two Johns. He himself had come from Asia and was familiar with the writings of Papias. In his famous *Adversus Haereses* (5.33,36) he refers several times to a group of people whom he names 'the presbyters, disciples of the Apostles'. He seems to be referring to 'those who had companied with Apostles, and had perhaps been placed in office by them' (Brooke), who thus 'formed a link between the apostles and the next generation' and 'transmitted ... the apostolic traditions' (Dodd). He also sometimes mentions such a presbyter in the singular (4.47,49; 1.8,7 and *Ecclesiastical History*, 5.8.8 'a certain apostolic elder, whose name he bequeaths to silence'), but there is no indication that he means the presbyter John, whom in fact he does not mention. He does, however, refer to the apostle John, and calls him a 'disciple of the Lord', which is the same title used by Papias for the seven apostles/elders, Aristion and 'John the elder'.

Dionysius of Alexandria in the third century was quoted by Eusebius (3.39.6; 7.25.16) in confirmation of his theory that there were two Johns: 'since it is said both that there were two tombs at Ephesus, and that each of the two is said to be John's'. This statement needs to be treated with considerable caution. To begin with, Eusebius does not appear to have any personal knowledge of these two tombs; he is merely quoting Dionysius. Dionysius claims no personal knowledge of them either, but only that 'it is said' there were two tombs and it 'is said' that both were John's. Further, Dionysius had a reason for wanting to distinguish two Johns: he was determined to find a John other than the apostle to whom he could attribute the book of Revelation, which he did not like. Finally, even if at one time there were two tombs at Ephesus bearing John's name, it is more likely that they were rival claimants for the tomb of the same John than separate tombs of two distinct Johns. Certainly Polycrates, who was Bishop of Ephesus at the end of the second century, and who sent to Bishop Victor of Rome a list of earlier Christian celebrities who had been buried in Asian cities, does not mention 'John the elder'; he does, however, mention the apostle John and Polycarp as having their graves in Ephesus. It is not until Jerome (d. 420) that a second tomb was said to be either an alternative site for the same John's grave, or the grave of another John 'the elder', who according to the opinion of many was the author of the shorter letters (*De Viris Illustribus* 9).

It is probable that Eusebius adopted the theory of two Johns for the same reason as Dionysius, namely that he disapproved of the Revelation for its supposed millenarian views and wanted to ascribe it to an author other than the apostle John. He therefore proposed 'John the elder' and quoted Papias and Dionysius in support of such a person.

It must be admitted that grounds for believing in a second John, 'the presbyter', are extremely scanty. Plummer does not hesitate to write: 'there is no independent evidence of the existence of a second John. Papias, as interpreted or misinterpreted by Eusebius, is our sole witness . . . We, therefore, give up the second John as unhistorical.'

Turning now from the vexed question of the historicity of a distinct 'presbyter John', let us suppose for a moment that such a person existed, and ask: Could he have been the author of these letters? Scholars find themselves in difficulties here because some want him as the author of the letters, while others want him as the author of the Gospel, and yet others as the author of the Apocalypse. Leaving aside this rather unseemly scramble for the patronage of the shadowy presbyter John, in order to attribute to him writings for which it is desired to relieve the apostle John of responsibility, is there any evidence that this presbyter wrote the letters? Westcott describes such a view as 'purely conjectural' and adds that 'there is not the least direct evidence external or internal in its favour'.

We agree, of course, that the author of the two short letters called himself 'the elder'. He must have done so, without adding his name, only because his identity was so well known and his authority so well recognized that he could use the title without needing to qualify or amplify it. Moreover, since the two letters were written to different churches, he was evidently known and acknowledged in a wide area of the province of Asia. It is plain, as we read his letters, that he is intimately acquainted with their affairs, and accepts responsibility for their spiritual oversight. He loves them, exhorts them, teaches them, warns them, commands them. Is it possible that a man of such prominence, who exercised such authority and wrote three letters which are included in the New Testament canon, should have left no more trace of himself in history than one dubious reference by Papias? It seems far more probable that this widespread authority was that of the apostle John, who, according to well-attested tradition, lived to a ripe old age in Ephesus. Eusebius says (3.23.1, 3, 4) that 'he whom Jesus loved, apostle alike and evangelist, even John' lived on in Asia, 'directing the churches there', according to Irenaeus 'until the time of Trajan' (reigned AD 98–117). Such was his far-flung 'diocese' that, in words of Clement of Alexandria also quoted by Eusebius, 'he used to go off, when requested, to the neighbouring districts of the Gentiles also, to appoint bishops in some places, to organize whole churches in others . . .' (3.23.6).

If the author was the apostle John, we still have to ask why he styled himself 'the elder'. To begin with, there is nothing strange about an apostle calling himself an 'elder'. The title had been taken over from the Jewish eldership, and elders were appointed in Christian churches at least from the time of Paul's first missionary journey (Acts 14:23). The apostle Peter used the title of himself, calling himself a 'fellow-elder' of those he was addressing in his letter (1 Pet. 5:1). And we have seen that the Papias quotation, whichever way it is interpreted, calls the apostles 'elders' also. But why did John use the absolute title '*the* elder'? Of course the word literally means an 'old man', 'senior' or 'veteran', and it is possible that John assumed, or was given, the title in his old age, much as Paul called himself 'Paul the aged' in his letter to Philemon (v. 9, AV; although there the word is the similar *presbytēs*, not *presbyteros*). It is not necessary to speak of the title as an 'affectionate nickname', like our 'The Old Man' (Dodd), which John would be unlikely to use in a formal and solemn pastoral letter. But as a serious title, it would be particularly appropriate to the apostle who had outlived the other apostles. He would not have dreamt of calling himself 'the apostle', for all the apostles shared the same special divine commission. He was only '*an* apostle', as Paul and Peter also styled themselves (*e.g.* Rom. 1:1; 1 Pet. 1:1). But he could be called *'the* elder' *par excellence.* There were other elders in Ephesus, but he was unique among them because he was an apostle as well, and a veritable patriarch in age. It is even conceivable that the later technical use of the title 'elders' for 'disciples of the apostles' was derived from John, who as the last surviving apostle and 'the elder' was the link between the apostolic and the sub-apostolic periods. As 'the elder', whose leadership was accepted, he exercised a widespread supervision of the Asian churches surrounding Ephesus, perhaps especially the six others named in the seven letters of Revelation 2 and 3.

We conclude, therefore, that although we can only guess how and why the writer came to style himself 'the elder' in this anonymous and absolute way, the use of the title tends to confirm the unique position of the person who held it. Such an exceptional position, together with the author's authoritative tone and claim to have been an eyewitness, are fully consistent with the early tradition of the church that these three letters were in fact written by the apostle John.

II. OCCASION

A number of authors have argued that the letters of John are to be regarded rather as pastoral than as polemical writings. There is some truth in this assertion. For John certainly exhibits a tender, pastoral care for his readers. His first concern is not to confound the false teachers, whose activities form the background of the letters, but to protect his readers, his beloved 'children', and to establish them in their Christian faith and life. Thus, he defines his own purpose in writing as being 'to make our joy complete', 'so that you will not sin', and 'so that you may know that you have eternal life' (1:4; 2:1; 5:13). Joy, holiness, assurance: these are the Christian qualities the pastor desires to see in his flock. John's first letter is 'a masterpiece in the art of edification' (Findlay).

Nevertheless, John also has a polemical purpose. His first letter is not a theological treatise written in the academic peace of a library, but a tract for the times, called forth by a particular and urgent situation in the church. This situation concerns the insidious propaganda of certain false teachers. 'I am writing these things to you about those who are trying to lead you astray' (2:26), or 'about those who would deceive you' (RSV). Again, 'Dear children, do not let anyone lead you astray' (3:7). The apostle Paul's prophecy to the Ephesian elders about 'savage wolves' (Acts 20:29–30), later repeated to Timothy (2 Tim. 3:1–7; 4:3–4), has evidently come true. John describes them by three expressions, which draw attention to their diabolical origin, evil influence and false teaching. First, they are 'false prophets' (4:1). A prophet is a teacher who speaks under the inspiration of a supernatural power. The true prophet was the mouthpiece of the Spirit of truth, the false of the spirit of error. This is why examining the teaching of prophets is called 'testing the spirits' (4:1–6). Secondly, they are 'deceivers' (2 Jn. 7), because they are leading people astray. Thirdly, they are 'antichrists' (2:18, cf. v. 22; 4:3; 2 Jn. 7), because the substance of their teaching is to deny the divine-human person of Jesus Christ. In each case they are 'many' – 'many false prophets', 'many deceivers', 'many antichrists'. Once they passed as loyal members of the church, but now they have seceded (2:19) and 'gone out into the world' (4:1; cf. 2 Jn. 7) to spread their pernicious lies. It seems probable that their secession was due to their failure to convert the rest of the congregation, who by their loyalty to the truth had 'overcome them' (4:4). Yet some who remained must have been left in a wavering and insecure state, so that John needs to write to reassure and strengthen them. His great emphasis is on the differences between the genuine Christian and the spurious, and how to discern between the two.

A. INTERNAL EVIDENCE: THEOLOGICAL AND ETHICAL ERROR

The internal evidence furnished by the letters discloses not only the diabolical origin and damaging activity of the false teachers, but to some extent the nature of their perverted system as well. We can learn it both from John's direct references to their teaching which he contradicts and from the positive emphasis he feels it necessary to make in order to counteract it. Moreover, the context of his double mention of deceivers shows that their error was both theological (2:26; *cf.* 2 Jn. 7) and ethical (3:7).

Their theological error concerned the person of Jesus. They denied that Jesus was the Christ (2:22). This does not seem to mean, however, that they disbelieved in Jesus of Nazareth as the Christ of Old Testament expectation. John's argument has little in common with the earliest apostolic reasoning with the Jews that Jesus was the Christ (*e.g.* Acts 9:22; 17:3; 18:5).[1] What John's opponents denied was not the Messiahship, but the incarnation of Jesus. In their case, to deny that he was 'the Christ' was equivalent to a denial that he was 'the Son' (2:23; 4:15; 2 Jn. 9). Similarly he 'who believes that Jesus is the Christ' is identical with him 'who believes that Jesus is the Son of God' (5:1, 5, and *cf.* vv. 9, 13). It is the same in the Gospel (Jn. 20:31).

In two important verses John is more precise. The heretical teaching is either a denial that 'Jesus Christ has come in the flesh' or a denial of Jesus as 'Christ come in the flesh' (4:2; 2 Jn. 7, see comments *ad loc.*). But whether John uses this more elaborate expression or the very simplest, namely to 'acknowledge Jesus' (4:3), he means the same thing. He is asserting the reality of the incarnation, the coming in flesh of Jesus Christ, which the heretics apparently denied. Moreover, although they thus denied the incarnation, they evidently claimed to be progressive thinkers (2 Jn. 9) still to have the Father without the Son (2:22–23; 2 Jn. 9). Against these false teachers John emphasizes the historical manifestation of 'that which was from the beginning' to the ears, eyes and hands of witnesses (1:1–3; 4:14). He also appeals against the 'progressive' thought of the heretics to the original apostolic gospel which his readers have received 'from the beginning' (2:7, 24).

Smalley argues that the denial of the incarnation took two complementary forms, since the Johannine community was being disturbed by two distinct heretical groups. On the one hand there was a group of ex-Jews, who did not accept the divine *Messiahship* of Jesus, and on the other a group of ex-pagans, who did not accept his full *humanity*. In consequence,

---

[1]Brooke and Barclay, however, think that John did have Jews in mind, who, especially after the destruction of Jerusalem in AD 70, were even more vigorous in their rejection of the Messiahship of Jesus.

'At the heart of the fourth evangelist's theology is his balanced understanding of the person of Jesus: that he is both one with man and (in some sense) one with God.' John therefore addresses both those 'who thought of Jesus as less than God, to remind them of his divinity' and those 'who thought of Jesus as less than man, to assure them of his humanity' (p. xxiii; cf. pp. xxvi, 101). Since these two heretical tendencies are known to have arisen early in the church's history, there is no *a priori* reason why they should not both have been represented in the Johannine churches. John's full-orbed Christology of 'Christ come in the flesh' repudiated them both.

Turning now to the ethical error of the false teachers, we are not told explicitly what it was. But the implication is plain, for it is their claims which appear to be in view whenever John uses the formulae 'if we claim' and 'anyone who claims'. The three 'if we claim' sentences of 1:6–10 are a denial either that sin exists in our nature, or that it has erupted in our behaviour, or that it interferes with our fellowship with God. Those who make such assertions, John says bluntly, either lie or deceive themselves or make God a liar (1:6, 8, 10). God's self-revelation is ethical, and there can be no fellowship with him without righteousness. Similarly, 'the man who says' he knows God is a liar if he disobeys his commands; while 'whoever claims' to live in Christ ought to give evidence of it by walking as Christ walked (2:4, 6). And what do the commands of God and the walk of Christ involve? In a word, love. 'Anyone who claims' to be in the light and yet hates his brother is still in darkness (2:9; cf. 4:20). John does not mince his words. The false teachers are claiming to 'know God', to 'live in Christ' and to 'be in the light' (perhaps their very expressions or catchprases), while living themselves in unrighteousness and uncharitableness. Such people are 'liars'. They cannot claim to 'be' righteous unless they actually 'do' righteousness (2:29 – 3:10).

John does not rest content with negatives, however. The first letter is a great positive affirmation that 'God is light' (1:5) and 'God is love' (4:8, 16), and that therefore the darkness of sin and hatred is incompatible with any claim to know God. It is only if we obey God's commandments and love our brothers and sisters that we can know that we know him (2:3; 3:14). Further,

Jesus Christ appeared to put away sin and to destroy the works of the devil. Therefore sin and lovelessness are as much at variance with the mission of Christ as they are with the nature of God (3:4–10). All sin is 'lawlessness' and 'wrongdoing' (3:4; 5:17), and wholly inconsistent with the profession and conduct of a Christian. The letter expounds in successively profound and elaborate arguments the indispensable necessity of righteousness and love in the child of God. Moreover, John appeals against the heretics' ethical error, as he does against their Christological error, to the original apostolic teaching which his readers had 'heard from the beginning', namely, 'We should love one another' (3:11).

B. EXTERNAL EVIDENCE: DOCETISM, GNOSTICISM, CERINTHIANISM

From this internal evidence it emerges that, if we are to identify the heresy against which John writes, we must find a system which denied that Jesus was the Son or the Christ come in the flesh and which also viewed righteousness and love as indifferent. Some writers have argued that this system is the doctrine known as 'docetism'. Derived from the Greek verb *dokein*, to seem, it describes the view that Jesus was not a man in reality but only in appearance. He 'seemed' to the eyes of witnesses to be truly human, but it was a disguise similar to that of the Old Testament theophanies when God (or the angel of the Lord) appeared in the form of a man. We know of this error from several patristic writers, who also used the letters of John to refute it. It was condemned, for instance, by Ignatius, Polycarp and Tertullian.

But a careful study of the phraseology of John shows that he is concerned not just with the reality of the 'flesh' of Jesus, but with the relation between the human 'Jesus' and the divine 'Son' or 'Christ'. 'The emphasis is not upon the real humanity of Jesus so much as upon the personal identity of the pre-existent Divine Christ with Jesus' (Law).

This has led a majority of commentators to discover the heretics in the ranks of semi-Gnostics whose preoccupation was with deliverance from the 'flesh', which they regarded as the soul's material imprisonment. 'Gnosticism' is a broad term embracing various pagan, Jewish and semi-Christian systems, which did not come to full development until the second century. It was pagan in origin, combining elements of 'Western intellectualism and Eastern mysticism' (Law). Thoroughly syncretistic in its genius, a 'theosophical hotchpotch' (Dodd), it did not hesitate to fasten upon and to corrupt first Judaism and then Christianity. Plummer sums up its two main principles as 'the impurity of matter' and 'the supremacy of knowledge'. The notion that matter is inherently evil was both oriental and Greek. It led to speculations about the origin of the material universe and how it could in any sense have been created by the Supreme Being who is good. The Gnostics posited a series of 'aeons' or emanations from the Supreme, each more removed from him than its predecessors, until there emerged one sufficiently remote to create the material world.

The controversy which John's letters reflect, however, concerns the doctrine of the incarnation rather than that of creation. Those proto-Gnostics who believed that matter was evil were obsessed with the problems raised not just by the world in general but by the body in particular. They were immediately in difficulties with the Christian religion because it is such an essentially 'material' religion. It asserts that the Son of God clothed himself with a body, and that the Christian's body is the temple of the Holy Spirit. What could they make of the body of Christ and of the body of Christians? We have already seen that they denied the former. They did not deny that the man Jesus had a body, but that the Christ was to be personally identified with the bodily man Jesus. They could not conceive how the 'Christ' could have become incarnate, still less have assumed a body subject to suffering and pain. As for the Christian's body, it was fundamental to their thought that the body was a base prison in which the rational or spiritual part of human beings was incarcerated, and from which it needed to be released by *gnōsis*, knowledge. They believed in salvation by enlightenment. This enlightenment could come by the imparting of an esoteric knowledge in some secret initiation ceremony. The initiated were the *pneumatikoi*, the truly 'spiritual' people, who despised the uninitiated as *psychikoi*, doomed to an animal life

49

on earth. The better Gnostic systems of the second century combined these views of spiritual enlightenment and release with a strict asceticism; the worst systems asserted that evil could not harm the enlightened spirit, that morality was therefore a matter of indifference, and that the grossest forms of licence were quite permissible. Such *pneumatikoi* claimed also to be *dikaioi*, 'righteous', irrespective of their behaviour.

The earliest traditions associate the letters of John with Asia, especially Ephesus, and it is clear from other parts of the New Testament (*e.g.* the letters to the Colossians and Timothy, and those to Pergamum and Thyatira in Revelation 2) that incipient Gnostic views had begun to infiltrate the churches of Asia. One resident in first-century Ephesus, who could justly be described as a 'pre-Gnostic' or 'proto-Gnostic', was a certain Cerinthus. True, none of his writings has survived. But he is known to have been both a contemporary and an opponent of John. We learn about him chiefly from Irenaeus and Eusebius. Irenaeus records in *Adversus Haereses* the famous anecdote told by Polycarp, Bishop of Smyrna, that 'John, the disciple of the Lord, going to bathe at Ephesus, and perceiving Cerinthus within, rushed out of the bath-house without bathing, exclaiming "Let us fly, let even the bath-house fall down, because Cerinthus, the enemy of the truth, is within!" '[1] Irenaeus has already given an account of the heretical views of Cerinthus in Book 1 of this same great work *Against Heresies*. He says that Cerinthus 'represented Jesus as having not been born of a virgin, but as being the son of Joseph and Mary according to the ordinary course of human generation, while he nevertheless was more righteous, prudent and wise than other men. Moreover, after his baptism, Christ descended upon him in the form of a dove from the Supreme Ruler, and that then he proclaimed the unknown Father, and performed miracles. But at last Christ departed from Jesus, and that then Jesus suffered and rose again, while Christ remained impassible,[2] inasmuch as he was a spiritual being.'[3] Epiphanius' account of the heresy in his *Refutation of All Heresies* is substantially the same, except that he identifies the divine aeon

---

[1] 3.3.4. Eusebius also records the story in the *Ecclesiastical History*, both in 3.28.6 and in 4.14.6.
[2] *I.e.* 'not liable to pain or injury' (*OED*).   [3] *Against Heresies*, 1.26.1.

descending upon the man Jesus as 'the Spirit' rather than 'Christ'.[1] The essence of Cerinthus' error, then, seems to have been this severance of the man Jesus from the divine Christ or Spirit. Irenaeus refers to it again later when he alludes to those 'who separate Jesus from Christ, alleging that Christ remained impassible, but that it was Jesus who suffered',[2] and again 'the Son of the Creator was, forsooth, one, but the Christ from above another, who also continued impassible, descending upon Jesus, the Son of the Creator, and flew back again into His Pleroma'.[3]

John's arguments certainly make sense if they are understood as directed against Corinthus and his disciples. He defines the false teaching as a denial 'that Jesus is the Christ' (2:22), a denial that the two are to be identified. More precisely, it is a denial that 'Jesus Christ has come in the flesh', which perhaps could be translated 'that Jesus is the Christ-come-in-the-flesh' (4:2; 2 Jn. 7). An ancient reading of 4:3 renders the heretical position not as 'denying' but as 'loosing' Jesus Christ. (See the Additional Note, 'The interpretation of 1 John 4:2', on pp. 158–159.) It is mentioned in the RV margin. Irenaeus evidently knew this variant, for he quotes 4:3 as 'every spirit which *separates* Jesus Christ is not of God'.[4] The Vulgate has *solvit*. Although the reading is not original, it bears witness to an early recognition that the Gnostic rejection of the incarnation was a sundering or 'loosing' of Jesus from Christ. John goes further in his refutation of Cerinthus when he describes Jesus as 'the one who came by water and blood – Jesus Christ. He did not come by water only, but by water and blood' (5:6). See the commentary on this verse, where it is argued that 'water' here refers primarily to the baptism of Jesus Christ, and 'blood' to his death. Cerinthus taught that the Christ descended upon Jesus *after* his baptism and departed from him *before* his death; John asserts that on the contrary 'Jesus Christ', one person, passed *through* both baptism and death.

Irenaeus and Eusebius tell us about the ethical, as well as the Christological, leanings of Cerinthus. According to Irenaeus

---

[1]*Refutation of All Heresies*, 28.1.   [2]*Against Heresies*, 3.11.7.   [3]*Ibid.*, 3.11.1.
[4]*Ibid.*, 3.16.8.

the error of Cerinthus had been 'disseminated among men . . . a long time previously by those termed Nicolaitans',[1] and these Nicolaitans are mentioned in Revelation 2:6, 14–15 as having been guilty of immorality. Both Tertullian and Clement of Alexandria said that they were unrestrained in their dissolute ways. This is further confirmed by two passages in Eusebius' *Ecclesiastical History*, which has strong anti-millenarian views and criticizes Cerinthus for the thoroughly sensual millennium he seems to have been anticipating.[2]

There is no clear evidence in John's letters that the false teachers John is opposing held such extreme carnal views, but there is abundant evidence, as we have already seen, that they regarded righteousness of conduct as a matter of indifference. So John lays repeated emphasis on the necessity of holy living and obedience to the commands of God. He shows that the practice of sin is wholly inadmissible in the Christian. He also denies the possibility of a dual standard of morality by which the élite are spared the moral obligations demanded of the common herd. '*Everyone* who has this hope in him [Christ] purifies himself,' he writes. Again, '*No-one* who is born of God will continue to sin . . .' (see 3:3, 9). The *dikaioi*, the self-styled 'righteous' ones, can show themselves worthy of the title only by *doing* righteousness (3:7). If they sin, they show that, whatever they may claim, they have neither seen nor known God (3:6).

A third characteristic of the false teachers, who had Gnostic tendencies, Cerinthus no doubt included, seems to have been their lovelessness. Claiming to be a spiritual aristocracy of the enlightened, who alone had come to know 'the depths', they despised the ordinary run of Christians. John cuts across this dangerous outlook by asserting that there are not two categories of Christians, the enlightened and the unenlightened, for 'God is light', continuously revealing himself to all. 'All of you know', he writes (see 2:13–14, 20; 5:20). His readers have all received the same 'anointing' and the same message which 'you have heard from the beginning' (see 2:20–27). It is argued in the commentary on this paragraph that John is referring to the Spirit and

---

[1] *Against Heresies*, 3.11.1.   [2] *Ecclesiastical History*, 3.28.1–2; 7.25.2–3.

the Word. If all Christians have received both the Word of God and the Spirit of God, there is no room for cliques claiming a superior illumination.

Nor is there any justification for an unloving spirit among the members of God's family, such as characterized the proto-Gnostics. Bishop Ignatius of Antioch describes them in his letter to the Smyrnaeans. Having quoted the 'new commandment . . . that ye love one another', he goes on: 'Do ye, therefore, notice those who preach other doctrines, how they affirm that the Father of Christ cannot be known, and how they exhibit envy and deceit in their dealings with one another. They have no regard for love. . . .' The apostle Paul had written in 1 Corinthians of the dangers of knowledge without love (8:1–3; 13:2). It is very apparent in the letters of John. So he affirms that God is in his very being love, and that we have come to know love only because God sent his Son to be our Saviour and because Christ laid down his life for us (4:8, 10, 14; 3:16). Since God is love and has loved, and since all love is of God, he reasons, 'beloved, let us love one another' (4:7, RSV); 'Whoever does not love does not know God' (4:8).

In his commentary on Galatians 6:10 Jerome tells a famous story of 'blessed John the evangelist' in extreme old age at Ephesus. He used to be carried into the congregation in the arms of his disciples and was unable to say anything except 'Little children, love one another'. At last, wearied that he always spoke the same words, they asked: 'Master, why do you always say this?' 'Because', he replied, 'it is the Lord's command, and if this only is done, it is enough.'[1]

Some recent commentators, however, have questioned the precise identification of the false teaching as Cerinthianism. Marshall, for example, points out that some of the known features of the teaching of Cerinthus are not reflected in what John writes in his letters, while some of the features of the heresy which John rejects are not found in what is known of Cerinthianism.[2] The fact is that among scholars there is still 'considerable difference of opinion regarding the identity of

---

[1]Longer Version, Chapter VI.
[2]See his discussion on pp. 14–22. See also Smalley's hesitations on pp. 111–113 and 278–279. Brown, *Epistles*, has an Appendix II entitled 'Cerinthus' (pp. 766–771).

John's opponents'. At the same time, Marshall accepts that they had 'probably adopted a view like that of Cerinthus' (p. 21).

Other contemporary scholars have distanced themselves further from this suggestion. They are agreed on two preliminaries. First, they consider the link with Cerinthus somewhat anachronistic, and secondly they feel more sympathy towards John's adversaries than he did. They find his dismissal of them as 'antichrists' and accomplices of the devil altogether too harsh. Brown refers to them by the neutral word 'secessionists', while Houlden and Grayston call them 'dissidents' (which in contemporary usage is usually an honourable term). What was their position?

Houlden, who writes of the adventurous, speculative quality of the Fourth Gospel (p. 19), characterizes the dissidents as wanting to go further in that direction, while the letters are 'a rearguard action' to reassert traditional doctrine. He finds their theology conservative, style repetitious and grammar monotonous. The elder is too reactionary to tolerate diversity; so the dissidents drop out. Grayston similarly sees John's letters as 'a defense of the (Johannine) tradition against the view of a dissident group which had left the community' (p. 3). He thinks they combined a claim to be 'anointed by the Holy One' with a denial that Jesus had been similarly anointed. They are 'no longer interested in Jesus come in the flesh because they themselves possess the Spirit' (pp. 78–79). They are convinced that 'by possessing the Spirit they can dispense with Jesus' (p. 134).

Brown, who describes himself as having had 'a quarter–century love affair' with John's Gospel and letters, has engaged in some very ingenious 'detective work' in attempting to reconstruct the history of the Johannine community (Community, pp. 5, 7). He too attributes the letters to the life-situation which followed the writing of the Gospel. Not only does the first letter presuppose in its readers, as Westcott argued, a familiar acquaintance with the teaching of the Gospel; it reveals the 'internal struggles' of two groups within the Johannine community in relation to the Gospel. They were not divided in their acceptance of the Gospel's teaching, but in their understanding of it. 'Both parties knew the proclamation of Christianity available to us through the Fourth Gospel, but they interpreted it differently' (*Community*, p. 106; *cf. Epistles*, p. 69). In *The Community of the Beloved Disciple* Brown suggests that the four 'areas of dispute' between John and the secessionists were 'christology, ethics, eschatology and pneumatology' (pp. 109–144), but in his *The Epistles of John* he focuses on the first two. (See especially *Epistles*, pp. 71–79, and 79–86.) In their Christology both groups accepted the Gospel's exalted teaching about the pre-existent Son of God, but the secessionists 'negated the importance of Jesus' (Brown's rendering of 1 Jn. 4:3), by denying not the reality of the incarnation but its significance for salvation. To them 'the very coming or sending of the Son of God, not his life or ministry or death, was what brought salvation' (*Epistles*, p. 180). As for ethics, the secessionists taught perfectionism, which indeed (Brown argues) the Gospel encouraged by its teaching on receiving the Spirit, overcoming the world and being kept from the evil one; what John criticized was 'their failure to draw behavioural implications from the claimed relationship to God' (*Epistles*, p. 80). Brown then sees the 'aftermath' of the Johannine community's internal struggle: the secessionists 'drifted off into various "heretical" movements' like the 'Cerinthianism, Montanism, docetism and/or gnosticism' of the second century, while John's adherents (whom one might style the 'loyalists'), 'were swallowed up by the "great church" ', which Bishop Ignatius of Antioch at the beginning of the second century called 'the catholic church' (*Epistles*, pp. 103–115; *cf.* also pp. 69–71).

Brown admits that the attempt to reconstruct the secessionists' views from John's polemics against them is a precarious procedure. The resulting reconstruction is bound to contain a large element of conjecture. His own 'theory', as he modestly calls it, will doubtless continue to be debated. For myself I have to confess that it has not dislodged me from the more traditional view. I would prefer to conclude that, over against the Christological heresy, the moral indifferentism and the arrogant lovelessness of an embryonic Cerinthian Gnosticism, John lays his emphasis on three marks of authentic Christianity, namely belief in Jesus as the Christ come in the flesh, obedience to the commands of God and brotherly love.

III. MESSAGE

The middle and end of the twentieth century are an epoch of fundamental insecurity. Everything is changing; nothing is stable. New nations have constantly been coming to birth. New social and political patterns are continually evolving. The very survival of civilization is in doubt before the threat of a nuclear war. These external insecurities are reflected in the world of the mind and of the spirit. Even the Christian church, which has received 'a kingdom that cannot be shaken' and is charged to proclaim him who is 'the same yesterday and today and for ever' (Heb. 12:28; 13:8), now often speaks its message softly, shyly and without conviction. There is a widespread distrust of dogmatism and a preference for agnosticism or free thought. Many church members are filled with uncertainty and confusion.

Against this background, to read the letters of John is to enter another world altogether, for its marks are assurance, knowledge, confidence and boldness. The predominant theme of these letters is Christian certainty. Their characteristic verbs are *ginōskein*, 'to perceive' (twenty-five times) and *eidenai*, 'to know' (fifteen times), while a characteristic noun is *parrēsia*, 'confidence of attitude' or 'boldness of speech'. The certainty of Christian people is twofold – objective (that the Christian religion is true) and subjective (that they themselves have been born of God and possess eternal life). Both are expounded by John, who takes it for granted that this double assurance is right and healthy. His teaching about these certainties, their nature and the grounds on which they are built, urgently needs to be heard and heeded today.

A. CERTAINTY ABOUT CHRIST

John asserts of Christians, as a result of the anointing which we have received, that we 'all know' (2:20), absolutely. This does not mean, of course, that we know all things, as the AV (following an alternative reading) mistakenly suggests, for some things God has not yet revealed (*e.g.* 3:2). Nevertheless, we 'know the truth' (2:21; *cf.* 2 Jn. 1 and 4:6), which includes the truth about the world and its condition (5:19; *cf.* 2:18; 3:15), and about ourselves, our duty and destiny (2:10–11, 29; 3:2; 5:18). Above all, we know the truth about God and Christ. 'We know . . . that the Son of God has come and has given us understanding, so that we may know him who is true' (5:20). We thus know both God (2:13–14; 4:6–7) and Christ (3:6; *cf.* 3:1). We know, moreover, that the cause of Christ's coming was love (3:16; 4:16) and its purpose to 'take away our sins' (3:5).

But how do we know these things, especially who Jesus Christ is and why he came? John's clear answer is in three stages. First, there is the historical event, Christ's being 'sent' (4:9–10, 14), his 'coming' (5:20), his 'manifestation' or 'appearing' (*ephanerōthē* in 1:2; 3:5, 8; 4:9). His coming was 'in the flesh' (4:2; 2 Jn. 7) and 'by water and blood' (5:6). That is, it was real, and involved him in the definite historical experiences of birth, baptism and death. Next, there is the apostolic witness. The event did not pass unnoticed. The one who came in the flesh was seen, heard and touched, so that those who saw could testify from their own first-hand experience (1:1–3; 4:14). Thirdly, there is the 'anointing' of the Holy Spirit, by whom we are taught and therefore know (2:20, 27; *cf.* 3:24; 4:13). This testimony of the Spirit is within the believer (5:10) and corroborates the external witness of 'the water and the blood' (5:6, 8–9).

The ground of our certainty about Christ has not changed. The fact that we read the letters of John in the twentieth century rather than the first makes no difference. The Christian religion is still firmly attached to the historical event of Christ and the witness which the apostles bore to it. In this 'teaching of Christ' we must 'continue' (2 Jn. 9). To advance beyond it will inevitably lead us into error and therefore into ruin. The duty of Christian ministers today is to follow the apostle John, not the false teachers. We are not to lead the congregation into novel doctrines, but to recall them to what they have heard 'from the beginning' (2:7, 24; 3:11; 2 Jn. 5). Further, those who believe in the historical Jesus on the unique testimony of the apostolic eyewitnesses, which is now preserved in the New Testament and expounded by the church, are granted the contemporary and confirmatory witness of the Spirit within themselves (5:10).

B. CERTAINTY ABOUT ETERNAL LIFE

The kind of Christian knowledge which is distinctively treated in these letters, however, is subjective as well as objective. It concerns not only the truth about God and Christ but also the truth about our own Christian standing, which John describes by four favourite expressions. First, we know 'that we . . . know him' (2:3; cf. 5:20). Secondly, we know that 'we are in him' and 'that we live in him and he in us' (2:5; 4:13; cf. 3:24). Thirdly, we know 'that we are children of God' (5:19; cf. 3:19, 'belong to the truth'). Fourthly, we know 'that we have passed from death to life' and that therefore we have eternal life (3:14; 5:13). To be a Christian, then, in the language of John, is to have been born of God, to know God, to live in him, and to enjoy that intimate, personal communion with him which is eternal life (5:20; cf. Jn. 17:3). Of this heavenly birth and life-giving relationship we have no doubt. Indeed, John declares that his purpose in writing his first letter is that those who 'believe' may also 'know' (5:13).

John's argument is double-edged. If he seeks to bring believers to the knowledge that they have eternal life, he is equally at pains to show that unbelievers have not received life. His purpose is to destroy the false assurance of the counterfeit as well as to confirm the right assurance of the genuine. He is conscious throughout the letters of these two companies, 'you' and 'they' (e.g. 2:18–20; 4:4–5). The same two groups exist today. Some are cocksure and boast of what they may well not possess; others are conventional churchgoers who have no assurance of salvation, and even say it is presumptuous to claim any. But there is a true Christian assurance, which is neither arrogant nor presumptuous, but is on the contrary, as these letters show, the plainly revealed will of God for his people (5:13). So John urges his readers to examine themselves, and he supplies tests by which they (and we) may do so.

Law called his studies in the first letter *The Tests of Life* (1885), because in it are given what he terms 'the three cardinal tests' by which we may judge whether we possess eternal life or not. The first is theological, whether we believe that Jesus is 'the Son of God' (3:23; 5:5, 10, 13), the Christ 'come in the flesh' (4:2; 2 Jn. 7). No system of teaching which denies either the eternal divine pre-existence of Jesus or the historical incarnation of the Christ can be accepted as Christian. 'No-one who denies the Son has the Father' (2:23). The second test is moral, whether we are practising righteousness and keeping the commands of God. Sin is shown to be wholly incompatible with the nature of God as light (1:5), the mission of the Son to take away sins (3:5) and the new birth of the believer (3:9). Now, as then, any claim to mystical experience without moral conduct is to be rejected (1:6). The third test is social, whether we love one another. Since God is love and all love comes from God, it is clear that a loveless person does not know him (4:7–8).

It is important to see that John's three tests are not arbitrarily selected. On the contrary, they possess an inner coherence, which he particularly unfolds in the second half of chapter 4 in relation to the gospel. This in brief is that 'the Father has sent his Son to be the Saviour of the world' (4:14), an affirmation which implies the divine-human person of the Son who was sent, the love of the Father who sent him, and the righteousness of those who receive his salvation. The three tests belong to each other also, because faith, love and holiness are all the works of the Holy Spirit. It is only if God has given us his Spirit that we are able to believe, to love and to obey (3:24; 4:13). So everyone who believes that Jesus is the Christ, and loves, and does righteousness, thereby gives evidence that he has been 'born of God'. This identical expression occurs in the Greek text of 2:29; 4:7 and 5:1. 'The tenses sufficiently show', writes Law, referring to the change from the present to the perfect, 'that in each case the Divine Begetting is the necessary antecedent to the human activity.' Further, if belief, holiness and love betray a birth of God, they are marks also of the continuing reciprocal indwelling of God and his people (3:24; 4:12–13, 16; 4:15).

To fail to pass these tests is to stand self-exposed. We may still claim to be Christian, to know God and to have life, but John insists that our verbal profession is negatived by the facts (*e.g.* 1:6, 8, 10; 2:4, 6, 9; 4:20). Indeed, he who says he knows and loves God, while disobeying his command or hating his brother, or denying that Jesus is the Christ, is 'a liar' (2:4; 4:20; *cf.* 2:22). On the other hand, 'this is how we know' that we know God, are in him and have life, if we keep his commands, love our brothers and sisters and believe in Jesus Christ (2:3–4; 3:14, 18–19, 24).

A fresh certainty about Christ and about eternal life, based upon the grounds which John gives, can still lead Christian people into that boldness of approach to God and of testimony to the world which is as sorely needed as it is sadly missing in the church today.

1 JOHN: ANALYSIS

1 JOHN: COMMENTARY

I. THE PREFACE (1:1–4)

The opening of the letter is remarkable in that it lacks any salutation or personal reference. In this it differs from all the other New Testament letters except Hebrews. For the bearing of this on the question of authorship see Introduction, p. 17. All commentators have found this first paragraph involved in syntax and abstruse in meaning. It is, in fact, a 'grammatical tangle' (Dodd). We must try to disentangle it. The main verb, which does not occur until verse 3 (*apangellomen, we proclaim*), shows that the preface is concerned essentially with the apostolic proclamation of the gospel – what it was, and why it was made. In outline the first sentence begins with four relative clauses in apposition to each other (*That which was from the beginning, which we have heard, which we have seen with our eyes, which we have looked at and our hands have touched*), followed by the phrase *concerning the Word of life*. Verse 2 is a parenthesis, explaining how that which was from the beginning could have been heard, seen and handled, namely because *the life appeared*, and elaborates what is meant by *life* in the expression *Word of life*. This parenthesis so interrupts the flow of the sentence that verse 3 opens with the resumptive relative clause *what we have seen and heard* before we finally reach the main verb, *we proclaim to you*. The rest of verse 3, and verse 4, describe the purposes, immediate and ultimate, of the apostolic proclamation, namely, *so that you also may have fellowship with us* and *to make our joy complete*. In brief, therefore, and omitting the parenthesis of verse 2, the sentence might be paraphrased: 'We proclaim to you, concerning the word of life, what was from the beginning, which we have seen, heard and touched, and the objects of our proclamation are fellowship and joy.'

Before considering the preface in detail, two questions about the phrase *concerning the Word of life* (*peri tou logou tēs zōēs*) need to be discussed. The first is whether *logos* is here personal or impersonal, that is whether it is the semi-technical designation of the Son found in the Prologue to the Fourth Gospel or whether it is rather a synonym for 'the message of the gospel' (Acts 15:7). The second question is whether the clause introduced by *peri* is in apposition to the four relative clauses which precede it, or whether it qualifies them (or they it). For a detailed consideration of these questions see Additional Note: 'The Word of life' (p. 72). The conclusion reached there is that *the Word of life* is not a title for the Son, the Word or *Logos* of the Fourth Gospel Prologue, but an expression for the gospel, the message of life; and, secondly, that this 'word of life' is the general subject of the apostolic proclamation, the particular emphasis of which concerns *that which was from the beginning, which we have heard . . . seen . . . and . . . touched*. In other words, what the apostle stresses in his proclamation of the gospel is the historical manifestation of the eternal.

We are now in a position to approach the preface as a whole. Its noble sweep unfolds the purpose of God from eternity to eternity, from *that which was from the beginning* (1) to the fullness of *joy* (4) experienced by Christian believers, which will not be finally consummated until the end. Five stages are discernible in the unfolding of this divine purpose, indicated by the words *beginning* (*archēs*, 1), *appeared* (*ephanerōthē*, twice in v. 2), *we proclaim* (*apangellomen*, 3), *fellowship* (*koinōnia*, twice in v. 3) and *joy* (*chara*, 4).

A. THE ETERNAL PRE-EXISTENCE

Dodd interprets the opening phrase of the beginning of the gospel. The author is announcing, he says, 'what has always ("from the beginning") been true about the word of life'. In other words, he is not introducing 'any innovation or afterthought' but proclaiming 'the unchanged, original content of the Gospel, over against novel forms of doctrine'.[1] Now, it is true that 'the beginning' is used in the Fourth Gospel with reference to the beginning of Christ's ministry (Jn. 6:64; 15:27; 16:4), which was virtually the beginning of the Christian era, and in the letters with reference to the individual's Christian experience (2:7, 24; 3:11; 2 Jn. 6).

Nevertheless, the similar expression at the opening of the Prologue to the Gospel ('In the beginning was the Word') suggests that here too the beginning of all things is meant. The phrase is so used of the eternal God in 2:13–14 and, with a less clear time reference, to the devil sinning 'from the beginning' in 3:8. Moreover, since the words precede the clauses *which we have heard . . . seen . . . touched*, we should expect the meaning to precede them logically too. The eternal Son was before his historical manifestation; the preaching of the gospel came after. Finally, the expression is parallel to that in the parenthesis of verse 2 *the eternal life, which was with the Father*. In both phrases the verb is imperfect (*ēn*) and expresses the Son's eternal pre-existence. The first says that he *was from the beginning*; the second that he *was with the Father*, just as in the Gospel Prologue it is written first 'In the beginning was the Word', and secondly 'and the Word was with God'. Since eternal life is to know God (Jn. 17:3), he who is eternal life does not enjoy immortal solitude but conscious, continuous, intimate communion as Son with the Father.

B. THE HISTORICAL MANIFESTATION

The contrast between the first and the next three relative clauses with which the letter begins is dramatic. The eternal entered time and appeared to human beings. The Word became flesh and thus presented himself to people's three higher senses (hearing, sight and touch). The four relative clauses proceed 'from the most abstract to the most material aspect of divine

---

[1]Dodd adds in a footnote, however, that it is not necessary to decide between this and 'the absolute Beginning of the universe', since 'the Gospel is by its nature, as the Word of God, an "eternal Gospel" (Rev. xiv. 6)'.

revelation' (Westcott). To have *heard* was not enough; people 'heard' God's voice in the Old Testament. To have *seen* was more compelling. But to have *touched* was the conclusive proof of material reality, that the Word 'became flesh, and lived for a while among us'. This word *touched* (*epsēlaphēsan*), the climax of the four relative clauses, describes more than a momentary contact. ' "*Psēlaphan*" is to *grope* or *feel after* in order to find, like a blind man or one in the dark; hence to *handle, touch* . . . It may also be used in the sense of "examine closely" ' (Brooke). Although this 'touching' is the climax of the sentence, the emphasis is on the 'seeing' (which is repeated four times in the first three verses), presumably because it is sight in particular which qualifies people to witness (2). Two verbs are used for sight, *horan* three times and *theasthai* once. 'If *blepein* is to "look", and *horan* to "see", *theasthai* is to "behold" intelligently, so as to grasp the meaning and significance of that which comes within our vision' (Brooke). This is the verb used in the fourth clause, where it is associated with *our hands have touched* by one relative (*ho*). Whereas the two earlier verbs *have heard* and *have seen* are in the perfect tense, suggesting the abiding possession which results from the hearing and seeing, these two are both aorists, and seem therefore to refer to a particular time, perhaps after the resurrection, when the apostles had an opportunity both to gaze thoughtfully upon the Lord Jesus and to handle him (*cf*. Lk. 24:39; Jn. 20:26–29). These two verbs express a 'definite investigation by the observer' (Westcott). The latter is also used in John 1:14, where John writes that the glory of the Son, the Word become flesh, was 'seen'.

The proclamation of what had been heard, seen and felt was part of *the Word of life*, the gospel of Christ. It would seem most natural to take the genitive *of life* as indicating the content of *the Word*, as in Philippians 2:16 (*cf*. Jn. 6:68). The gospel announces and offers life in Christ. Compare 'the word of the kingdom' (Mt. 13:19, RSV), 'the word of this salvation' (Acts 13:26, AV), 'the word of reconciliation' (2 Cor. 5:19, AV), and similar expressions used in the New Testament to describe the gospel. Nevertheless, the genitive *of life* in the Fourth Gospel means 'life-giving' (*e.g*. 'light of life', 'bread of life' in 8:12; 6:35, 48; *cf*. 'living water' in Jn. 4:10–11 and 'water of life' in Rev. 21:6; 22:1, 17). Perhaps it is not necessary to choose between these alternatives, however, since 'the revelation proclaims that which it includes; it has, announces, gives life' (Westcott).

This audible, visible and tangible apprehension of that which was from the beginning was possible to human beings only because (*for*) *the life appeared*. The aorist verb *ephanerōthē*, indicating the historic fact of the incarnation, is repeated twice, at the beginning and end of the parenthesis. First it occurs absolutely; then *to us* is added. We could not have seen the one who was eternally with the Father unless he had taken the initiative deliberately to manifest himself. Human beings can apprehend only what God is pleased to make known.

This stress on the material manifestation of Christ to human ears, eyes and hands is of course directed primarily against the heretics who were troubling the church. The followers of Cerinthus are shown that *the Word of life*, the gospel of Christ, is concerned with the historical incarnation of the eternal Son. He who is from the beginning is he whom the apostles heard, saw and touched. It is impossible to distinguish between Jesus and the Christ, the historical and the eternal. They are the same person, who is both God and man. Such an emphasis on the historical revelation of the invisible and intangible is still needed today, not least by the scientist trained in the empirical method, the radical who regards much in the Gospels as 'myths' (but you cannot 'demythologize' the incarnation without thereby contradicting it) and the mystic who becomes preoccupied with his subjective religious experience to the neglect of God's objective self-revelation in Christ.

C. THE AUTHORITATIVE PROCLAMATION

The historical appearance of the eternal life was proclaimed, not monopolized. The revelation was given to the few for the sake of the many. They were to declare it to the world. The manifestation *to us* (2) becomes a proclamation *to you* (3). John desires his readers to enjoy 'the same advantageous position which he himself and his fellow-apostles enjoyed, as regards the knowledge of God in Christ' (Candlish).

John uses two verbs to describe the apostolic announcement, *we . . . testify* (*martyroumen*, 2) and *we proclaim* (*apangellomen*, 2 and 3). The apostolic ministry involved both a testimony and a proclamation. Both words imply an authority, but of a different kind. *Martyreisthai* indicates the authority of experience. To testify is an activity which belongs properly to an eyewitness. He must *be* a witness before he is competent to *bear* witness. (Compare Lk. 24:48, 'You are witnesses of these things', with Acts 1:8, 'you will be my witnesses'.) True witnesses speak not of what they have gathered second-hand from others, but of what they have themselves personally seen and heard. It is for this reason that the verbs to 'see' and to 'testify' are so commonly associated with each other in the New Testament, as they are in verse 2. (For the bearing of this on the authorship of the letter see Introduction, pp. 30 ff.) Since John introduces the letter with relative clauses describing what had been heard, seen and felt, concerning the Word of life, it is natural that the first verb he uses for the apostolic preaching is the word *we . . . testify*.

If *martyreisthai* is the word of experience, *apangellein* indicates the authority of commission. The experience is personal; the commission is derived. In order to testify, the apostles must have seen and heard Christ for themselves; in order to proclaim, they must have received a commission from him. It is true that, although *apangellomen* occurs in verses 2 and 3, the verb in verse 5 is *anangellomen*, and that *apangellein* means strictly 'to report with reference to the source from which the message comes', while *anangellein* is 'to report with reference to the persons addressed' (Law, Brooke). But it is also significant that in verse 5, where *anangellein* is used, the phrase 'we have heard from him' (*ap' autou*) is added. The verbs in both passages, therefore, the one from its own prefix and the other from its explicit additional clause, seem to direct the reader's attention to the source from which the message was derived, namely Christ himself (*cf.* 1 Cor. 2:13; 11:23; 15:3). He not only showed himself to the disciples to qualify them as *eyewitnesses*, but gave them an authoritative commission as *apostles* to preach the gospel. Our author insists that he possesses these necessary credentials. Possessing them, he is very bold. Having heard, seen and touched the Lord Jesus, he now testifies to him. Having received a commission, he proclaims the gospel with authority. For the Christian message is neither a philosophical speculation, nor a tentative suggestion, nor a modest contribution to religious thought, but a confident affirmation by those whose experience and commission have qualified them to make it.

D. THE COMMUNAL FELLOWSHIP

The proclamation was not an end in itself; its purpose, immediate and ultimate, is now defined. The immediate is *fellowship* (*koinōnia*, 3), and the ultimate *joy* (*chara*, 4). The fellowship created by Christ in the days of his flesh within the apostolic band, and deepened by the coming of the Spirit at Pentecost, was not to be limited to them. It was to extend to the next generation (*that you also may have fellowship with us*), and so on down the ages. 'The last of the apostles points to the unbroken succession of the heritage of Faith' (Westcott).

The purpose of the proclamation of the gospel is, therefore, stated in terms not of salvation but of *fellowship*. Yet, properly understood, this is the meaning of salvation in its widest embrace, including reconciliation to God in Christ (*fellowship . . . with the Father and with his Son, Jesus Christ*), holiness of life (see v. 6), and incorporation in the church (*you . . . with us*). This fellowship is the meaning of eternal life (Jn. 17:3). Just as the Son, who is *the eternal life*, was (eternally) with the Father (2), so he purposes that we should have fellowship with them and with each other (*cf.* Jn. 17:21–22). 'Fellowship' is a specifically Christian word and denotes that common participation in the grace of God, the salvation of Christ and the indwelling Spirit which is the spiritual birthright of all believers. It is our common possession of God, Father, Son and Holy Spirit, which makes us one. So John could not have written *that you also may have fellowship with us* without adding *and our fellowship is with the Father and with his Son, Jesus Christ*, since our fellowship with each other arises from, and depends on, our fellowship with God.

This truth, although expressed in different language, is an echo of our Lord's prayer 'that all of them may be one' and that they may 'also be in us' (Jn. 17:21). As there our oneness depends on our being in them, so here our fellowship with each other is impossible without fellowship with the Father and the Son. John does not here mention the fellowship of the Holy Spirit, which occurs twice in Paul's letters (2 Cor. 13:14; Phil. 2:1), no doubt because the false teachers against whom he is writing make him concentrate on the Son, whom their heresy dishonoured, and on the Father whom they thereby forfeited. He here states not just that our fellowship is with the Father through the Son, and that we may have the Father only by confessing the Son (2:23), but that our fellowship is both *with the Father and with his Son*. The phrase 'marks emphatically the distinction and equality between the Son and the Father' (Plummer). The use of the full title *his Son, Jesus Christ* (as in 3:23; 5:20, and 2 Jn. 3; *cf.* 1 Cor. 1:9) also, perhaps, contains a side-glance at the heretics, who denied that the man Jesus was the Christ, the Son of God.

This statement of the apostolic objective in the proclamation of the gospel, namely a human fellowship arising spontaneously from a divine fellowship, is a rebuke to much of our modern evangelism and church life. We cannot be content with an evangelism which does not lead to the drawing of converts into the church, nor with a church life whose principle of cohesion is a superficial social camaraderie instead of a spiritual fellowship with the Father and with his Son Jesus Christ. The doctrine and behaviour of the heretics were threatening to disrupt the church; the true *angelia* ('message', 5), on the other hand, produces a true *koinōnia*.

E. THE COMPLETED JOY

Verse 4, like verse 3, contains a final clause introduced by *hina*, meaning 'in order that'. In verse 3 the clause depends on *we proclaim*, and in verse 4 on *write*. Do these verbs refer to the same message, in one case oral and in the other written, or are they different messages? Most commentators seem to take the proclamation of verses 1–3 to refer to the author's 'whole apostolic ministry' (Westcott) and especially his written Gospel (Ebrard), and the writing mentioned in verse 4 to his present letter. 'The preceding verses have reference to the writer's habitual oral proclamation of the Gospel, or to its literary embodiment. These words now introduce the Epistle itself' (Law). Westcott also adds that, whereas the relative *ho* (*that which* in v. 1 and *what* in verse 3) denotes 'the apostolic message . . . in its unity', *tauta* (literally 'these things') in verse 4 points by contrast to certain special aspects of it. At the same time, the distinction can be overpressed. Verse 4 is the first occasion in the letter when the adjective *houtos* ('this') occurs. It comes frequently later in such expressions as 'this is' (*houtos estin* and *touto estin*) and 'by this we . . .' (*en toutō, ek toutou* and *dia touto, etc.*). In nearly every case it is uncertain whether the phrase points backwards to what has just been written or forwards to what is about to be written. According to Brooke 'the reference forward would seem to be his prevailing custom' (*e.g.* 1:4; 2:3; 3:8, 10, 16, 23, 24; 4:2, 9, 13, 17; 5:4, 11, 14). But it is not always so (*e.g.* 2:22; 4:6; 5:20, and especially 2:26 and 5:13, where the similar phrase 'I write these things' occurs and in each case refers to the previous paragraph). Moreover, when the reference is forward, it points to what *immediately* follows. It is possible, therefore, and seems to me more natural, to take *we write this* (4) as referring not to the whole letter which follows but to the statements just made in the preface about the apostolic proclamation. In this case *we proclaim* (3) and *we write* (4) refer to the same message.

The purpose of the writing is now given. It is *to make our joy complete* (NIV, RV, RSV) or *to make your joy complete* (AV, NIV mg.). It is difficult to decide between these alternatives. Indeed, since both are well supported, Westcott declares that 'a positive decision on the reading here is impossible'. Johannine usage is no more determinative than the evidence of the manuscripts, since John 15:11 (*cf.* 16:24) has 'that *your* joy may be complete', while 2 John 12 has 'so that *our* joy may be complete'.

So what about the sense in its context? If, as seems probable, John begins verse 4 with '*we* write these things' (*tauta graphomen hēmeis*), not with 'we write these things *to you*' (*tauta graphomen hymin*), then one would expect his emphatic 'we' to be contrasted with 'you' or 'your', as throughout this opening paragraph, not to mention the rest of the letter. In this case, the conclusion 'to make *your* joy complete' would be more likely. On the other hand, in the previous verse (3) John clearly moves from 'we' to 'you' to 'our', so that a parallel movement of thought would be natural in verse 4. Just as the purpose of the proclamation is *so that you . . . may have fellowship with us*, so the purpose of the writing is *to make our joy complete*. The fellowship and the joy are both to be a common possession between the apostle and his readers. This 'seems to suit best the generous solicitude of the author, whose own joy would be incomplete unless his readers shared it' (Metzger, p. 708). Brooke quotes John 4:36 in this connection, where Jesus spoke of the sower and the reaper rejoicing together. And NEB captures the sense well by translating 'we write this in order that the joy of us all may be complete'.

And what is the secret of fullness of joy, 'the complete and perfect felicity which we obtain from the Gospel' (Calvin)? It is in the fellowship which the proclamation creates; for if the immediate purpose of the proclamation is the establishment of fellowship, the ultimate purpose is the completion of joy. This is the divine order – *angelia, koinōnia, chara*.

The idea of fullness of joy is not uncommon in the Johannine literature (*cf.* Jn. 3:29; 15:11; 16:24; 17:13; 2 Jn. 12), and it is significant that in each case there is some allusion to the subject of fellowship with God or with each other. Yet 'complete joy' is not possible in this world of sin, because perfect fellowship is not possible. So verse 4 must be understood also to look beyond this life to the life of heaven. Then consummated fellowship will bring completed joy. 'You will fill me with joy in your presence, with eternal pleasures at your right hand' (Ps. 16:11). It is to this ultimate end that he who *was from the beginning . . . appeared* in time, and that what the apostles heard, saw and touched they have proclaimed to us. The substance of the apostolic proclamation was the historical manifestation of the eternal; its purpose was and is a fellowship with one another, which is based on fellowship with the Father and the Son and which issues in fullness of joy.

Additional Note: 'The Word of life' (1:1)

A. The meaning of 'logos'

The Greek word *logos* can be translated either as 'reason' or as 'word' or 'speech'. It is used in the Prologue to the Fourth Gospel as a designation of the Son who is the revelation of the Father.[1] That the word is also a descriptive title of the eternal Son in the preface to the first letter has been held by many commentators. Thus, Moffatt transliterates the Greek word into English and coins the expression 'Logos of Life'. There is certainly a parallel to be drawn between the Gospel and the letter, although the Prologue is considerably longer and more elaborate than the preface. Both open with a reference to the beginning (vv. 1–2/v. 1); both speak of the Logos in connection with the Father and with life (vv. 1, 4/vv. 1–2); both declare that the eternal entered history (vv. 10–11, 14/v. 2); both add that the divine manifestation was seen (v. 14, 18/vv. 1–3); both mention testimony resulting from what people saw (vv. 7–8, 15/v. 2); both speak of Christ as the Father's Son (vv. 14, 18/v. 3); both describe the result of responding to Christ in terms of a new relationship with God (vv. 12–13/v. 3). And yet the similarity between the two passages can be overdrawn. The general sequence of thought is the same, and there are verbal echoes, but Westcott is right in saying that 'the two passages are complementary and not parallel'. Two differences must be mentioned:

First, in the Prologue 'the Word' is used absolutely four times (three times in v. 1 and once in v. 14), while in the preface the phrase is 'the Word of life'.

Secondly, it is plain from the parenthesis which immediately follows the use of this expression (v. 2) that the emphasis in it in the author's mind is not on 'Word' but on 'life', for the word *logos* is not used in the preface, or indeed in the whole letter, whereas 'life' is repeated twice in verse 2 and five times more in the rest of the letter (2:25; 3:14; 5:11–12, 20). It is significant that

[1]See R. V. G. Tasker, *The Gospel According to St John*, Tyndale New Testament Commentary (Tyndale Press, 1960), pp. 41–42.

what the author writes is not 'concerning the Word of life – the word became flesh' but 'concerning the Word of life – the life appeared'. What he means by 'the eternal life, which was with the Father' is clear: it is a plain personification of the Son. It cannot be otherwise, because the expression 'with the Father' (*pros ton patera*) implies personal communion. Besides, both Gospel and letter declare not only that life is in Christ (Jn. 1:4; 1 Jn. 5:11–12) but that he is himself the life (Jn. 11:25; 14:6; *cf.* 5:26; 1 Jn. 5:20). It is this life, he says, which was eternally in communion with the Father and historically appeared to us, which we proclaim.

Now what is stated briefly in verse 2 as the subject of the proclamation is stated more elaborately in verses 1 and 3. John is concerned to make known what is eternal ('that which was from the beginning') and historical ('which we have heard . . . seen . . . touched') concerning 'the Word of life'. What then does 'the Word of life' mean? Westcott renders it 'the revelation of Life' and understands it as referring generally to 'the whole message from God to man, which tells of life, or, perhaps, out of which life springs, which beginning to be spoken by the prophets, was at last fully proclaimed by one who was His Son'. With this Brooke agrees. Dodd is more particular and translates the phrase 'the Gospel', since 'the word of life' in Philippians 2:16 (although without the definite article), 'the . . . message of this new life' in Acts 5:20 and 'the words of eternal life' (Jn. 6:68) are similar expressions for the gospel. But in view of the personal meaning given to 'life' in verse 2, we desire to be more particular still, and say that 'the Word of life' means 'the gospel *of Christ*'. What John proclaims is Christ, who is the life (2), and in this proclamation concerning the word of life he lays his emphasis on his eternal being and historical manifestation (1, 3).

B. *The meaning of* 'peri'

In discussing the precise meaning of the expression 'the Word of life' we have already begun to solve the second problem which concerns the relation of the phrase 'concerning the Word of life' to the whole paragraph in which it is embedded. Moffatt and other commentators have taken the phrase *peri tou logou tēs zōēs* as being in apposition to the four preceding relative clauses and as adding another aspect of the proclamation to the four already mentioned. The proclamation would then be concerned equally with 'that which was from the beginning', with that which was 'heard', 'seen' and 'touched', and with 'the Word of life'. But this is very awkward and is rejected by Westcott, Law, Dodd and others, both because it would bring four neuter relative pronouns into apposition to the masculine *logos*, and because it pays no attention to the change of construction from relative clauses to the use of the preposition *peri*.

The alternative is to take *peri tou logou tēs zōēs* as an independent adverbial clause. In this way, 'the Word of life' becomes the 'subject' (Westcott, Law) of the announcement, while the four relative clauses 'declare the substance' of it (Law). Similarly, 'the clause "concerning the word of life" indicates the *theme* of the announcement, and the clauses "that which was from the beginning . . . our hands felt" state the *contents* of the announcement' (Dodd). It is essentially about eternal life in Christ that John is concerned (Jn. 20:31; 1 Jn. 5:12–13). What he seems to be saying here is: 'In our proclamation concerning the message of life in Christ we concentrate on the historical appearance of the eternal. We do this partly because we are uniquely qualified to be witnesses to the incarnation. Our own eyes have seen, and our own hands have touched him. We have heard and looked at him for ourselves. Or, to put it otherwise, the very life itself (with which our message is concerned), the eternal life which was eternally with the Father, appeared to us, and we saw it. So we testify to it. Our announcement is a testimony. We also make this our particular emphasis because of the false teaching of the heretics who deny the truth of the incarnation either by affirming that the body of Jesus was not real (the docetists) or by distinguishing the divine *Logos* or Spirit or Christ from the man Jesus upon whom he came at the baptism and from whom he departed before the cross. In contradiction of these errors we stress that his body was real (because we heard, saw and touched him) and that this historical Jesus was the same person as the eternal Word.' This apostolic purpose would explain the clumsy syntax which leaves the main verb to near the end of the sentence and begins with the emphatic clauses 'that which was from the beginning, which we have heard . . . seen . . . and . . . touched'. It is these aspects of the Word of life that the proclamation underlines. 'St. John employs the neuter (*that which . . . which* . . .) as the most comprehensive expression to cover the attributes, words and works' (Plummer) of the incarnate life.

II. THE APOSTOLIC MESSAGE AND ITS MORAL IMPLICATIONS (1:5 – 2:2)

5. The link between this paragraph and the foregoing preface is in the word *message*. John has already used the verb *apangellomen* ('we proclaim', v. 3); he now uses the similar verb *anangellomen*, *we . . . declare*, in conjunction with the noun *angelia*, *message*. This message has not been invented by himself or the other apostles, but is what they *have heard from him*. It is unlikely that he is quoting any specific saying of Jesus that *God is light*, as no such saying has survived. Rather he is summarizing the Lord's teaching according to the emphasis he gives to it in his own Gospel. 'The Word of life' (v. 1), with which his proclamation is concerned, can be condensed into the single great affirmation *God is light; in him there is no darkness at all* (*cf.* Jn. 1:4). The statement is absolute and anarthrous. The Logos is 'the light' (*to phōs*); but God is *light* (*phōs*), just as he is 'love' and 'spirit' and 'consuming fire'. In none of these statements is the article used (1 Jn. 4:8, 16; Jn. 4:24; Heb. 12:29).

Of the statements about the essential being of God, none is more comprehensive than *God is light*.[1] It is his nature to reveal himself, as it is the property of light to shine; and the revelation is of perfect purity and unutterable majesty. We are to think of God as a personal being, infinite in all his perfections, transcendent, 'the high and lofty One . . . he who lives for ever, whose name is holy' (Is. 57:15), yet who desires to be known and has revealed himself. The miserable errors of the heretics were due to their ignorance of God's ethical self-revelation as light. They could never have laid claim to a private, esoteric

[1]For the symbolic use of 'light' in Scripture, and particularly in the Johannine literature, see the Additional Note overleaf.

gnōsis into which they had been initiated if their conception of God had been of one who is light, diffusive, shining forth and manifesting himself, in whom *there is no darkness at all*, no secrecy, no hiding in the shadows. And if God is also light in the sense of possessing an absolute moral perfection, their claim to know him and have fellowship with him despite their indifference to morality is seen to be sheer nonsense, as the author goes on to demonstrate.

Additional Note: The symbolism of light in Scripture (1:5)

The categories of light and darkness belong to the universal language of religious symbolism. They are common to most religions, not least the revealed religion of the Bible.[1] They are used metaphorically in Scripture in several senses. Intellectually, light is truth and darkness ignorance or error. Morally, light is purity and darkness evil. One or two examples will suffice to illustrate this double use. God's self-revelation through the law and the prophets is described in terms of light. 'For these commands are a lamp, this teaching is a light'; 'Your word is a lamp to my feet and a light for my path'; and 'the word of the prophets' is 'a light shining in a dark place' (Pr. 6:23; Ps. 119:105, 130; 2 Pet. 1:19). God said he would make his servant 'a light for the Gentiles' and his 'salvation to the ends of the earth' (Is. 42:6; 49:6), phrases which are applied by Simeon to the infant Jesus (Lk. 2:30–32; *cf.* Lk. 1:79), and by Paul and Barnabas to their own ministry (Acts 13:46–47; *cf.* Acts 26:18, 23). The apostle Paul also wrote to the Corinthians of 'the light of the knowledge of the glory of God in the face of Christ', which had shone in their hearts (2 Cor. 4:6).

The second use of light, namely to symbolize righteousness, is already plain in Isaiah 5:20, where the inhabitants of Judah are so morally perverse that they 'call evil good and good evil . . . put darkness for light and light for darkness'. In the ethical instruction contained in his letters Paul employs this metaphor (see Eph. 5:8–14; Rom. 13:11–14; *cf.* 1 Thes. 5:4–8; 1 Cor. 4:5).

---

[1]See, *e.g.*, Ex. 40: 34–38; Ps. 104:2; 1 Tim. 6:16; Jas. 1:17; 1 Pet. 2:9; Rev. 21:23; *cf.* Rev. 22:5. See also Mt. 8:12; 22:13; 25:30.

This double use of the symbolism of light and darkness is found in the Fourth Gospel, particularly in four passages. In three of these the emphasis is undoubtedly on light as the revelation of truth. See the Prologue to the Gospel, especially verses 4–5 and 9,[1] John 8:12, a passage which is related to the healing of the man born blind (cf. Jn. 9:4–5), and John 12:35–36, 46 (cf. also 11:9–10). In this last passage, however, a moral element is also discernible. The effect of the light is not just to make people see, but to enable them to *walk*. Right conduct, not just clear vision, is the benefit which light bestows. This brings us to John 3:19–21, where the relation between light and purity, darkness and evil, is made explicit. In this passage the good person, opposed to one 'who does evil', is actually described as 'whoever lives by the truth'. Truth, like light, in Scripture has a moral content. We are not just to *know* the truth, but to *do* it, just as we are not only to *see* the light, but to *walk* in it. So it is not uncommon, as here, for 'truth' to be contrasted not with 'error' but with 'wickedness' or unrighteousness (cf. Rom. 1:18; 2 Thes. 2:12).

The moral implications of light are apparent also in 1 John 2:8–11. Here the statement is made that 'the true light is already shining' (8). This light diffuses righteousness, and in particular love. A person's claim to be 'in the light' (9) can be credited only if he is walking in love, for 'whoever loves his brother lives in the light', while 'whoever hates his brother is in the darkness and walks around in the darkness; he is so blind that he does not know where he is going' (10–11).

(End of Additional Note)

In 1:6 – 2:2 three of the spurious claims of the false teachers are exposed and contradicted. Each is introduced by the formula *if we claim* (6, 8, 10). Dodd thinks the writer is 'alluding all through to certain maxims which were used as watchwords by heretical teachers'. Whether or not John is quoting their actual slogans, he is certainly representing some of their pernicious teaching,

---

[1] In the Prologue the Logos is distinguished from John the Baptist. John 'was not the light; he came only as a witness to the light' (8). True, in 5:33–35, John's witness to the truth is described in terms of light, which people 'chose for a time to enjoy'; yet he was himself not the light, but 'a lamp that burned and gave light' (v. 35).

and, having stated it, he immediately proceeds to brand it as deceitful error. A person's verbal profession is not necessarily to be believed. It must be tested in itself, in its relation to the fundamental truth that God is light, and in its bearing upon his behaviour. Similar expressions are used in 2:4, 6, 9 (*the man who says*) and in 4:20 (*if anyone says*). *Cf.* James 2:14–18. This is the dominant theme of the letter. John supplies searching tests by which to judge those who profess and call themselves Christians. The supreme question is whether their teaching and behaviour are consistent with each other and with the apostolic proclamation that God is light. This affirmation is still the test of the truth and reality of our Christian profession.

The symmetry of these seven verses is evident. John repeats the same pattern three times. First, he introduces the false teaching with the words *if we claim*. Next, he contradicts it with an unequivocal *we lie* or a similar expression. Finally, he makes a positive and true statement corresponding to the error he has refuted, *but if we . . .*, although in the last of the three examples the ending is different (*cf.* vv.7, 9 with 2:1–2).

The introductory phrase *if we claim* is noteworthy because with it the identity of the *we* has subtly changed. See Introduction, p. 47. The 'we – you' relationship of the authoritative apostle to his readers seen in 1:1–5 has faded; John now humbly identifies himself with them. Naturally, he is not suggesting that he has ever himself said or thought the errors he is rebutting. He uses the first person plural only because he is stating general principles which are applicable to all people equally.

The three errors he treats concern the fact of sin in our conduct, its origin in our nature, and its consequence in our relationship to God. They are the misconceptions of people who want fellowship with God on easy terms. They have never learnt the indissoluble marriage of religion and ethics; they are seeking a divorce between them. They have a thoroughly inadequate doctrine of sin and its sinfulness in relation to God who is light. So, in each of the three examples he gives, John faces the fact and the problem of sin before proceeding to state the solution. He not only denies the erroneous view, but indicates the divine remedy which is offered if people will only acknowledge their need of it. Each time he describes the cleansing and forgiveness which God has made possible through the death of Jesus Christ his Son (7, 9 and 2:1–2). Christianity is the only religion which, by emphasizing that God is light, first insists on taking sin seriously and then offers a satisfactory moral solution to the problem of sin. The way to have fellowship with a God who is light is not to deny the fact or effects of sin, but to confess our sins and thankfully appropriate God's provision for our cleansing.

A. THE DENIAL THAT SIN BREAKS OUR FELLOWSHIP WITH GOD (1:6–7)

6. The false claim here is the assertion that we have *fellowship* with God, while at the same time we *walk* (that is, habitually live) *in the darkness* (*cf.* 2:11; Is. 9:2; Jn. 8:12; Rom. 2:19). Some of the early Gnostics were guilty of such blatant antinomianism. They thought of the body as a mere envelope covering the human spirit, which, they further maintained, was inviolable; it could not be contaminated by the deeds of the body. Others, according to Irenaeus, taught that if a person had become truly 'spiritual', he had progressed beyond the possibility of any defilement. You could, they said, *be* righteous without necessarily *doing* righteousness (*cf.* 3:7, where John denies this). Consequently, the communion of the spirit with God was independent of the morality of the body. Still today, although Gnostic notions are outmoded, it is not uncommon for people to claim fellowship with God who see no necessity either first to go to the cross of Christ for cleansing and forgiveness or thereafter to lead a consistently holy life. We are right to be suspicious of those who claim a mystical intimacy with God and yet *walk in the darkness* of error and sin, paying no regard to the self-revelation of an all-holy God. Since God is light, such claims are ludicrous. Religion without morality is an illusion. Sin is always a barrier to fellowship with God (*cf.* Ps. 5:4; 66:18; Is. 59:1–2), for 'what fellowship can light have with darkness?' (2 Cor. 6:14).

If we make such a claim *we lie*, deliberately, knowingly, self-evidently, and we 'do not the truth' (AV). That is, we not only contradict the truth in our words, but deny it by our inconsistent lives. We 'do not live according to the 'truth' (RSV). 'Our words and our lives are a lie' (NEB).

79

7. The error having been refuted, John now affirms a complementary truth. He has shown the consequence of walking in darkness; he now describes what happens *if we walk in the light*. Any interpretation of this phrase must be consistent both with the symbolic meaning of light and with the following phrase *as he is the light*. God *is* eternally and necessarily in the light because he *is* himself light; we are called to walk in the light. God is in the light because he is always true to himself and his activity is consistent with his nature. 'He cannot disown himself' (2 Tim. 2:13). We must walk in the light of his holy self-revelation, and in his presence, without deceit or dishonesty in our mind or consciously tolerated sin in our conduct. 'Walking in the light' describes 'absolute sincerity . . . to be, so to speak, all of a piece, to have nothing to conceal, and to make no attempt to conceal anything'.[1] Two results of this are given.

First, *we have fellowship with one another*. Since in verse 6 John has declared that to walk in darkness prevents fellowship with God, one would have expected him in verse 7 to express the opposite truth that if we walk in the light, we enjoy fellowship with God. This is no doubt true, but characteristically he moves one step further, and states that walking in the light leads to that fellowship with each other which, as he has already said in verse 3, is grounded upon our fellowship with the Father and the Son.

The second result of walking in the light is that *the blood of Jesus, his Son, purifies us from all sin*. The verb suggests that God does more than forgive; he erases the stain of sin. And the present tense shows that it is a continuous process. But what sin needs to be cleansed *if we walk in the light*? Alford, aware of this difficulty, insists that here and in verse 9, cleansing indicates 'sanctification distinct from justification'. Ebrard also thinks this interpretation 'conclusively decided by the ninth verse'. But it would be unusual to ascribe this benefit to *the blood of Jesus*. Law, to whom 'light' means revelation rather than holiness, sees nothing inconsistent about the presence of sins in those who 'walk in the light'. He goes further and writes: 'to "walk in the light" is, first of all, to confess sin; to walk in the darkness, to

---

[1] Stephen Neill, *Christian Holiness* (Lutterworth Press, 1960), p. 35.

ignore or to deny sin'. But if 'light' signifies holiness as well as revelation, to walk in it is to live not only in honesty, but, at least to some degree, in purity also. This being so, the reference here must be to cleansing not from deliberate sins but either from 'every sin' (NIV mg.), even those committed unconsciously, or, as may be suggested by the use of the singular *sin*, from the defilement of our fallen nature. What is clear is that if we walk in the light, God has made provision to purify us from whatever sin would otherwise mar our fellowship with him or each other. This provision is *the blood of Jesus, his Son*, that is to say, the virtue of his death for our sins.[1] This is the only explicit reference in the letter to the saving power of the death of Jesus Christ, although an allusion is implied when it is written that the Son came 'to be the Saviour of the world' (4:14), 'to be the propitiation for our sins' (4:10, AV; *cf.* 2:2)[2] and 'that we might live through him' (4:9). The efficacy of this death for our sins is due to the unique person of him who died. He was both man (*Jesus*) and God (*his Son*). The condition of receiving cleansing through the blood of Christ and of enjoying fellowship with each other is to walk in the light, to be sincere, open, honest, transparent.

B. THE DENIAL THAT SIN EXISTS IN OUR NATURE (1:8–9)

8. The second claim of the heretics was one stage worse than the first, namely to *be without sin*, 'to be sinless'. (NEB). The first

---

[1] Westcott argues in an Additional Note (pp. 34–37) that 'by the outpouring of the Blood the life which was in it was not destroyed, though it was separated from the organism which it had before quickened'. Thus, 'participation in Christ's Blood is participation in His life . . . the simple idea of the Death of Christ, as separated from His Life, falls wholly into the background in the writings of St. John'. With this Brooke agrees, describing the blood of Christ as 'the power of Christ's life . . . set free by death for wider service than was possible under the limitations of a human life in Palestine at a definite date'. But this view has been refuted by A. M. Stibbs in *The Meaning of the Word 'Blood' in Scripture* (Tyndale Press, 1948), where he clearly shows that 'blood' in the Bible (*e.g.* Lv. 17:11) signifies not 'life' merely, but 'life violently ended; it is a sign of life either given or taken in death' (p. 33).

[2] The NIV translation 'as an atoning sacrifice' is better than either 'expiation' (RSV) or 'the remedy for the defilement of our sins' (NEB). But it is still inadequate, for it omits any allusion to God's wrath against sin, which is implied in the word 'propitiation' (AV). See both the commentary on 2:2 and the Additional Note on 'The biblical concept of propitiation', pp. 89–93.

heretical claim at least appeared to concede the existence of sin, while denying that it had the effect of estranging the sinner from God. Now the very fact of sin is denied. These people cannot benefit from the cleansing effects of the blood of Jesus because they *claim to be without sin*. 'Sin' is again in the singular and refers to the inherited principle of sin or self-centredness. The heretics are now saying that, whatever their outward conduct may be, there is no sin inherent in their nature.[1] Perhaps they asserted that in those enlightened with *gnōsis* the sinful nature was eradicated, and claimed a kind of sinless perfection, as some still do today. Alternatively, John is referring to the Gnostic subtlety that sin was a matter of the flesh and did not touch or defile the spirit. Whatever their exact pretensions, John repudiates it. To claim that we have no sin means that *we deceive ourselves*, that is, we are self-deceived rather than deliberate liars, and *the truth is not in us*. Not only do we fail to live by the truth (v. 6); we are void of it. For if it did indwell us we should inevitably be aware of our sinfulness. John's affirmation is equally applicable today to those who deny the fact or guilt of sin by seeking to interpret it solely in terms of physiological, psychological or social causes.

9. The proper Christian attitude to sin is not to deny it but to admit it, and then to receive the forgiveness which God has made possible and promises to us. *If we confess our sins*, acknowledging before God that we are sinners not only by nature (*sin*) but by practice also (*our sins*), God will both *forgive us our sins and purify us from all unrighteousness*. In the first phrase sin is a debt which he remits and in the second a stain which he removes. In both he is said to be *faithful and just*. The first word may mean that he is faithful to his nature and character (*cf.* 2 Tim. 2:13). But the faithfulness of God in Scripture is constantly associated with his covenant promises (*e.g.* Ps. 89; Heb. 10:23). He is true to his word and faithful to his covenant. Since the new covenant

[1] Other commentators argue that to 'have sin' in the Johannine literature means to 'have guilt' or 'be guilty'. It is thus translated by RSV in Jn. 9:41 (*cf.* Jn. 15:22, 24; 19:11), and Moffatt translates 1 Jn. 1:8: 'If we say, "We are not guilty" . . .' Law urges that in the Fourth Gospel the phrase 'specifically denotes the guiltiness of the agent'. In this case the denial here would not be so much of sin itself as of responsibility for it.

includes the pledge, 'I will forgive their wickedness and will remember their sins no more' (Je. 31:34), it is not difficult to see why God is said to be 'faithful' in forgiving our sins. But how can he also be described as *just* when he forgives us our sins? Some commentators relate God's justice to his faithfulness and suggest that it is by being faithful to his promises that God is just to forgive. Even so it is a strange adjective to use. Justice is associated in our minds with punishment or acquittal, not with forgiveness. If God visits upon the sinner his sin and 'does not leave the guilty unpunished' (Ex. 34:7), how can he forgive sins? This is the divine dilemma. The Judge of all the earth cannot lightly remit sin. The cross is, in fact, the only moral ground on which he can forgive sin at all, for there the blood of Jesus his Son was shed that he might be 'the atoning sacrifice for our sins' (2:2). *Cf.* Romans 3:25, another passage in which the justice of God is related to the atoning sacrifice of Christ. So we may say that in forgiving our sins and cleansing us from them, God displays loyalty to his covenant – his faithfulness because of the word which initiated it and his justice because of the deed which ratified it. More simply, he is *faithful* to forgive because he has promised to do so, and *just* because his Son died for our sins.[1]

This forgiveness and cleansing, issuing from the faithfulness and justice of God, are conditional upon confession. There are many warnings in Scripture about the danger of concealing our sins, and many promises of blessing if we confess them. Moreover, what is required is not a general confession of sin but a particular confession of *our sins*, as we deliberately call them to mind, confess and forsake them (*cf.* Ps. 32:1–5; Pr. 28:13).

C. THE DENIAL THAT SIN SHOWS ITSELF IN OUR CONDUCT (1:10–2:2)

10. The third heretical claim is indicated by the words *if we claim we have not sinned*. We may concede in theory that sin would

[1] Some commentators interpret differently the relation between the faithfulness and the justice, or righteousness, of God, drawing attention to the fact that in the Old Testament God's righteousness is often not an attribute but an activity equivalent to 'salvation' (*e.g.* Is. 51:5). Thus Dodd writes: 'For "John" as for Paul ... the mercy or forgiveness of God is a function of His righteousness ... If we confess our sins ... God forgives ... because no

break our fellowship with God if we did sin, and that sin does exist in our nature as an inborn disposition, and yet deny that we have in practice sinned and thus put ourselves out of fellowship with God. This is the most blatant of the three denials. The heretics maintained that their superior enlightenment rendered them incapable of sinning. But John is as clear about the outbreak of sin in our behaviour as he is about its origin in our nature and its consequences in preventing our fellowship with God. To say that we have not sinned is neither just to tell a deliberate lie (6), nor to be deluded (8), but actually to accuse God of lying, to *make him out to be a liar* and to reveal clearly that *his word has no place in our lives*. This is because his word frequently declares that sin is universal (*e.g.* 1 Ki. 8:46; Ps. 14:3; Ec. 7:20; Is. 53:6; 64:6), and the word of the gospel, which is a gospel of salvation, clearly assumes the sinfulness of man.

2:1. The symmetrical construction of this paragraph now changes, lest it should be thought that the frank admission and full forgiveness of our sins (1:9–10) allowed us to think lightly of them. On the contrary, the author's purpose is 'to prevent sin, not to condone it' (Brooke). So instead of adding 'if', as on the two previous occasions, John begins a new sentence in order to enlarge on the subject of sin in the Christian. He does this first negatively (*so that you will not sin*) and then positively (*But if anybody does sin*). It is important to hold these two statements in balance. It is possible to be either too lenient or too severe towards sin. Too great a lenience almost encourages sin in the Christian by stressing God's provision for the sinner. An exaggerated severity, on the other hand, either denies the possibility of a Christian sinning or refuses him forgiveness and restoration if he falls. Both extreme positions are contradicted by John.

The phrase *my dear children* is suggestive both of the author's advanced years and of the affectionate, tender relationship which exists between him and his readers. Usually he calls

---

other course would be consistent with the perfectly good will by which the whole universe is created and sustained.' But God's righteousness (*dikaiosynē*) is also displayed against sin, and 'the perfectly good will' of God does not exclude his 'wrath' or antagonism to sin and the consequent need of a 'propitiation'. See the Additional Note, 'The biblical concept of propitiation', pp. 89–93.

them just 'children', either *paidia* (2:13, 18) or *teknia* (2:12, 28; 3:7, 18; 4:4; 5:21), both of which NIV renders *dear children*; here alone (2:1) John adds the possessive adjective *my dear children*. Both words also occur in the Gospel on the lips of Jesus himself, *teknia* in 13:33 and *paidia* in 21:5. The purpose of his letter, John says, is to keep them from sinning. His references to the cleansing blood of Jesus (1:7) and to the forgiveness of God (9) are not intended to give them a light view of the gravity of sin. Far from it. 'Horror, hatred, fear, repudiation of sin pervade the whole Epistle' (Law). He longs that they shall be preserved from the evil teaching of the heretics and that they shall not fall into sin. The Christian may never escape the specific command of Jesus, 'Stop sinning' (Jn. 5:14; *cf.* 8:11). But, on the other hand, he adds that, *if anybody does sin*, God has graciously made provision for his restoration. The clause is significant. It clearly indicates the author's conviction that acts of sin (the aorist *hamartē* implies this), as opposed to the continuous sinful habit, are possible in the Christian, which some have supposed John denies in 3:9 and 5:18. 'The thought is of the single act (*hamartē*) into which the believer may be carried against the true tenor of his life, as contrasted with the habitual state (*hamartanei*, iii. 6, 8, 9, v. 18)' (Westcott).

The provision which God has made for the sinning Christian is now unfolded. It is to be found in him who is described first as *one who speaks to the Father in our defence* (in most English versions simply 'advocate with the Father'), secondly as *Jesus Christ, the Righteous One*, and thirdly (in v. 2) as 'the atoning sacrifice for our sins'.

In form the word *advocate* in both its Latin and Greek equivalents (*advocatus* and *paraklētos*) is passive not active. It means literally not 'comforter' but 'called alongside' and describes anybody summoned to the assistance of another, in other words, a 'mediator, intercessor, helper' (BAGD). More rarely it was used in the particular, legal sense of a barrister, whose special responsibility it is, as counsel for the defence, to plead the cause of the person on trial. Although the verb *parakalein*, 'to encourage, exhort or comfort', is used quite frequently in the New Testament, the noun *paraklētos* occurs only in the Johannine literature. Indeed, apart from this verse, where it applies to

Jesus, its use is restricted to the upper-room discourse in the Fourth Gospel, where Jesus made it a title for the Holy Spirit (Jn. 14:16, 26; 15:26; 16:17). At the same time, he called him 'another' Paraclete (14:16), thereby implying that he himself was the first. A comparison of the two uses is instructive. If we have an advocate in heaven, Christ has an advocate on earth. The Holy Spirit is Christ's Paraclete, as the Lord Jesus is ours. But whereas the Holy Spirit pleads Christ's cause before a hostile world, Christ pleads our cause against our 'accuser' (Rev. 12:10) and *to the Father*, who loves and forgives his children. He is not now to be regarded as our Judge. The person who believes in Christ already 'has eternal life and will not be condemned; he has crossed over from death to life' (Jn. 5:24; *cf.* 1 Jn. 3:14; 5:12 and Rom. 8:1, 33–34). Once the sinner has been justified by God his Judge, he has entered the family of God and become related to God as his Father. If he should sin, he does not need another justification from the divine Judge. He is a child of God; he needs the Father's forgiveness. This is assured to him through the advocacy of *Jesus Christ, the Righteous One*, a composite expression indicating his human nature (*Jesus*), messianic office (*Christ*) and righteous character. In the picture of a righteous advocate standing before the Father on our behalf, 'the case is not that of love pleading with justice'. Rather the opposite: 'Justice pleads with love for our release!' (Findlay).

This reference to Christ being *the Righteous One*, like the description of God in 1:9 as being 'just' (the adjective is *dikaios* in both cases), is unexpected. Yet the similarity between the two verses can be exaggerated. The righteousness, purity and sinlessness of Christ's character are mentioned several times, directly or indirectly, in this letter (2:6, 29; 3:3, 5, 7). It is self-evident that only through a *righteous* Saviour could we be cleansed from 'all unrighteousness' (1:9). *Cf.* 2 Corinthians 5:21 and 1 Peter 3:18. For the relation between Christ's intercession and his holiness see Hebrews 7:25–26. There are many similarities between the teaching of this letter and of the letter to the Hebrews on the subjects of atonement and intercession. In both books the doctrines are closely linked, although in Hebrews Christ intercedes as priest, in this letter as paraclete.

2. John now proceeds to describe our righteous advocate as *the atoning sacrifice for our sins*, since it is this alone which qualifies him for the position. 'Our advocate does not plead that we are innocent, or adduce extenuating circumstances. He acknowledges our guilt and presents his vicarious work as the ground of our acquittal' (Smith). 'Christ's intercession is the continual application of his death to our salvation' (Calvin). In Greek writings the noun *hilasmos* (translated 'propitiation' in AV and *atoning sacrifice* in NIV) and its cognate verb *hilaskesthai* were generally used for the appeasement of an angry deity by offerings. So base and corrupt was this heathen conception that many modern scholars have altogether rejected the notion of a Christian propitiation. It is incompatible, they say, with the revelation of God through Jesus Christ. They argue that the barrier to fellowship with God is not in him but in us and our sins, and that the atoning work of Christ removes the barrier by dealing with our sins. They point out, in support of their view, that the verb *hilaskesthai* is very seldom used in the Old Testament with God as its object (only Zc. 7:2; 8:22; Mal. 1:9), and never in the New Testament. It is not God who is the object of Christ's atonement but our sin and defilement, which is thereby 'covered' (the probable root meaning of the Hebrew word *kipper*, translated by *hilaskesthai* in the LXX), 'neutralized' (Westcott), even 'sterilized' (Dodd). For this reason they propose to translate the word by 'expiation' (RSV), and assume that what is meant is not the placating of the wrath of God but the annulling of the guilt of sin. Thus 'He is himself the remedy for the defilement of our sins' (NEB). But this is too summary a dismissal of the idea of propitiation. Although it is true that nowhere in the New Testament is God explicitly said to be 'propitiated', this does not settle the matter, for there are other biblical words and phrases which indicate that in some senses he does need to be propitiated. His 'wrath' abides upon all sin and must somehow be averted or appeased if the sinner is to be forgiven.

Moreover, the notion of the propitiation of God by the death of his Son is not at all inconsistent with the revelation we have been given of his character in his Son and in his word, if it is rightly understood. It needs to be safeguarded, and distinguished from pagan conceptions, in two particulars.

First, God's wrath is not arbitrary or capricious. It bears no resemblance to the unpredictable passions and personal vengefulness of the pagan deities. Instead, it is his settled, controlled, holy antagonism to all evil. Secondly, the means by which his wrath is averted is not a bribe, either from us or from a third party. On the contrary, the initiative in the propitiation is entirely God's. In the LXX he is himself sometimes the subject of the verb to 'propitiate' – a usage unknown in pagan writings. Similarly, in this letter the whole initiative is ascribed to God. 'The action of which, in some sense, God is Himself the object, has God Himself as its origin' (Law). This origin is his love, the spontaneous, uncaused love of Father and Son together. We must not imagine either that the Father sent his Son to do something which the Son was reluctant to do, or that the Son was a third party intervening between the sinner and a reluctant God. Both these views are excluded by the teaching of this letter. It is not reluctance but love which is attributed to both Father and Son. 'This is love: not that we loved God, but that he loved us and sent his Son as an atoning sacrifice for our sins' (4:10). 'By this we know love, that he laid down his life for us' (3:16, RSV).[1]

Having distinguished between the pagan and Christian concepts of propitiation in these two major respects, we must now ask: What was or is the propitiation? John's answer is that it is 'Jesus Christ, the Righteous One' himself (2:1), the Father's sent Son (4:10). In both verses he is described not as the 'propitiator', but as the 'propitiation'. This is significant because it emphasizes 'the thought that He is Himself the propitiatory offering . . . A propitiator might make use of a means of propitiation outside Himself. But Christ is our propitiation . . .' (Westcott), which is implied by the prominent *he (autos)*. But in what sense is he *the atoning sacrifice for our sins*? No direct answer is given in this verse, but if John writes of 'propitiation' here and in 4:10, and of forgiveness in 1:9, it is because he has stated in 1:7 that what cleanses sinners from their guilty stains is the blood of Jesus, God's Son, that is the laying down of his life in a

---

[1]See the Additional Note, 'The biblical concept of propitiation', pp. 89–93, for a fuller discussion of the linguistic and theological questions involved in the idea of propitiation.

violent death. 'In these passages we have a concatenation of ideas – propitiation, blood, cleansing, forgiveness – which are directly derived from the sacrificial system of the Old Testament, which are expressed, indeed, in technical Levitical terms' (Law; cf. Lv. 16:30; Heb. 9:22 and commentary on 1:7).

Moreover, Christ still *is* the propitiation, not because in any sense he continues to offer his sacrifice, but because his one sacrifice once offered has an eternal virtue which is effective today in those who believe. And the propitiation for our sins is *not only for ours but also for the sins of the whole world*. This cannot be pressed into meaning that all sins are automatically pardoned through the propitiation of Christ, but that a universal pardon is offered for (the sins of) the whole world and is enjoyed by those who embrace it; cf. 4:9, 14 and John 1:29; 3:16; 5:24. 'For no man in the whole world is there any other way of being reconciled than that of the propitiation of Christ' (Ebrard).

Thus, the Father's provision for the sinning Christian is in his Son, who possesses a threefold qualification: his righteous character, his propitiatory death and his heavenly advocacy. Each depends on the others. He could not be our advocate in heaven today if he had not died to be the propitiation for our sins; and his propitiation would not have been effective if in his life and character he had not been Jesus Christ, the Righteous One.

Additional Note: The biblical concept of propitiation (2:2)

The only two occurrences in the New Testament of the noun *hilasmos*, 'propitiation', are in this letter (2:2 and 4:10). The verb *hilaskesthai* occurs twice also (Lk. 18:13; Heb. 2:17), while *hilastērion* is found in Hebrews 9:5 for the 'mercy seat', and in Romans 3:25 either in the same sense or, more probably, signifying 'a means of propitiation'.

The AV translation of *hilasmos* as 'propitiation' comes from the Vulgate, but is regarded by many modern writers as 'infelicitous' (Dodd). Thus the RSV prefers 'expiation' and the NEB the rather clumsy periphrasis 'the remedy for the defilement of'. The main contemporary objection to the vocabulary of 'propitiation' is theological. It is said to conjure up notions of an irritable and capricious deity who needs to be appeased with bribes. Such ideas are rightly dismissed as pagan; they are inconsistent with the revelation of God in Jesus Christ. Apparently unwilling to concede that there may be a biblical and Christian concept of propitiation quite distinct from crude pagan views, some scholars proceed to support their theological rejection of propitiation with linguistic arguments.

It is quite true, they say, that in pagan Greek from Homer onwards the verb *hilaskesthai* meant to make somebody propitious to oneself, to propitiate or pacify an offended person, and especially to placate the angry gods by gifts or sacrifices. This is incontrovertible. But, the argument goes, secular Greek had a rarer, secondary use of the same verb, meaning 'to perform an act by which defilement (ritual or moral) is removed; to "expiate" ' (Dodd). In these cases the object is not personal (God) but impersonal (sin's defilement). It was, in fact, a universal belief of the ancient world that certain rituals acted as a 'powerful disinfectant' (*ibid.*). Further, it is maintained, this second, expiatory meaning of the verb is found in the Greek Old Testament. It is true that on three occasions, God himself is the object of *exilaskesthai* (Zc. 7:2; 8:22; Mal. 1:9, where the RSV renders the Hebrew 'entreat the favour of the Lord'; *cf.* Gn. 32:20 of Jacob and Esau), but nowhere else. The commonest use of the verb is with an impersonal object, translating the Hebrew *kipper*, to 'cover' and so to 'make atonement' or 'expiate'. Indeed, so far from being the object of the verb in the LXX, God is sometimes its subject, a usage unknown in pagan Greek. Similarly, in the LXX of Psalms 65:3; 78:38 and 79:9 God is the subject of the non-compound verb *hilaskesthai*, while its object is the sins or ungodliness of men (in the accusative in the first case and the dative in the other two). In these verses the AV translation is 'forgive' or 'purge away', so that Dodd can write, 'the meaning is virtually indistinguishable from "to forgive"; the defilement of sin can be removed, in the last resort, only by divine forgiveness'. Therefore, in 1 John 2:2, to say that Jesus is 'the propitiation for our sins' is just another way of saying that through Christ God both 'cleanses' and 'forgives' us, as has already been stated in 1:7, 9 (*cf.* Lv. 4:20; 12:7). We have thus come full circle. The notion conveyed by *hilasmos* and its cognates, we are told, is not an action by which God is propitiated, but one by which man is cleansed and his sin 'neutralized' (Westcott, Dodd). The thought is 'not that of appeasing one who is angry . . . against the offender; but of altering the character of that which from without occasions a necessary alienation, and interposes an inevitable obstacle to fellowship' (Westcott). The *hilasmos* changes man not God; it annuls his sin and thus removes the barrier to fellowship with God.

Leon Morris has subjected to a close and critical analysis the linguistic arguments by which this reconstruction is buttressed.[1] He shows that the only two possible secular Greek passages in which *exilaskesthai* is said to mean to 'expiate' are quite capable of being translated in a propitiatory sense; that the eleven occurrences of *hilaskesthai* in LXX, which are all in the middle or passive, with God as the subject, either must or may convey the sense 'propitiate' or 'be propitious to'; that the compound verb *exilaskesthai* (commoner in LXX, but not found in New Testament) translates the Hebrew *kipper* eighty-three times, and that the latter from its context normally means either 'to avert punishment, especially the divine anger, by the payment of a *kopher*, a ransom', or in its cultic use 'to accomplish reconciliation between God and man' by sacrifice; and that, contrary to what has often been asserted, this compound verb *exilaskesthai* 'is never followed by an accusative of sin in the canonical Scriptures of the Old Testament', but most commonly (fifty-eight times) by *peri* with a genitive of person, meaning 'to make propitiation concerning a person'. Morris's conclusion from this linguistic study, briefly summarized here, is that 'it would seem impossible for anyone in the first century to have used one of the *hilaskomai* group without conveying to his readers some idea of propitiation'.

Turning from linguistics to theology, and in particular to the two Johannine verses in which the noun *hilasmos* occurs (2:2 and 4:10), three points may be made. The first concerns *the need for the propitiation*. This is indicated in the expression 'the atoning sacrifice for our sins' (*peri tōn hamartiōn hemōn*) common to both verses. If what John had in mind was in reality an expiation, of

[1] Leon Morris, *The Apostolic Preaching of the Cross* (IVP, [3]1965), pp. 144–178.

which our sins were the object, the construction would surely have been a simple genitive, 'the expiation *of* our sins'. Instead he uses the preposition *peri*. The need for a *hilasmos* is seen not in 'our sins' by themselves but 'concerning our sins', namely in God's uncompromising hostility towards them. The pagan was wrong to see the need for propitiation in the wrathful character of his god, arbitrary and without ethical cause. Some modern commentators, in their proper reaction against this travesty, are equally wrong to see it in sin and its taint alone. Christ 'has made possible the removal of the sin which keeps men from God', writes Brooke. But what is this 'removal' of sin which takes no account of the divine judgment upon it? The need for propitiation is constituted neither by God's wrath in isolation, nor by man's sin in isolation, but by both together. Sin is 'lawlessness' (3:4), a defiant disregard for the law of God which deserves the judgment of God. It is this divine judgment upon human rebellion which constitutes the barrier to fellowship with God; and there can be no expiation of man's sin without a propitiation of God's wrath. God's holy antagonism to sin must somehow be turned away if sin is to be forgiven and the sinner restored. These concepts are not foreign to John, the apostle of love. Although he does not mention God's wrath in his letters, he does in his Gospel, where he writes that 'God's wrath remains' on the disobedient unbeliever (Jn. 3:36). And in his first letter the concept is implied. The condition of the unbeliever is 'death', which is the result of sin (3:14; 5:16); and 'life', which is fellowship with God, is available only in Christ, who came to win it for us (4:9; 5:11–12). Moreover, the fact that Jesus Christ, the Righteous One, is our advocate in heaven, implies the need for his advocacy. It is on the ground of his propitiation that his advocacy is effective.

Secondly, both verses indicate that *the nature of the propitiation* is Jesus Christ himself. God 'sent his Son as an atoning sacrifice for our sins' (4:10). 'He (*autos*) is the atoning sacrifice . . .' (2:2). No direct mention is made in either verse of his death, but John has already written that what cleanses from sin is the blood of God's Son (1:7), that is, the virtue of his sacrificial death. He died the death which was the just reward of our sins. And the efficacy of his death remains, so that he is today himself the propitiation. 'Christ is said to be the "propitiation" and not simply the "propitiator" (as He is called the "Saviour", iv.14), in order to emphasise the thought that He is Himself the propitiatory offering as well as the priest (comp. Rom. iii.25)' (Westcott).

Thirdly, *the source of the propitiation* is clearly taught in 4:10, namely the love of God. This was so in Old Testament days, since the propitiatory offerings were divinely instituted and prescribed as the means by which the sinner might be forgiven. 'The life of a creature is in the blood, and I have given it to you to make atonement for yourselves on the altar . . .' (Lv. 17:11). The sacrifices were not a human arrangement, but a divine gift. So with the sacrifice of Christ. God gave his Son to die for sinners. This gift was not only the result of God's love (Jn. 3:16), nor only the proof and pledge of it (Rom. 5:8; 8:32), but the very essence of it: 'This is love . . . that he loved us and sent his Son as an atoning sacrifice for our sins' (1 Jn. 4:10).

There can, therefore, be no question of human beings appeasing an angry deity by their gifts. The Christian propitiation is quite different, not only in the character of the divine anger but in the means by which it is propitiated. It is an appeasement of the wrath of God by the love of God through the gift of God. The initiative is not taken by us, nor even by Christ, but by God himself in sheer unmerited love. His wrath is averted not by any external gift, but by his own self-giving to die the death of sinners. This is the means he has himself contrived by which to turn his own wrath away (*cf.* Pss. 78:38; 85:2–3; 103:8–10; Mi. 7:18–19).

III. FIRST APPLICATION OF THE TESTS (2:3–27)

So far John has given a general introduction to his theme of Christian consistency. He has defined the nature of the apostolic proclamation concerning the word of life in Christ. It centres first on the historical manifestation of the eternal, and secondly on the fact that God is light. These two truths are fundamental and must control and condition our lives if we call ourselves Christian. Indeed, all Christian profession may be judged in relation to these truths. No thought or action can be condoned which is inconsistent either with God's nature as light, pure and self-giving, or with his historical, palpable self-disclosure in Christ.

This general introduction to the essential relation between our life and God's truth is now particularized in three tests – moral (the test of obedience), social (the test of love) and doctrinal (the test of belief in Christ). The rest of the letter contains three successively elaborate expositions and applications of these.

A. OBEDIENCE, OR THE MORAL TEST (2:3–6)

In the preceeding section the author has recorded three false claims of the heretics, each introduced by the phrase 'if we claim'. He now expresses two right and positive assurances which the true Christian may have, introduced by the formula *en toutō ginōskomen hoti*, meaning literally 'by this we know that'. They occur in verse 3 (*we know that . . .*) and verse 5b (*this is how we know . . .*). Each of these statements is in the first person plural, *we know*, and is followed by an application in the third person singular, *ho legōn*, literally 'he who says' (4, 6). Indeed, there is a third *ho legōn* in verse 9, although the NIV obscures the fact by translating each occurrence differently (*the man who says*, v. 4; *whoever claims*, v. 6; and *anyone who claims*, v. 9). The repetition is emphatic. The claim to be a Christian may be variously stated, in terms of knowing God (4), or living in Christ (6) or being in the light (9), but invariably, if it is an authentic claim, it will show itself in a new life of obeying God (4), imitating Christ (6) and loving our brothers and sisters (9–10). Without such a moral authentication, the claim is seen to be bogus.

3. *We know that* is a characteristic phrase of this letter. John uses two verbs for to 'know' which often, though not always, have subtly different nuances. Sometimes, as here, the word is *ginōskomen*, a present tense meaning 'we come to know' or 'we perceive' (twenty-five times in this letter, in present, aorist and perfect tenses); sometimes it is *oidamen*, the perfect tense of the verb *eidenai*, and generally means 'we know as a fact', not by perception but as something self-evident (fifteen times in this letter). The repetition of these expressions in the letter shows that the author's purpose is to supply tests by which the genuine Christian may be discerned from the spurious and vice versa (*cf.* 5:13). 'Here is the test by which we can make sure that we know him' (NEB). The Gnostics in particular laid claim to the knowledge of God. They had been enlightened with the true *gnōsis*. John does not deny the possibility of knowing God, since both the Old Testament and the Gospel promise it (*e.g.* Je. 31:34; Jn. 17:3). But he insists that no religious experience is valid if it does not have moral consequences (*cf.* Tit. 1:16). It is not the person who claims to be a Christian and to know God who is presumptuous, but the person whose claim is contradicted by his conduct. He is a *liar* (4).

How may we 'be sure that we know him' (RSV)? By this answer John provides the first test, which he has already adumbrated in the first chapter and now forcefully clarifies. It is the test of moral obedience. We may know that we have come to know him (perfect tense, *egnōkamen*) only *if we obey his commands.* Only if we obey him can we claim to *know* him, not to have accurate information about him merely, but to have become personally acquainted with him. If it is objected that in this case no-one knows God, because no-one is perfectly obedient, we may reply with Calvin: 'he does not mean that those who wholly satisfy the Law keep His commandments (and no such instance can be found in the world), but those who strive, according to the capacity of human infirmity, to form their life in obedience to God'. The verb John uses in relation to God's commands (*tērein*) indicates more than a merely external conformity to moral standards; it 'expresses the idea of watchful, observant obedience' (Law).

4. The positive principle of the previous verse is illustrated by a negative example. A person's words must be tested by his works. If he disobeys God's commandments, his claim to have come to know God is a lie (*cf.* 1:6). His conduct contradicts his profession and proves it to be false.

5a. On the other hand, *if anyone obeys his word* (observing not only his commands in particular but his word in general, regarded as a single and compete revelation of his will), he is shown by his obedience to be indeed a true Christian, whether he lays claim to be one or not. *God's love* is in him, and that so fully as to be described as *truly made complete*. The genitive in the expression *God's love* could be subjective (God's love for him), qualitative (love like God's love) or objective (his love for God). The RSV is almost certainly right to take it in the latter sense here and to render the phrase 'love for God', although various commentators have questioned whether obedience really supplies evidence of a love for God that is *made complete*. True love for God is expressed not in sentimental language or mystical experience but in moral obedience (*cf.* 5:3 and our Lord's teaching in Jn. 14:15, 21, 23; 15:10). The proof of love is loyalty. For love expressed in confidence towards God rather than in obedience to him, see 4:17–18.

John now states the same general principle in a slightly different form, and adds another and more positive illustration of it. The whole context, and especially verse 6, suggests that the phrase *in him* refers to Christ. To be 'in Christ' is Paul's characteristic description of the Christian. But John uses it too. To be (or to 'live', 6) 'in' him is equivalent to the phrase to 'know' him (3, 4) and to 'love' him (5). Being a Christian consists in essence of a personal relationship to God in Christ, knowing him, loving him, and living in him as the branch lives in the vine (Jn. 15:1ff.). This is the meaning of 'eternal life' (Jn. 17:3; 1 Jn. 5:20).

5b–6. It is never easy in this letter to decide whether expressions like *'this is how we know'* look back to what precedes or forward to what follows. Usually the look is forward; once or twice it is clearly backward; while sometimes the expression is what Alexander calls a 'swing-door' because it appears to move in both directions! In this case the symmetry between verses 3–4 and 5–6 suggests that the NIV punctuation is correct, making the reference a forward one, namely *This is how we know we are in him*: *Whoever claims* . . . A second time the author adds a more specific example to the general principle he has stated. This time the formula *whoever claims* introduces not a false claim but an obligation to righteous conduct which alone can make the claim credible. It is not enough to obey 'his word' (5a); we must *walk as*

Jesus did. The name 'Jesus' is absent from the Greek sentence. But the NIV is surely right to add it, for in this letter the pronouns *ekeinos* (here, 3:3, 5, 7, 16; 4:17) and often *autos* (2:8; 12, 27, 28; 3:2, 3; 4:21) refer to Jesus. Christian conformity is to the example of Jesus as well as to his commands (*cf.* 2:29; 3:3, 7; Jn. 13:15; 1 Pet. 2:21). We cannot claim to live in him unless we behave like him.

B. LOVE, OR THE SOCIAL TEST (2:7–11)

7. John now applies to professing Christians his second test, which is not moral but social. As he is about to write of brotherly love, he appropriately addresses them as his *agapētoi* (literally 'beloved', NIV 'dear friends'; the AV 'brethren' renders a less well-supported reading). In urging them to love one another, he assures them of his own love for them. See also 3:2, 21; 4:1, 7, 11 and 3 John 2, 5, 11. He has been writing about the Christian obligation to keep God's commandments (3–4); he now singles out one of them which in one sense is *old* (7) and in another is *new* (8). He does not explicitly reveal what the nature of this commandment is; but since the subject of verses 9–11 is love, and since the 'new commandment' which Jesus gave was 'As I have loved you, so you must love one another' (Jn. 13:34; *cf.* 15:12, 17), it is plain that the command concerns brotherly love. *Cf.* 2 John 4–6. John has told them they must walk as Jesus walked (6); and that was a walk in love.

Is this commandment new or old? It is both. To begin with, what John was writing to them was *not . . . a new command but an old one*. They had learnt it before, because John had taught it before. Indeed, they had known it from the outset of their Christian life (*cf.* 2:24; 3:11 and 2 Jn. 6 for this meaning of *since the beginning*). It was part of the ethical instruction they received from the day of their conversion. So basic was it to the teaching they received that John could even equate it with *the message you have heard*, literally 'which you heard' (*ēkousate*, aorist; *since the beginning* is not repeated in the better MSS). Brotherly love was part of the original message which had come to them. John was not now inventing it. It was not an innovation such as the heretics claimed to teach. It was as old as the gospel itself.

8. Nevertheless, or *yet*, what was old to them, because they had heard it before, was in itself also new, in fact *a new command*, whose *truth* (especially its newness) *is seen in him and you*. That is, its novelty was a fact when he called it 'a new command' (Jn. 13:34) and himself exemplified it, and it remains a fact for us, who are required to obey it. The idea of love in general was not new, but Jesus Christ invested it in several ways with a richer and deeper meaning. First, it was new in the emphasis he gave it, bringing the love commands of Deuteronomy 6:5 and Leviticus 19:18 together and declaring that the whole teaching of the Law and the Prophets hung upon them. Secondly, it was new in the quality he gave it. A disciple was to love others not just as he loved himself but in the same measure as Christ had loved him, with selfless self-sacrifice even unto death. Thirdly, it was new in the extent he gave it, showing in the parable of the Good Samaritan that the 'neighbour' we must love is anyone who needs our compassion and help, irrespective of race and rank, and includes our 'enemy' (*cf.* Mt. 5:44). It was also, fourthly, to continue new by our fresh apprehension of it, 'for though doctrinal Christianity is always old, experimental Christianity is always new' (Candlish). In these ways it was 'a new command', and will always remain new. It is new teaching for the new age which has dawned, new . . . *because the darkness is passing and the true light is already shining*.

All Jews were familiar with the division of history into 'the present age' and 'the age to come' (*cf. e.g.* Mt. 12:32). But the New Testament teaches that 'the age to come' came with Jesus. He inaugurated it, so that the two ages now overlap one another. Christians have been delivered out of this present evil age (Gal. 1:4) and have already begun to taste the powers of the age to come (Heb. 6:5; *cf.* 1 Cor. 10:11). *The darkness* is the present age or the 'world' which in verse 17 is also said to be passing away (*paragetai* again). The *true light*, which *is already shining*, is Jesus Christ, with whom light came 'into the world' (Jn. 3:19; *cf.* Is. 9:2; Mt. 4:16 and Lk. 1:79). He is *true* (*alēthinos*) not in the sense in which a statement is true as opposed to false (*alēthēs*, the word used at the beginning of this verse), but in the sense in which the real differs from the unreal, the substance from the shadow and the prototype from the type. The adjective is a favourite of John's. Christ is the true, or real, light, of which physical light is but a reflection, just as he is the true bread and the true vine (Jn. 1:9; 6:32; 15:1). The true idea of light, vine, bread, *etc.*, is the heavenly reality; the earthly material things which we call 'light', 'vine', 'bread' are copies of the true (*cf.* Heb. 8:5; 9:23–24; 10:1). So the new command remains new because it belongs to the new age which has been ushered in by the shining of the true light.

9. John now shows that Jesus Christ, the true light, is the light of love, and that therefore to be, or to live, or to walk *in the light* (9, 10; *cf.* 1:6) is to walk in love. Light and love, darkness and hatred belong together. In verses 3–6 the general principle preceded the specific example. Here the example comes first. The Gnostic claim was as much to have been 'enlightened' as to possess the 'knowledge' of God. The falsity of their claim to *be in the light* was betrayed not now by disobedience, but by hatred. The true Christian, who knows God and walks in the light, both obeys God and loves his brother. The genuineness of his faith is seen in his right relation to both God and his fellow human beings.

10–11. Now follows the general principle, stated first positively and then negatively. The contrast is stark and absolute. Love and hatred are set in opposition to each other with no alternative, just as we are said to be either *in the light* or *in the darkness*, and there is no twilight. The first part of the contrast is simple. What follows shows, however, that our love and hatred not only reveal whether we are already in the light or in the darkness, but actually contribute towards the light or the darkness in which we already are. Thus, of the loving Christian who abides in the light it may be said that *there is nothing in him* (or perhaps 'in it') *to make him stumble* (*en autō* could refer either to the person or to the light in which he lives). The light shines on our path, so that we can see clearly and so walk properly. If we love people, we see how to avoid sinning against them. The person with hatred in his heart, however, because he *is in the darkness*, also *walks around in the darkness; he does not know where he is going, because the darkness has blinded him* (11; *cf.* Pr. 4:19).

Hatred distorts our perspective. We do not first misjudge people and then hate them as a result; our view of them is already jaundiced by our hatred. It is love which sees straight, thinks clearly and makes us balanced in our outlook, judgments and conduct. *Cf.* John 8:12; 11:9–10; 12:35.

C. A DIGRESSION ABOUT THE CHURCH (2:12–14)

John has abruptly concluded his exposition of his second test. He does not mean to give his readers the impression that he thinks they are in darkness or that he doubts the reality of their Christian faith. It is the false teachers whom he regards as spurious, not the loyal members of the church. So he digresses to tell them his view of their Christian standing. His purpose in writing is as much to confirm the right assurance of genuine Christians as to rob the counterfeit of their false assurance. They are in the new age all right, and are enjoying the forgiveness, the knowledge of God and the power to overcome which had been prophesied of the new covenant (*e.g.* Je. 31:33–34).

So John makes six statements about them, introducing each with the words *I write to you*. In the first three the tense of the verb is present, *graphō hymin* (*I write* or 'I am writing' *to you*), whereas the remaining three verbs are aorists, *egrapsa hymin* ('I wrote' or 'I have written' to you). Some commentators have thought the aorist verbs refer either to a former letter (and the present verbs to this) or to the first part of the letter already written (and the present verbs to the whole letter). Law makes the ingenious suggestion that 'the author was interrupted' at the end of verse 13 and that, when he resumed, he repeated what he had just written, changing the tense of the verbs from the present to the aorist. But this is pure conjecture. It seems more probable that the tense of the second trio is an epistolary aorist referring to the present letter, in which case there is really no difference in meaning between the two tenses, as the NIV rightly indicates by translating all six *I write to you*. John first 'writes' and then confirms what he 'has written'. His message is sure and steadfast; he does not change his mind; this is his 'full and final testimony' (Candlish).

The author divides his readers into three groups, whom he names *dear children, fathers* and *young men*, and addresses each group twice. He is indicating not their physical ages, as some have thought, but stages in their spiritual development, for God's family, like every human family, has members of differing maturity. In view of John's use of the title *dear children* elsewhere in this letter to embrace all his readers, many (including the Greek fathers, Calvin and Luther) have thought that here the phrase has the same inclusive reference to all church members who are subsequently divided into two groups only, namely fathers and young men, the mature and the immature, corresponding to the familiar Pauline 'babes in Christ' and 'mature in Christ' (*e.g.* 1 Cor. 3:1; Col. 1:28, RSV). Certainly the order (children, fathers, young men) may also suggest this. But the distinctive content of the message addressed to the three groups favours the view of some ancient Latin commentators such as Augustine that they represent three different stages of spiritual pilgrimage. The *dear children* are those newborn in Christ. The *young men* are more developed Christians, strong and victorious in spiritual warfare; while the *fathers* possess the depth and stability of ripe Christian experience. Since the description of each group is similar on both occasions when it is addressed, it will be simplest to take the corresponding pairs together. The repetition of the three groups and of the messages addressed to them, which if not the same are similar, is no doubt intended for emphasis.

12, 13c. The *dear children* are called first *teknia* (12) and then *paidia* (13c). If any distinct flavour is preserved between them, *teknia* emphasizes the community of nature between the child and its parent (from *tiktō*, to bear or give birth to), while *paidia* refers to the child's minority as one under discipline (*paideuō*, to train or chastise). *Paidia* differs from *teknia* 'by emphasizing the idea of subordination and not that of kinsmanship' (Westcott). By being born of God John's readers had become children of God. Their *sins have been forgiven on account of his name* (12), that is, they have been and remain forgiven (perfect tense, *apheōntai*) because of the name of Christ, our atoning sacrifice and advocate (1–2), whose *name* represents both his person and his saving work (*cf.* Acts 4:12). Further, they *have known the Father* (13c), literally, 'have come to know' (another perfect tense) God as their Father. These are the earliest conscious experiences of newborn Christians. They rejoice in the forgiveness of their sins through Christ and in their consequent fellowship with God. The Holy Spirit within them makes them aware of their filial relationship to God and causes them to cry '*Abba!* Father!' (Rom. 8:15–16; Gal. 4:6).

13a, 14a. The *fathers*, to whom John now addresses himself, are the spiritually adult in the congregation. Their first flush of ecstasy in receiving forgiveness and fellowship with the Father was an experience of long ago. Even the battles of the young men, to which he will next refer, are past. The fathers have progressed into a deep communion with God. Both times he addresses them, John uses identical words: *you have known him who is from the beginning*. The verb is the same as that used of the little children. All Christians, mature and immature, have come to know (*egnōkate*) God. But their knowledge of him ripens with the years. The children know him as 'the Father' (13c); the fathers have come to know him as *him who is from the beginning*, which is probably a reference, not to the Logos (though see 1:1; Jn. 1:1), but to the immutable, eternal God who does not change (as humans change) with advancing years, but who is for ever the same. Time hurries on, but in all generations they find a refuge in him who from everlasting to everlasting is God (Ps. 90:1–2; *cf.* Mal. 3:6). They are already consciously living in eternity.

13b, 14b. In between the children and the fathers are the *young men*, busily involved in the battle of Christian living. The Christian life, then, is not just enjoying the forgiveness and the fellowship of God, but fighting the enemy. The forgiveness of past sins must be followed by deliverance from sin's present power, justification by sanctification. So in both messages to the *young men* it is asserted that they *have overcome* (NEB 'mastered') *the evil one*. Their conflict has become a conquest. Possibly John uses a deliberate assonance: *neaniskoi . . . nenikēkate* (13b). It is significant that in each of these six messages the verb is in the perfect tense, which indicates the present consequence of a past event. John is laying emphasis on the assured standing into which every Christian has come, whatever his stage of spiritual development. A hint is given as to the secret of the young men's victory. *You are strong*, he says, and your strength is due to the fact that *the word of God lives in you* (14b). They have grasped the Christian revelation. They are seeking to conform their lives to its ethical demands, for 'How can a young man keep his way pure?' Only 'by living according to your word' (Ps. 119:9; *cf.* v. 11). Alternatively, the reference may be to their overcoming of the antichrists' false teaching, which was diabolical (*cf.* 4:1–4; 5:4–5).

D. A DIGRESSION ABOUT THE WORLD (2:15–17)

John turns now from a description of the church to a description of the world, and to instruction about the church's attitude to it. In so doing he changes from affirmations about the Christians' standing to warnings about their behaviour. The characteristic tense of this paragraph is not the perfect indicative but the present imperative: *do not love the world*. Christian people have entered into a great inheritance in the forgiveness of sins, fellowship with God and the conquest of the evil one, but their temptations have not come to an end.

What is *the world*? John here mentions it for the first time, but he refers to it many times later. His teaching about it in the letter, supplemented by our Lord's recorded teaching on this subject in the Fourth Gospel, is summarized in an Additional Note (pp. 106–108). Suffice it to say here that sometimes John simply means 'the universe' (Jn. 1:10) or 'life on earth' (Jn. 3:17; 1 Jn. 4:17), but usually he is referring to 'the life of human society as organized under the power of evil' (Dodd), 'the order of finite being regarded as apart from God' (Westcott). In these verses in which the world is mentioned six times, the sequence of thought is clear. The command not to love the world is grounded on two arguments; first, the incompatibility of love for the world and love for the Father (15–16) and secondly, the transience of the world as contrasted with the eternity of those who do God's will (17).

15. *Do not love the world.* Some people have been puzzled as to how this command not to love the world can be reconciled with the statement of God's love for the world in John 3:16. There are two possible explanations. The first is that *the world* has a different connotation in these verses. Viewed as people, the world must be loved. Viewed as an evil system, organized under the dominion of Satan and not of God, it is not to be loved. The second explanation is that it is the verb 'to love', not its object 'the world', which has a different shade of meaning. In the one it is 'the holy love of Redemption'; in the other it is 'the selfish love of participation' (Alford). The first aims 'to save the sinner's person'; the second, 'to share his sin' (Ebrard). So NEB: 'Do not set your hearts on the godless world . . .' Perhaps there is a subtle change of emphasis in both words. The command is uncompromising. The Christian is to love God (5) and his brother or sister (10), but he is not to love the world. And love is a fit subject for such commandment and prohibition because it is not an uncontrollable emotion but the steady devotion of the will. The reason why we are enjoined not to love the world is because 'love for the Father' (RSV) and love for the world are mutually exclusive. If we are engrossed in the outlook and pursuits of the world which rejects Christ, it is evident that we have no love for the Father. 'Friendship with the world is hatred towards God' (Jas. 4:4). 'No-one can serve two masters' (Mt. 6:24; Lk. 16:13), and if we cannot serve God and mammon, neither can we love the Father and the world.

16. If there were some things *in the world* (in the technical sense in which John uses this phrase) which were *from the Father*, that is, which owed their origin and existence to him, we might love them. But since *everything in the world . . . comes . . . from the world*, we may not love any of it. John selects for special mention *the cravings of sinful man, the lust of his eyes and the boasting of what he has and does*. These appear to him 'the essential marks of the pagan way of life' (Dodd). The first describes the desire of our fallen and sinful nature. It may be said to be *in the world*, because the world, where the devil rules, is the sphere of its free operation. It is noteworthy that within the space of three verses, John mentions the world, the flesh and the devil (14–16).

The second seems to indicate temptations which assault us not from within, but from without through our *eyes*. This is 'the tendency to be captivated by the outward show of things, without enquiring into their real values' (Dodd). Eve's view of the forbidden fruit as 'pleasing to the eye', Achan's covetous sight among the spoil of a 'beautiful robe from Babylonia', and David's lustful looking after Bathsheba as she bathed, are obvious examples (Gn. 3:6; Jos. 7:21; 2 Sa. 11:2). It will include 'the love of beauty divorced from the love of goodness' (Law). What the AV and the RSV render 'the pride of life' (*hē alazoneia tou biou*) is the most difficult of these three expressions. The NIV translates it *the boasting of what he* (*sc. sinful man*) *has and does*. While *zōē* means 'life in its essential principle', *bios* is 'life in its present concrete manifestation' (Westcott). It occurs again in 3:17 in the expression *ton bion tou kosmou*, translated 'material possessions'. The *alazōn* is a braggart (Rom. 1:30; 2 Tim. 3:2; Jas. 4:16), 'a conceited, pretentious humbug' (Dodd), who seeks 'to impress everyone he meets with his own non-existent importance' (Barclay). He boasts *of what he has and does*. His arrogance relates to his external circumstances, whether wealth or rank or dress; it is a 'pretentious ostentation' (Plummer), 'the desire to shine or outshine others' in luxurious living (Ebrard).

Some commentators have seen 'this trinity of evil' (Plummer, Findlay) exemplified in our Lord's three temptations in the wilderness, and even in the threefold attraction of the forbidden fruit to Eve (Gn. 3:6). But neither parallel is sufficiently close to suppose a deliberate allusion to be intended. Nor is there a very obvious correspondence between these aspects of the world and the 'three master vices which occupy a prominent place in ancient and medieval ethics' (Westcott), namely *voluptas*, *avaritia* and *superbia*. Findlay summarizes John's three as 'two lusts and one vaunt, two forms of depravation arising from our needs and one from our possessions – unholy desire for things one has not, and unholy pride in things one has'. Dodd's summary is 'base desires, false values, egoism'.

17. The second reason for not setting our love on the world is that the new age has arrived, and the present age is doomed. The world, like the darkness that is in it, is already disintegrating (*paragetai* is used both here and in v. 8). *Cf.* 1 Corinthians 7:31. And those consumed with worldly lusts will pass away with it. Only one kind of person will remain: *the man who does the will of God lives for ever*. Jesus had said that 'whoever does God's will' was his 'brother and sister and mother' (Mk. 3:35). John draws the logical conclusion that those thus related to Christ live as he lives (*cf.* Jn. 8:35; 12:34). The same choice between God and the world, or more particularly between the lust of the world and the will of God, still confronts Christians. We shall more readily obey the command 'do not love the world' if we remember that while *the world and its desires* are transient, God's will and those who do it are alike eternal (*cf.* 2 Cor. 4:18).

Additional Note: The meaning of 'the world' (2:15–17)

In the New Testament the Greek word *kosmos* denotes now the whole material order, the universe, now the planet earth, and now the totality of its human inhabitants. But in John's Gospel and letters it constantly refers to fallen humanity, hostile to God. The word occurs so often that it may be helpful to summarize John's teaching on this topic.

A. The world and Satan

'The world' is under the dominion of Satan. He is 'the prince of this world' (Jn. 12:31; 14:30; 16:11), and 'the whole world is under the control of the evil one' (5:19). Indeed, the devil is entitled 'the one who is in the world' (4:4). The world is his sphere of influence. Similarly, the 'spirit of the antichrist' which is coming, is 'even now . . . already in the world' (4:3), and 'many false prophets have gone out into the world' (4:1). 'The world', therefore, is an inclusive term for all those who are in the kingdom of darkness and have not been born of God. Though 'the whole world is under the control of the evil one', 'we know that we are children of God' (5:19). Because we are the children of God, 'the world does not know us', for 'it did not know him', Christ (3:1–2). Nor does it know the Father (Jn. 17:25). The world and the church are thus portrayed in sharp contrast to each other, two entirely separate and distinct groups of people, the one under the dominion of Satan, the other born of God and knowing God. Since the world's prince is 'driven out' and 'stands condemned' (Jn. 12:31; 16:11), it follows that the world itself is doomed. Indeed already it is passing away (2:17).

B. *The world and God*

This sinful 'world', ruled by Satan, is nevertheless the object of God's love and saving activity. Not, of course, that he condones its materialism and sin, but his compassion embraces the poor creatures the devil has enthralled. 'God so loved the world, that he gave his one and only Son . . .' (Jn. 3:16). God 'sent his one and only Son into the world that we might live through him' (4:9). 'The Father has sent his Son to be the Saviour of the world' (4:14), and Jesus Christ died to be 'the atoning sacrifice for our sins, and not only for ours but also for the sins of the whole world' (2:2).

C. *The world and the Christian*

Christians know themselves to have been chosen 'out of the world' (Jn. 17:6) in such a way that they no longer belong to it. They are still 'in this world' (4:17; *cf.* Jn. 17:11, 15), yet distinct from it, so that we and the world are set over against each other. John writes: 'Do not be surprised, my brothers, if the world hates you' (3:13; *cf.* Jn. 15:18–19; 17:14). Hatred is characteristic of the world, as love is of the Christian (3:14). The world not only hates us but will not listen to us. It listens to false prophets. 'They are from the world and therefore speak from the viewpoint of the world, and the world listens to them' (4:5). But 'we are from God', and 'not of the world' (Jn. 17:14, 16), and so 'whoever knows God listens to us', whereas 'whoever is not from God does not listen to us' (4:6; *cf.* Jn. 15:19). Though the world hates the Christian, the Christian must not hate the world. Nevertheless, he must 'not love the world or anything in the world' (2:15). He is to be neither conformed to it, nor contaminated by it. What then is to be the Christian's attitude to the world? He is not to escape out of it; he is to remain in it. He is to be 'unworldly' without becoming 'otherworldly', living 'in' it without being 'of' it. Indeed he is 'sent into the world' as Jesus was (Jn. 17:18), and, above all, 'everyone born of God overcomes the world'. Not only does he resist the allurements of the world (2:15–16), but he positively overcomes it; and 'this is the victory that has overcome the world, even our faith. Who is it that overcomes the world? Only he who believes that Jesus is the Son of God' (5:4–5). The devil, through the spirit of antichrist, holds the world in unbelief; it is by faith in Jesus as the Son of God that we escape from the devil and thus overcome the world.

E. BELIEF, OR THE DOCTRINAL TEST (2:18–27)

After his two brief digressions, John reverts to his principal thesis, namely discrimination between the true and the false by means of tests. To the moral and social tests which he has already expounded (3–11), he now adds his doctrinal test. He first draws a clear distinction between the heretics and the genuine Christians (18–21); then defines the nature and effect of the heresy (22–23); and finally describes the two safeguards against heresy which his readers already have (24–27).

1. *The heretics and the genuine Christians* (2:18–21)

Twice he tells his *dear children* that *this is the last hour*. Since the new age had dawned with the coming of Christ (see commentary on vv. 8 and 17), Christians knew themselves to be living 'in the last days'. The age to come had already come; the world and the darkness were already passing away (8, 17). John was convinced not only that it was the last days, but that within this end period 'the last hour' (*eschatē hōra*) had struck.[1]

The evidence for this was that *even now many antichrists have come*. The word 'antichrist' occurs in the Bible only in the Johannine letters (1 Jn. 2:18, 22; 4:3; 2 Jn. 7), but the conception is found elsewhere. The appearing of the antichrist was regarded

---

[1]For a more detailed consideration of John's use of this term see the Additional Note, 'The last hour' (pp. 112–114).

as a sign of the approaching end. Daniel's prophecy of 'the abomination that causes desolation' (Dn. 11:31; 12:11), which was partly fulfilled when Antiochus Epiphanes desecrated the Temple in *c.* 168 BC, was not thought to have been finally fulfilled even when the Temple was defiled and destroyed by the Roman army under Titus in AD 70, to which event Jesus had referred Daniel's phrase (Mk. 13:14; *cf.* Lk. 21:20–21). Paul taught that a further outbreak of evil sacrilege would precede the end, but that even now 'the secret power of lawlessness is already at work' (see 2 Thes. 2:1–12). In the same way John writes that, *as you have heard that the antichrist is coming* (because this was part of the apostolic teaching; *cf.* 2 Thes. 2:5), *even now many antichrists have come.*[1] The 'spirit of the antichrist' is already at work in the world (4:3). It is not necessary to say that John 'rationalizes (demythologizes?) the myth and boldly identifies the heretics with the foretold Antichrist' (Alexander) or that to John 'antichrist is not so much a person as a principle' (Barclay); what John means is that the *many antichrists* are forerunners of the one still to come.

It is tempting to interpret the prefix 'anti' in the word 'antichrist' as meaning not 'against' but 'instead of', on the analogy of *antibasileus*, 'viceroy', and to regard the antichrist as being essentially a substitute-Christ, a lying pretender, rather than an opponent of Christ – 'a kind of diabolical parody of God's Messiah' (Dodd), active 'not in the world, but in perversions of Christianity' (Law). Certainly Jesus warned the disciples of 'false Christs' (*pseudochristoi*, Mt. 24:24; Mk. 13:22), and it is characteristic of the antichrist that he is described as he that *is coming*. He makes himself out to be 'the coming one', thus aping the Christ, of whose first coming in the flesh and second coming in glory John has much to say (*e.g.* 4:2; 2 Jn. 7 and 2:28). Nevertheless, the early commentators understood the word to signify an 'adversary' of Christ, and if John had meant a 'false' Christ, he probably would have used the term *pseudochristos* as he does *pseudoprophētēs* in 4:1. Certainly the antichrist's teaching is here recognized as being fundamentally against Christ and a

[1] The verb (*gegonasin*) may be contrasted with *was* (*ēn*), which is used of the eternal Son in 1:1. 'Christ the Word *was* from all eternity; antichrists have arisen, have come into existence in time' (Plummer on 1:1).

denial of Christ (22). Perhaps both ideas are present in the word, 'counterfeiting and opposing' (Plummer), as in the case of Paul's 'man of lawlessness' (see especially 2 Thes. 2:3–4).

19. The many antichrists who have already come (in contrast to the one antichrist who shall come) are now identified as human teachers. They are no doubt the same as the 'many false prophets' of 4:1 (*cf.* our Lord's combination of 'false Christs and false prophets' in Mk. 13:22). They have left the church to which John is writing, perhaps because they have failed to win over the church leaders to their viewpoint. They have excommunicated themselves. John distinguishes sharply between the *they* who have left and the *us* who remain. *They went out (exēlthan) from us.* By their defection they have given clear evidence of their true character. In fact, their withdrawal was 'anticipated by Judas Iscariot, who "went out" (*exēlthen*) from the company of Jesus and the disciples in the upper room (Jn. 13:30*a* . . .)' (Smalley, p. 102). Just so, the false teachers *did not really belong to us.* So certain is John of this fact that he adds the hypothesis: *if they had belonged to us, they would have remained with us.*

John not only relates the fact of their departure from the fellowship, but discerns a purpose in it. The heretics went out of their own volition, but behind the secession was the divine purpose that the spurious should be 'made manifest' (AV) (*phanerōthōsin*) lest the elect should be led astray (Mt. 24:24). Their departure was 'their unmasking' (Law). What is counterfeit cannot remain for ever hidden (*cf.* 1 Cor. 3:13; 4:5). 'There is nothing concealed that will not be disclosed, or hidden that will not be made known' (Lk. 12:2).

Light is shed by this verse upon two important doctrines: the perseverance of the saints and the nature of the church. 'He who stands firm to the end will be saved' (Mk. 13:13), not because salvation is the reward of endurance, but because endurance is the hallmark of the saved. If the false teachers *had belonged to us, they would have remained with us.* This is stated as a principle. Those who belong to us stay with us. Future and final perseverance is the ultimate test of a past participation in Christ (*cf.* Heb. 3:14). 'Those who fall away', on the other hand, 'have never been thoroughly imbued with the knowledge of Christ but only had a slight and passing taste of it' (Calvin).

This verse also gives biblical warrant for some distinction between the visible and the invisible church. Granted that God intends his church to be visibly manifest in local worshipping, witnessing fellowships, this does not mean that all the professing baptized, communicant members of the church are necessarily members of Christ. Only the Lord knows 'those who are his' (2 Tim. 2:19). Perhaps most visible-church members are also members of the invisible church, the mystical body of Christ, but some are not. They are *with us* yet do *not really belong to us*. They share our earthly company but not our heavenly birth. Only on the final day of separation will the wheat and the tares be completely revealed. Meanwhile, some are shown up in their true colours by their defection. *Cf.* 3:10 for a manifestation in moral behaviour.

20. *All of you know the truth.* By this translation *all of you* NIV opts for the reading *pantes*, 'understanding the passage to be directed against the claims of a few to possess esoteric knowledge' (Metzger, p. 709). The alternative reading *panta* is well supported, but in view of the ignorance which John declares in 3:2, it is improbable that he would have written that his readers 'know all things' (NIV mg.). Whichever is correct, his readers' loyalty to the truth is contrasted with the heretical teaching of those who have departed from the church, and is traced to the fact that they possess *an anointing (chrisma) from the Holy One*, the latter title designating either God (*e.g.* Hab. 3:3) or Christ (*e.g.* Jn. 6:69). There seems to be here a deliberate play on words. Protection against the 'antichrist' is in the 'chrism' they had received. The word literally means 'not the act of anointing, but that with which it is performed' (Westcott). This was commonly oil. When the Messiah ('the Lord's Anointed') came, however, in fulfilment of Isaiah 61:1 he was anointed at his baptism not with oil but with the Holy Spirit (Lk. 4:18; Acts 4:27; 10:38). It is likely, therefore, that the anointing which we have received from God is the same Holy Spirit. In contrast to the false teachers who were antichrists, the true Christian has received the same spiritual 'chrism' as Christ (*cf.* 2 Cor. 1:21–22). It is through the illumination of the Spirit of truth that we *know the truth*, as is elaborated in verse 27. As Tyndale put it, 'Ye are not anointed with oil in your bodies, but with the Spirit of Christ in your souls: which Spirit teacheth you all truth in Christ, and maketh you to judge what is a lie, and what truth, and to know Christ from antichrist.' Nor are we an esoteric, enlightened minority, such as the heretics claimed to be. It is probable that they used the word *chrisma* as a technical term for initiation into a special *gnōsis*. If so, it is in direct contradiction to their exclusive claim that John says *all* his readers have the same *gnōsis* because they have all received the same *chrisma*, the Spirit of truth (*cf*. Col. 1:28). 'You, no less than they, are among the initiated' (NEB).[1]

21. John emphasizes his assurance concerning their orthodoxy. His purpose in writing, he says, is not to inform them of new truth, but to confirm them in the truth they already know (*cf*. Rom 15:14–15). Not only do they *know the truth*, but they know the character of truth, that it is wholly true and self-consistent, and that *no lie comes from the truth*. On the contrary, lies emanate from the devil (Jn. 7:44).

Additional Note: 'The last hour' (2:18)

The New Testament writers do not have an exact vocabulary to describe the chronology of the last time or the end, and it is not always easy to discern to what eschatological period or event they are alluding. What is clear is that they regarded the first coming of Christ as having inaugurated the new age and settled the doom of the old. 'The age to come' had come, and 'the present age' was therefore drawing to a close. It was not, of course, anticipated that this period would last for ever. It was a stage of transition called both the 'last days' (Mi. 4:1; Acts 2:17; *cf*. Joel 2:28; Heb. 1:1–2) and the 'last times' (1 Pet. 1:20; *cf*. 1 Cor. 10:11).The New Testament writers who describe its beginning are already looking forward to its consummation. The 'last days' will themselves have 'last days', a period of grievous moral and

---

[1]See also the Additional Note, 'The meaning of *"chrisma"* ', pp. 114–115.

religious decadence (2 Tim. 3:1ff.; 2 Pet. 3:3). Similarly, the 'last times' will have a 'last time' in which ungodly scoffers will arise (Jude 18; *cf*. 1 Tim. 4:1). Nor is this all. The 'last time' of the 'last times' will have a culminating 'last time' when our eternal inheritance will be revealed (1 Pet. 1:5; *cf*. Jas. 5:3).In the same way, 'the last days' of the 'last days' will themselves have a final 'last day' when Christ raises the dead and judges the world (Jn. 6:39–40, 44, 54; 11:24; 12:48).

In this progressive unfolding of the last things, to what does John's unique reference to a 'last hour' refer?

1. Some commentators are quite definite about the proper interpretation. 'The "last hour" is the last period of the interval between the first and second coming of Christ' (Brooke). Those who hold this view (*e.g.* Dodd and Barclay) add logically that in this John has proved to be mistaken.

2. A second interpretation draws attention to the fact that *eschatē hōra* is anarthrous and that the phrase could or should be rather translated 'it is *a* last hour'. Westcott makes much of this and writes that the omission of the definite article 'seems to mark the general character of the period and not its specific relation to "the end". It was a period of critical change.' Other writers have endorsed this view. Lewis, after pointing out that 'in the history of Christendom there have been many last hours and new beginnings', goes on to suggest that the time of John's writing, with 'widespread heresy . . . massing its forces against the Christian faith and threatening its survival', was 'one of the ultimate crises in the history of Christendom'. Although Plummer is very scornful of such an interpretation, declaring roundly that 'there can be only one last hour', it cannot be lightly dismissed. Even Dodd, who is clear that John is mistaken, allows a secondary application to that greatest 'last hour', the crucifixion and resurrection of Jesus, into whose meaning, he writes, the church was now entering.

3. There is a third possible interpretation, namely that John did mean the end of the old era and the consummation of the new, the last hour of the last days, but that he was not thereby dogmatizing that the end was imminent. He was expressing a theological truth rather than making a chronological reference. In view of our Lord's clear words about the uncertainty of the

day and the hour (Mk. 13:32) and of 'times or dates' (Acts 1:7), it is *a priori* most unlikely that the apostles would have presumed to speculate precisely *when* the end would come.[1] John could state on theological grounds that the last hour had struck, but this was not the same as affirming chronologically when the last hour would end. It was generally believed, and Jesus had taught, that a period of tribulation and apostasy would precede the end, including the rise of 'false Christs and false prophets' (Mk. 13: 22). It was because 'many antichrists have come' that John could affirm that he knew it was 'the last hour'. This is not 'a curious argument' (Dodd); it is sound reasoning. The powers of darkness were closing their ranks. The forces of evil were rallying. If the first coming of Christ evidenced the arrival of 'the last days', the coming of *many antichrists* proved that it was 'the last hour'. A last desperate stand on the part of Christ's enemies was expected before the consummation. This was taking place. The stage was now set for the end. 'No more remained but for Christ to appear for the redemption of the world' (Calvin). 'This is the last hour.' What John wrote was true. And it is still true. The fact that nearly 1,900 years have elapsed since he wrote these words does not invalidate his argument or contradict his affirmation. 'Nothing is so damaging in the study of New Testament prophecy . . . as to imagine that the Eternal God, who stands above and outside of time, is bound by the clocks and calendars of men' (Blaiklock). It is still 'the last hour', the hour of final opposition to Christ. Although there may yet be a special time of tribulation before the denouement, the whole Christian era consists of 'the great tribulation' through which all the redeemed must pass (Rev. 7:14). We still await the end.

Additional Note: The meaning of '*chrisma*' (2:20)

Dodd has a long passage about the interpretation of *chrisma* (pp. 58–64). He quotes from Hippolytus a document of the Gnostic 'Naassenes' sect in which reference is made to an initiation by anointing into some esoteric mystery. From it he argues

---

[1]Compare John's references to the appearing of Christ in 2:28 and 3:2, where the Greek conjunction *ean*, translated 'when', strictly means 'if'. ' "If" implies no doubt as to the *fact*; it merely implies indifference as to the *time*' (Plummer).

that the use of *chrisma* in these verses has a background of Hellenistic rather than Hebrew religion and signifies initiation not consecration. He also quotes a sentence from Ignatius' *Letter to the Ephesians* which speaks of anointing with 'doctrine'. He then refers to baptism as a rite of initiation 'which *all* Christians undergo', and concludes 'that the "chrism", which confers knowledge of God, and is also a prophylactic against the poison of false teaching, is the Word of God, that is, the Gospel, or the revelation of God in Christ, as communicated in the rule of faith to catechumens, and confessed in Baptism. This is the Christian's initiation, by water and the Word.' Barclay appears to be in substantial agreement.

But this interpretation, attractive as it is in some respects, seems to confuse the relation between the *chrisma* and the *gnōsis*, the anointing or initiation and the knowledge into which the Christian is initiated. Is the knowledge the means by which, or the benefit into which, the Christian is initiated? In the Ignatius passage it is the former, the 'doctrine' being the actual oil of anointing. In Dodd's reconstruction, however, it is both, the gospel being the *chrisma* by which Christians are initiated into the knowledge of God. But would John's readers have appreciated this rather subtle distinction between the gospel and the knowledge of God? It seems more probable that John would have insisted on equating the gospel and the *gnōsis*, denying that there was a further knowledge into which the gospel initiated people. Otherwise, would he not be playing into the hands of the heretics? He makes it plain in his second letter that his readers are to 'continue in the teaching of Christ' and not 'run ahead' beyond it (2 Jn. 9). It is more likely, therefore, that, if the concept of initiation is present, the benefit into which Christians are initiated is the eternal gospel, which is itself the true *gnōsis*, while the *chrisma*, the means of initiation into it, is the Holy Spirit of truth.

2. The nature and effect of the heresy (2:22–23)

The false teaching of those who have left the church is now revealed. It is a denial *that Jesus is the Christ*. A study of John's letters makes it plain that by this phrase he does not simply mean a denial that Jesus was the Messiah of Old Testament expectation (*cf.* Acts 5:42; 9:22; 17:3; 18:28). In the second part of this verse and in verse 23 he refers to Jesus as *the Son*. For a similar linking of the two expressions see 5:1 and 5:5 and *cf.* John 20:31; Mt.16:16. In 4:2-3 (*cf.* 2 Jn. 7) the theological error he is combating is defined more precisely as a denial that 'Jesus Christ has come in the flesh', or, as perhaps this expression should be translated, a denial that 'Jesus is the Christ come in the flesh'. The antichrists probably taught (as some later Gnostics certainly taught) that Jesus was born and died a man, and that 'the Christ', by which they meant a divine emanation, was within him only during his public ministry, descending upon him at his baptism and leaving him before the cross. They thus denied that Jesus was or is (*estin*, 22) the Christ or the Son. They made him a mere man who for a brief period was invested with divine powers or even adopted into the Godhead, but they denied that the man Jesus and the eternal Son were and are the same person, possessing two perfect natures, human and divine. In a word, they denied the incarnation.

John's black and white contrasts are healthily clearsighted. Opposing views are not to him 'complementary insights' but 'truth and error' (*cf.* vv. 21, 27). If we claim to enjoy fellowship with God while we walk in darkness, 'we lie' (1:6). He who says he knows God but disobeys his commands 'is a liar' (*pseustēs*, 2:4). So is the person who claims to love God but hates his brother (4:20). But what shall be said of him who denies that Jesus is the Christ? We must pronounce him 'the' liar (*ho pseustēs*, 22, RV, RSV, NEB, NIV), the liar *par excellence*. Indeed, you can tell that this is the arch-lie, because he who perpetrates it is none other than *the antichrist*, not the personal antichrist who is still to come (see v. 18), but a living embodiment of the spirit of antichrist (4:3; *cf.* 2 Jn. 7). The heretics' theology is not just defective; it is diabolical. The fundamental doctrinal test of the professing Christian concerns his view of the person of Jesus. If he is a Unitarian, or a member of a sect denying the deity of Jesus, he is not a Christian. Many strange cults which have a popular appeal today can be easily judged and quickly repudiated by this test. The extreme seriousness of the lie is that a second denial is implicit in the first: he *denies the Father and the Son*.

23. Having disclosed the nature of the heresy, John now elaborates its dreadful effect, which he has already mentioned at the end of the previous verse. He states the truth in absolute and unequivocal terms, first negatively, then positively. No-one who denies *the Son*, he declares, *has the Father*, while *whoever acknowledges the Son has the Father also*. John has in mind more than a private belief and disbelief. As when the same verbs are used by Jesus, a public confession and denial of him 'before men' are implied (*cf.* Mt. 10:32–33; Jn. 12:42; Rom. 10:9–10). On such a confession or denial depends not just our conception of, but our possession of, the Father. The verb *has* (*echei*) is the same in both parts of the verse. *Cf.* 5:12; 2 John 9. We cannot possess, *i.e.* have fellowship with, the Father if we do not confess the Son. Only the Son can reveal the Father to us (Mt. 11:27; Jn. 1:18; 12:44–45; 14:9); only the Son can represent and reconcile us to the Father (2:1–2; Jn. 14:6; *cf.* 1 Tim. 2:5).

3. Safeguards against heresy (2:24–27)

Having distinguished between the false teachers' and the true believers, and having exposed the nature and consequences of the heresy, John now draws attention to the two safeguards which will protect his readers from being led astray. If they are to be guarded against error, two things must 'remain' in them, first the message which 'you have heard from the beginning' (24) and secondly 'the anointing you received from him' (27).

24. *What you have heard from the beginning* is the gospel, the apostolic teaching, the original message which had been preached. It had not changed and would not change. They must *see that it remains in* them. It would not do so automatically – they must take steps to ensure that it does. Christians should always be 'conservative' in their theology. To have 'itching ears', ever running after new teachers, listening to anybody and never arriving at a knowledge of the truth, is a characteristic of the 'terrible times' which shall come 'in the last days' (2 Tim. 3:1, 7; 4:3). The continuous obsession for 'the latest ideas' is a mark of the Athenian not the Christian (Acts 17:21). Christian theology is anchored not only to certain historical events, culminating in the saving career of Jesus, but to the authoritative apostolic witness to, and interpretation of, these events. The Christian can never weigh anchor and launch out into the deep of speculative thought. Nor can he forsake the primitive teaching of the apostles for subsequent human traditions. The apostolic testimony is directed essentially to the Son. That is why it will keep them true to him if they remain true to it. Moreover, they will *remain in the Son and in the Father*, in the sense of experiencing an intimate spiritual communion with both. To *remain in* God (or 'abide in', RSV; Gk. *menein*) and to 'have' God (23) are virtually identical in meaning.

25. As a result of such loyalty to and communion with the Son and the Father, we shall enjoy the promised *eternal life* (*cf.* 5:11–12). The awful consequence of the heretical denial of the Son was a loss of life as well as of the Father.

26. But the apostolic teaching was not in itself enough to keep them in the truth. John does not underestimate the strength or the subtlety of the deceivers. The NIV is doubtless right to render the present participle here (*planōntōn*) as *those who are trying to lead you astray*. They have not succeeded, but they are in process of making the attempt. It is possible for Christians to be deceived by false teachers, as is implied here, by others (3:7) and by themselves (1:8) The devil himself is the primary deceiver, for he is in his very nature 'a liar and the father of lies' (Jn. 8:44).

27. Against such would-be deceivers John's readers had a second safeguard, namely, *the anointing* (*chrisma*) *you received from him* and which *remains in you*. See commentary on verse 20 and the Additional Note, 'The meaning of "*chrisma*"' (pp. 114–115), where it is argued that this is a reference to the Holy Spirit. Jesus himself had promised that the Spirit once given would remain with us for ever (Jn. 14:16). Possessing knowledge by the Spirit of truth's direct illumination, *you do not need anyone to teach you*. (*Cf.* Je. 31:34; 1 Thes. 4:9.) It would not be difficult to exaggerate this statement in an incautious and unbalanced fashion. True, in the last resort the Holy Spirit is our absolutely adequate teacher, and we maintain our right of private judgment by his illumination of the Word of God. But we must see this verse in the context of a letter in which John is, in fact, teaching those who, he says, have no need of human teachers! And other passages of the New Testament refer not only to the general ministry of teaching in the church (*e.g.* Acts 4:18; 5:28, 42; 2 Tim. 2:24) but also to specially gifted 'teachers' (1 Cor. 12:29; Eph. 4:11).

The competence of the Holy Spirit to teach them is indicated in the next phrases, namely both that *his anointing teaches you about all things* (*cf.* Jn. 14:26) and that it 'is true and is no lie' (the RSV contrast between 'true' and 'lie' is more accurate than the NIV *real* and *counterfeit*). If our God is 'the true God' (*e.g.* 2 Ch. 15:3; Je. 10:10; Jn. 17:3; 1 Thes. 1:9; *cf.* 1 Jn. 5:20) and Jesus Christ is 'the truth' (Jn. 14:6), the Holy Spirit also 'is true'. Indeed in 5:6 it is written, 'the Spirit is the truth'. Our Lord called him 'the Spirit of truth' (Jn. 15:26; 16:13), and promised that he would guide the apostles 'into all truth' (Jn. 16:13). With this knowledge of his nature, and with the further assurance that *it has taught you* in the past (*it*, neuter, because *chrisma*, anointing, is neuter, and not because the Holy Spirit is other than 'he', a person), John looks confidently into the future and ends the paragraph either with the statement that they 'shall abide in him' (AV) or with the command *remain in him* (or possibly 'in it', namely the *chrisma*). In either case, the imperative occurs at the beginning of the next verse, where the 'him' is clearly Christ: *And now, dear children, continue in him.*

Here, then, are the two safeguards against error – the apostolic Word and the anointing Spirit (*cf.* Is. 59:21). Both are received at conversion. 'You heard' (*ēkousate*, 24) the Word, he says, and 'you received' (*elabete*, 27) the Spirit, although indeed, he implies, the Word has come to you from us (1:2–3, 5), while you have received the Spirit direct *from him* (27), who is *the Holy One* (27). The Word is an objective safeguard, while the anointing of the Spirit is a subjective experience; but both the apostolic teaching and the heavenly teacher are necessary for continuance in the truth. And both are to be personally and inwardly grasped. This is the biblical balance which is too seldom preserved. Some honour the Word and neglect the Spirit who alone can interpret it; others honour the Spirit but neglect the Word out of which he teaches. The only safeguard against lies is to have remaining within us both the Word that we *heard from the beginning* and the *anointing* that we *received* from him. It is by these old possessions, not by new teachings or teachers, that we shall remain in the truth.

IV. SECOND APPLICATION OF THE TESTS (2:28 – 4:6)

John now reverts to his cycle of tests, expanding and enforcing them: the moral test of obedience or righteousness (2:28 – 3:10), the social test of love (3:11–18) and, after a digression about the relation between our assurance and our condemning heart (3:19–24), the doctrinal test of truth concerning Christ (4:1–6).

It is now, in the second exposition of the three tests, that for the first time the believer is described as having been 'born' of God (2:29). Previously he has been delineated as one who knows God (2:3–4, 13, 14), is in Christ (2:5–6) and in the light (2:9–10), and remains in the Father and in the Son (2:24, 27–28). But now there comes to the fore that birth from God which alone makes it possible for us to know God and remain in him. Such a spiritual 'birth' is due to a divine 'begetting', which is the imparting of the life of God. And it has manifest consequences in the life of the Christian, for he who has been born of God does not continue to sin (3:9), but practises righteousness (2:29), loves his brothers and sisters in God's family (3:10,14; *cf.* 4:7) and believes that Jesus is the Christ (5:1; *cf.* 4:1–6).

A. AN ELABORATION OF THE MORAL TEST: RIGHTEOUSNESS (2:28 – 3:10)

The moral test again comes first. The proof of being a Christian is not merely orthodoxy, but righteous conduct as well. This time, in unfolding the moral test, John associates it closely with the Lord's 'manifestations' or 'appearings'. The thought of manifestation, either as a noun, adjective or verb, occurs in this passage six times, four of which refer to Christ, two to his future appearing which is treated first (2:28 – 3:2) and two to his past appearing (3:5, 8; *cf.* 1:2). Such, then, is the theme of this paragraph. Unrighteous conduct is unthinkable in the Christian who has grasped the purpose of the two appearings of Christ. The fact of his first appearing and the hope of his second are both strong incentives to holiness.

1. Christ's future appearing (2:28 – 3:3)

We have already seen that the command in verse 28 to *continue in him* is probably a repetition of what John wrote at the end of the previous verse. But, whereas there the emphasis was upon remaining in Christ by acknowledging him as the incarnate Son, here the thought is rather of a personal relationship with Christ which has wholesome moral consequences, so that (*hina*, the purpose of continuing in Christ) *when he appears we* (he includes himself) *may be confident and unashamed before him*. There can be no mistaking this reference to our Lord's return. Some commentators have suggested that the vivid expectation of the parousia in Paul's letters has been replaced in the later writings of John by the coming of the Spirit and the present enjoyment of eternal life. Such a theory either ignores the teaching on the second coming which occurs in this letter or dismisses it as a concession to popular demand, which is a quite unwarrantable assumption. No: the doctrine of the Lord's return was part of the primitive apostolic faith. Four words (in verbal or substantive form) are used by Paul to describe it – his coming (*parousia*), appearing (*phanerōsis*), epiphany (*epiphaneia*), and revelation (*apokalypsis*). Of these John uses the first two in this verse. There is ample evidence in the papyri that in the East at that time 'the word (*parousia*) was the usual expression for the visit of a King or Emperor' (Brooke). *Parousia* means literally 'presence', and the two words together imply that our Lord's return will involve the personal presence of one now absent, the visible appearing of one now unseen.

People will react to his coming in one of two ways. Some will 'have confidence' (RSV; Gk. *parrēsia*); others will 'shrink from him in shame' (RSV; Gk. *aischynthōmen ap' autou*). In our English Bibles the noun *parrēsia* is usually translated 'confidence', 'assurance', 'courage' or 'boldness', while its adverbial use is rendered 'boldly', 'plainly' or 'freely'. It signifies literally 'outspokenness, frankness, freedom of speech' (LSJ) and is used to describe the

Christian's boldness of approach both to people (as a witness) and to God (as a suppliant). But in this letter, as in the letter to the Hebrews (4:16; 10:19), the word indicates the confidence with which the Christian may draw near to God in prayer now (3:21; 5:14), at the *parousia* (2:28) and on the judgment day (4:17). It is only if we *continue in him* today, however, that we shall *be confident* before him and not shrink from him on the last day. For a description of the shrinking of unbelievers from the presence of the divine Judge see Matthew 22:12 and Revelation 6:15–17.

29. *Born of him* may seem in this context to refer to Christ, but the consistent Johannine terms are to be born 'of God' or 'of the Spirit', and it is 'against the tenor of the New Testament to speak of Christians as "begotten of Christ"' (Law). We must therefore suppose that there is an abrupt change of person between verses 28 and 29, the *he* and *him* referring in verse 28 to Christ and in verse 29 to God. This would certainly be a better transition to the next chapter. Law takes it thus and devotes a long chapter to the relation between the Johannine statements 'God is righteous' and 'God is love'. If you know as a fact (*eidēte*) that God is righteous, John says, then you will perceive as a logical consequence (*ginōskete*) *that everyone who does what is right has been born of him.* The child exhibits the parent's character because he shares the parent's nature. A person's righteousness is thus the evidence of his new birth, not the cause or condition of it. The false teachers (in their incipient Gnosticism) may have called their initiation into *gnōsis* a 'regeneration'; John shows that righteousness, not knowledge, is the principal mark of the regenerate.

3:1 The mention of being 'born of him' leads John to an outburst of wonder at God's love in making us his *children* (*tekna*, derived from *tekein*, 'to beget'), the allusion being to the divine nature we have received through being born of God rather than to our filial status. The expression *how great* translates *potapēn* which meant originally 'of what country'. It is as if the Father's love is so unearthly, so foreign to this world, that John wonders from what country it may come. The word 'always implies astonishment' (Plummer). This love God has not only 'shown' us, but actually *lavished on us*. For *children of God* is no mere title; it is a fact. True, we are *called* 'children of God'. But God gives us this privileged designation only because *that is what we are* by his grace, whatever other people may think or say. The 'children of God' and the 'world' are so different from each other, that *the world does not know us* (*cf.* 1 Cor. 2:15–16). The reason for this is that *it did not know him*, which must surely here refer to Christ, as in verse 6. As his glory was veiled in flesh, so our 'life is now hidden with Christ in God' (Col. 3:3). Our filial status, though real, is not yet apparent (Rom. 8:19).

2. The author calls his readers *dear friends* (*agapētoi*, 'beloved') because those who are loved by the Father are loved by the apostle also. He then moves on from the reiteration *now are we children of God* (whether the world recognizes us or not) to a consideration of *what we will be*, for 'we look ... for an inheritance in virtue of that sonship' (Alford). At first he frankly admits that he does not know the precise character of this inheritance. What we are does not now appear to the world; what we shall be does not yet appear to us. It is important to note this apostolic confession of ignorance. His earlier statement that the 'anointing teaches you about all things' (2:27) is not to be pressed literally. The Christian is not omniscient. The New Testament apostles, like the Old Testament prophets, knew what it had been God's purpose to disclose to them, and no more (*cf.* Dt. 3:24; 1 Cor. 13:8–12). So here John confesses that the exact state and condition of the redeemed in heaven had not been revealed to him. This being so, it is idle and sinful to speculate or to pry into things which God has not been pleased to make known. Indeed, it is implied, it will appear only when he will appear.[1] The two revelations, of Christ and of our final state, will be made simultaneously. For then we shall 'share in his glory' (Rom. 8:17; *cf.* Col. 3:4).

This does not mean, however, that we know nothing about

---

[1] NEB ('when it is disclosed') and NIV mg. ('when it is made known') both follow RV mg. and many commentators in taking as the subject of the verb *phanerothē*, as of the previous *ephanerothē*, not Christ but 'what we shall be'. It could be either. No subject is supplied in the Greek.

our future state. We do know this, *that when he appears, we shall be like him, for we shall see him as he is.* The sequence is clear. First, he will appear; in consequence, we will see him as he is; and so we shall be like him. (For references to 'seeing' God or Christ in heaven *cf.* Mt. 5:8; Jn. 17:24; 1 Cor. 13:12; 2 Cor. 5:7; Heb. 12:14; 1 Pet. 1:8; Rev. 1:7; 22:4). Already the image of God, marred by the fall, has been stamped upon us again. The new nature, which we assumed at our conversion, was 'created to be like God in true righteousness and holiness' (Eph. 4:24; *cf.* 1 Col. 3:10). And since that day, in fulfilment of God's predestinating purpose that we should be 'conformed to the likeness of his Son' (Rom. 8:29), the Holy Spirit has been transfiguring us 'into his likeness with ever-increasing glory' (2 Cor. 3:18; *cf.* 1 Jn. 2:6). In this latter passage the transformation is said to be due to the fact that 'with unveiled faces' we 'all reflect the Lord's glory'. This being so, it is understandable that when we see him as he is, and not our face only but his too will be unveiled, we will be finally and completely like him, including our bodies (Phil. 3:21; *cf.* 1 Cor. 15:49). 'Vision becomes assimilation' (Law). This is all John knows about our final, heavenly state. Paul concentrates in his letters on the truth that in heaven we shall be 'with Christ' (2 Cor. 5:8; Phil. 1:23; Col. 3:4; 1 Thes. 4:17; *cf.* Lk. 23:43; Jn. 14:3; 17:24). It is enough for us to know that on the last day and through eternity we shall be both with Christ and like Christ; for the fuller revelation of what we are going to be we are content to wait.

3. John's reason for writing about the return of Christ and our final state is not theological but ethical. Like Paul he follows our Lord in teaching the practical implications of this glorious expectation. *In him* means 'in Christ', not 'in himself'. The RSV makes this plain by translating 'every one who thus hopes in him'. The Christian *hope* (the word is unique here in John's writings but common in Paul's and Peter's) has as its object or foundation (the preposition is *epi*, which usually means 'on', as in Rom. 15:12; 1 Tim: 4:10) the return of Christ and the glory which follows. It includes the three events already mentioned – his appearing, our seeing him, and our becoming like him. This is not an uncertain hope, like human hopes, because it is grounded upon the promise of Christ (*cf.* Heb. 10:23), and we know (verse 2) the truth for which we hope. Its very certainly adds to its challenge. Christians who fix their hope (their confident expectation) upon Christ's return, will purify themselves, not ceremonially but morally. Purity (*hagneia*) is primarily 'freedom from moral stain' and so 'that element in holy character which is wrought out by the discipline of temptation' (Law). John has already emphasized that, since Christ is righteous, we must practise righteousness if we do not want to be ashamed at his coming (2:28–29). Similarly, since he is pure, and when we see him we will be like him in his purity, we must ensure that the process of purification is begun now and purify ourselves. True, only the blood of Christ can cleanse us from the stain and guilt of sin (1:7), but we have a part to play in purifying ourselves from its power (*cf.* 2 Cor. 7:1; 1 Tim. 5:22; Jas. 4:8; 1 Pet. 1:22).

2. Christ's past appearing (3:4–10)

John now proceeds to the second part of his elaboration of the moral test, and this time links righteousness with Christ's past appearing. His argument for the indispensable necessity of holy living is drawn now, not from the expectation of the Lord's second coming, when we shall see him and become like him, but from the purpose of his first coming which was to remove sins and to destroy the works of the devil. The argument is repeated, each time with a different emphasis.

	Verses 4–7	**Verses 8–10**
The introductory phrase:	*Everyone who sins* (4)	*He who does what is sinful* (8)
The theme:	The nature of sin is lawlessness (4)	The origin of sin is the devil (8)
The purpose of Christ's appearing:	*. . . he appeared so that he might take away our sins* (5)	*The reason the Son of God appeared was to destroy the devil's work* (8)
The logical conclusion:	*No-one who lives in him keeps on sinning* (6)	*No-one who is born of God will continue to sin* (9)

To continue in sin is thus shown to be in complete contradiction to the whole purpose of Christ's first appearing, which is twice mentioned (5, 8), just as his second appearing has been mentioned twice in the previous section (2:28; 3:2).

i. The nature of sin: lawlessness (3:4–7)

4. *Everyone who sins.* John states a universal truth, from which there is no escape and to which there is no exception. This passage (and indeed the whole letter) is full of such generalizations, which are directed against the heretics' arrogant assumption that they constituted an initiated élite set apart from the rank and file. John will admit no such distinction. A dual standard of morality is quite foreign to the Christian religion. Thus, six times in this section he uses the expression *pas ho,* translated either 'everyone who' (with the negative, 'no-one who'), or 'anyone who' (2:29; 3:4, 6a, 6b, 9, 10b), and three times the simple relative *ho,* translated either 'he who' or 'anyone who' (7, 8, 10c). The gospel, with its moral implications, concerns all people, not just some.

There follows a definition of sin. *Everyone who sins breaks the law; in fact, sin is lawlessness (anomia).* There are other definitions of sin in the New Testament (*e.g.* Rom. 14:23; Jas. 4:17; 1 Jn. 5:17); but this, far from being 'somewhat superficial' (Dodd), is the clearest and most revealing. The statement 'sin is lawlessness' (that is, a defiant violation of God's moral law) so identifies the two as to render them interchangeable terms. Wherever one of them is read, it is possible to substitute the other. It is not just that sin manifests itself in disregard for God's law, but that sin is in its very nature lawlessness. Lawlessness is the essence, not the result, of sin. Thus exposed in its ugly reality, the seriousness of sin emerges. The heretics seem to have taught that to the enlightened Christian questions of morality were a matter of indifference; today our sins are excused either by euphemisms like 'personality problems' or by the plea of cultural relativity. In contrast to such underestimates of sin, John declares that it is not just a negative failure (*hamartia,* sin, meaning literally 'missing the mark', and *adikia,* unrighteousness, a deviation from what is right or just), but essentially an active rebellion against God's known will. It is important to acknowledge this, because the first step towards holy living is to recognize the true nature and wickedness of sin.

5. John appeals many times to the knowledge his readers already possess and urges them to conform their lives to it. In this case the knowledge to which he refers concerns not the nature of sin but the truth about Christ's person and work. He implies that if they have a right view of these, they will abhor evil. *He* (*ekeinos*, emphatic, meaning Christ) *appeared so that he might take away our sins. And in him is no sin.* Here Christ's work in removing our sins and his personal sinlessness are brought together. He came into the world to take our sins away (*arē*; the same word occurs in the Baptist's recognition of the Lamb of God, Jn. 1:29; *cf.* also Heb. 9:26). Other parts of the New Testament explain that he did this by taking them upon himself, bearing them in his own body (1 Pet. 2:24; Heb. 9:28; *cf.* Is. 53:11–12). And in removing our sins, he was himself entirely without sin. The sinlessness of Jesus is commonly mentioned in Scripture almost as an aside, in connection with his work of salvation (*e.g.* 2 Cor. 5:21; Heb. 7:26; 1 Pet. 1:19; 2:22). John stresses it much, stating it both positively, 'he is righteous', 'he is pure' (2:29; 3:3, 7) and negatively, 'in him is no sin'. In each case he uses the verb 'is' (*estin*), for the sinlessness of Christ does not belong only to his pre-existence, or to the days of his flesh, or to his present heavenly condition, but to his essential and eternal nature.

6. The logical deduction follows. If the eternal nature of the Son of God is sinless, and if the purpose of his historical appearing was to remove sin, then *no-one who lives in him keeps on sinning*, while, on the other hand, *no-one who continues to sin has either seen him or known him.* It is typical of John's method that he should drive the truth home by this double hammer-blow about sinning and not sinning. Since there is in him no sin, it is obvious that if we live in him we shall not sin either. If we do sin, it shows not only that we are not living in him (present tense) but that we can never have *seen him* (*cf.* 3 Jn. 11) *or known him* (perfect tenses). Not until he appears in glory shall we 'see him as he is' (2); yet every Christian has already seen him with the eye of faith. And the sight of Christ, both in present experience and in future prospect, is a strong incentive to holiness. These verses teach the utter incongruity of sin in the Christian. To see and to know Christ, the sinless Saviour of sinners, is to outlaw sin; to sin is to deny Christ and to reveal that one is not living in him. Sin and Christ are irreconcilably at enmity with each other. Christ in his sinless person and saving work is fundamentally opposed to it.

7. The first part of John's exposition of this theme ends with a solemn warning to his *dear children*. 'The tenderness of the address is called out by the peril of the situation' (Westcott). *Do not let anyone lead you astray*. The false teachers, tools of Satan the arch-deceiver, were seeking to lead them astray, not only theologically (2:26) but morally as well. So let them be on their guard. *He who does what is right is righteous, just as he is righteous.* The heretics appear to have indulged in the subtly perverse reasoning that somehow you could 'be' righteous without necessarily bothering to 'practise' righteousness. John roundly denies the possibility. The only person who is righteous in himself is he who does right like Jesus (*he*, the emphatic pronoun *ekeinos* again), who is righteous, as has already been stated several times (2:1, 29; *cf.* 3:3, 5). 'Doing is the test of Being' (Law).

ii. The origin of sin: the devil (3:8–10)

John follows the same pattern in the second exposition of his argument from Christ's first appearing. He again begins with a reference to the seriousness of sin; continues with the purpose of Christ's mission on earth; and concludes with a deduction about holiness. But this time his emphasis is rather on the origin than on the nature of sin, and he insists that for the Christian its practice is not merely incompatible, but impossible (9).

8. *He who does what is sinful is of the devil.* This second generalization links sin not with the law of God, which it breaks (5), but with the devil in whom it originates. *He has been sinning from the beginning* (*cf.* Jn. 8:44), meaning presumably, from the moment of his proud rebellion against God, from the beginning of his devilish career. Since sin is his characteristic activity (*has been sinning* translates *hamartanei*, a tense which conveys the thought of continuing activity), everyone who sins exhibits a character which must have been derived, at least ultimately, from him. The existence and malevolence of the devil are everywhere assumed in the Johannine literature.[1]

If the characteristic work of the devil is to sin, the characteristic work of the Son of God is to save. *The reason the Son of God appeared* (*ephanerōthē* again, as in v. 5), *was to destroy the devil's work.* The Greek text has 'works' in the plural, for the devil's activity is manifold. His works include all those things which he has insinuated into the perfect creation of God, in order to spoil it. Morally, his work is enticement to sin; physically, the infliction of disease; intellectually, seduction into error. He still assaults our soul, body and mind in these three ways; and Christ came to destroy his works. The destruction was a 'loosing' (*lysē*), as if these diabolical works were chains which bound us. Of course we know from experience that they are not in an absolute sense 'destroyed' (*cf.* Rom. 6:6; 2 Tim: 1:10; Heb. 2:14, where the verb *katargeō* evidently does not mean to liquidate or annihilate, but rather to deprive of force, render inoperative, conquer and overthrow). The devil is still busy doing his wicked works, but he has been defeated, and in Christ we can escape from his tyranny.

If, then, the whole purpose of Christ's first appearing was to remove sins and to undo the works of the devil, Christians must not compromise with either sin or the devil, or they will find themselves fighting against Christ. If the first step to holiness is to recognize the sinfulness of sin, both in its essence as lawlessness and in its diabolical origin, the second step is to see its absolute incompatibility with Christ in his sinless person and saving work. The more clearly we grasp these facts, the more incongruous will sin appear and the more determined we shall be to be rid of it.

9. John again draws a logical conclusion. He makes two searching statements of fact. The first says that the Christian

---

[1] See the Additional Note, 'John's teaching about the devil', pp. 141–142.

does not *continue to sin*, and the second that he *cannot go on sinning*. These expressions (especially because of their AV rendering 'doth not commit sin' and 'cannot sin') have sometimes been taken to teach that a true Christian, one who has been *born of God*, is constitutionally incapable of sinning. But such an interpretation cannot be maintained, unless we are prepared to say that John contradicts himself. In 1:8, 10 he described those who deny that they are sinners by nature and by practice as deceiving themselves and calling God a liar; and in 2:1, although he said he was writing 'so that you will not sin', he explicitly added that 'if anybody does sin' (evidently a possibility to be considered), gracious provision has been made for his forgiveness. It is plain, therefore, that John is not denying the possibility of sin in the Christian. The first way to reconcile his teaching in chapters 1 and 3 is to recognize that in each he is opposing a different error. Gnosticism led its adherents to different conclusions. Some supposed that their possession of *gnōsis* had made them perfect; others maintained that sin did not matter because it could not harm the enlightened. Both positions are morally perverse. The first is blind to sin and denies its existence; the second is indifferent to sin and denies its gravity. To the first John declares the universality of sin, even in the Christian; to deny sin is to be a liar. To the second he declares the incompatibility of sin in the Christian; to commit sin is to be *of the devil*. It is in order to confound these particular views of his opponents that John states the Christian position in such categorical terms.

What, then, does he mean in verse 9 when he writes that a Christian does not and cannot sin? An examination of his expressions will tell us. He uses three. First, he says that the Christian who lives in Christ does not *continue to sin* (6a and 5:18, *hamartanei*); this is a present tense, indicating a settled character like that of 'the devil' who 'has been sinning from the beginning' (8). *Cf. hamartanōn*, a present participle, in verse 6b, whereas the verbs in 2:1 are both aorists. The second statement is that he who has been born of God will not *continue to sin* (*hamartian ou poiei*, 9a). Again, it is not the isolated act of sin which is envisaged, but the settled habit of it, indicated by the verb *poiein*, to do or to practise, which is used of 'doing' sin in verses 4a, 8 and 9, of 'doing' lawlessness in verse 4b, and of 'doing' righteousness in 2:29; 3:7, 10a. The third expression is that the Christian 'cannot go on sinning' (*ou dynatai hamartanein*, 9), where 'to sin' is a present, not an aorist, infinitive. If the infinitive had been an aorist it would have meant 'he is not able to commit a sin'; the present infinitive, however, signifies 'he is not able to sin habitually'. In this whole section John is arguing rather the incongruity than the impossibility of sin in the Christian. If even isolated sins are incongruous, what is utterly impossible is persistence in sin, 'a character, a prevailing habit, and not primarily an act' (Westcott).

Wherein lies this 'impossibility'? John's answer is given in two phrases in verse 9: *because God's seed remains in him* and *because he has been born of God*. *God's seed* could be a collective noun for the children of God (*cf*. Jn. 8:33; Gal. 3:29), and *in him* could mean 'in God'. The whole phrase would then be translated 'the offspring of God abide in him, and they cannot sin because they are born of God' (RSV mg. and *cf*. Moffatt. The sense is parallel to v. 6). It is more probable, however, that *God's seed* is accurately rendered in the RSV text 'God's nature', or 'the divine seed' (NEB), and that *in him* refers to the child of God. In this way the two parts of verse 9 become exactly parallel, each part consisting of a statement that the Christian does not or cannot sin, to which is added the reason for such an assertion. The implication of both is this: the new birth involves the acquisition of a new nature through the implanting within us of the very seed or lifegiving power of God. Birth of God is a deep, radical, inward transformation. Moreover, the new nature received at the new birth remains. It exerts a strong internal pressure towards holiness. It is the abiding influence of *God's seed* within everyone who is *born of God*, which enables John to affirm without fear of contradiction that *he cannot go on sinning* (*cf*. 2 Cor. 5:17; 2 Pet. 1:4). Indeed, if he should continue to sin, it would indicate that he has never been born again. It was this conviction which enabled John to assert that the heretics, who not only persisted in sin but had seceded from the Christian fellowship altogether, were not true Christians at all (2:19).[1]

---

[1]See pp. 133–134 and pp.134–140 for the Additional Notes, 'The meaning of "God's seed"' and 'The interpretation of 1 John 3:4–9'.

10. This verse is at the same time a summary and conclusion of what has gone before and a transition to what follows. John has written twice of Christ's first appearing (3:5, 8) and twice of his second which is yet to come (2:28 and 3:2), but he also writes twice in this passage of the appearing or manifestation of human beings. Although it does not yet appear what we shall be in our final state, he has said (2), it already appears what we are, whether we are *children of God* or *of the devil*. The difference is apparent to the discerning, and John's purpose is to supply the test by which the two groups are recognized. And there are only two groups. There are not three. Nor is there only one. This 'very plain black-and-white' is not only true in itself, but also necessary, according to Dodd, because 'sophistry can as easily prove that evil is an aspect of good as that error is an aspect of truth. But truth and falsehood, good and evil, right and wrong, God and the devil are irreconcilable opposites'. Our parentage is either divine or diabolical. The universal fatherhood of God is not taught in the Bible, except in the general sense that God is the Creator of all (Acts 17:28). But in the intimate, spiritual sense God is not the Father of all people, and not all people are his children. Indeed, John here is only echoing what Jesus once said to certain unbelieving Jews: 'You belong to your father, the devil' (Jn. 8::44; *cf.* Mt. 13:38; Acts 13:10).

The way to become a child of God is, on the human side, by believing on or receiving Christ, and on the divine side, by new birth (Jn. 1:12–13). Meanwhile God's children (9) and the devil's (8) may be recognized by their moral behaviour. 'By their fruit you will recognise them' (Mt. 7:20). John now writes negatively, with the sinful and unloving heretics in his mind: *Anyone who does not do what is right is not a child of God; nor is anyone who does not love his brother.* The lack of righteousness and love proves the lack of a divine birth. Not that righteousness and love are entirely distinct. John adds the second phrase almost as an interpretation of the first. 'Love is righteousness in relation to others' (Plummer). The mention of love introduces the subject of the next paragraph.

We are in a position now to look back over the foregoing twelve verses (2:28 – 3:10), in which the moral test has been elaborated, and feel the compulsion of its argument. If Christ appeared first both to 'take away our sins' and to 'destroy the devil's work', and if, when he appears a second time, 'we shall see him' and, in consequence, 'we shall be like him', how can we possibly go on living in sin? To do so would be to deny the purpose of both his appearings. If we would be loyal to his first coming and ready for his second, we must purify ourselves, as he is pure. By so doing we shall give evidence of our birth of God.

Additional Note: The meaning of 'God's seed' (3:9)

Dodd (p. 76) gives a series of quotations from Hermetic tractates, Philo and Gnostic writings in which reference is made to the implantation of a divine 'seed' in man. In some of these the divine principle is in all human beings; in others it is planted into good souls only. In either case salvation was thought to consist of the liberation or redemption of this seed which was already imprisoned within them. It is possible that the heretics of John's day taught a similar doctrine about a divine element immanent in man; that they called it *sperma theou*, God's seed; and that John deliberately borrowed the expression from their vocabulary (as he may have borrowed *chrisma* in 2:20, 27, *q.v.*). If so, it is not necessary to suppose that he endorsed their theology. This should be clear from three questions. First, who is it in whom 'God's seed remains'? If the heretics were teaching that the divine principle is already resident by nature either in all people or in 'good souls' (Valentinus), John's position is rather that it is implanted into some by grace and that those who receive it are thereby 'born of God'. Secondly, what is the effect of the implantation of the divine principle? John insists in this passage that the reception of the divine *sperma* causes a new birth which asserts itself against sin and manifests itself in righteous conduct. Thirdly, what is the character of this *sperma*? In other New Testament passages the word of God is pictured as 'seed' (1 Pet. 1:23, 25; Jas. 1:18, 23; *cf.* Lk. 8:11). Is John's use of 'seed' a reference to the gospel also? Such was the view of Augustine, adopted by Bede, Luther, Alford (who emphasizes Jn. 5:38 as the 'key' to this interpretation) and others, and, more recently, by Dodd. Barclay favours it also. Dodd concludes that 'there is . . . a fairly well established association of the ideas "seed" and "word"', and that 'when our author speaks of divine "seed" he is thinking of the Word of God, or the Gospel'. Certainly the concept of the seed 'remaining in' Christians is reminiscent of 2:24, where what remains in them is 'what you have heard from the beginning'. Since Dodd regards 2:24 as referring to the *chrisma*, he thinks the *sperma* is identical with it, both being the gospel, the former initiating into knowledge, the latter 'producing in men the regenerate nature which does not sin'. Findlay makes the same identification between *chrisma* and *sperma* but regards them both as allusions to the Holy Spirit, who is the author of truth and holiness. That *sperma*, like *chrisma*, refers to the Holy Spirit is not impossible, since the new birth is clearly in the Fourth Gospel a birth 'of the Spirit' (Jn. 3:6, 8). We shall probably never know for certain precisely what John intended, or his readers understood, by *sperma autou*. But whether the implanted and abiding seed is the word of the gospel, or the Holy Spirit, or the divine nature thus imparted (*cf.* 2 Pet. 1:4), John's meaning is the same, namely that it is the Christian's supernatural birth from God which keeps him from habitual sin.

Additional Note: The interpretation of 1 John 3:4-9

The difficulty which commentators have experienced in interpreting this paragraph is evidenced in the variety of explanations which have been offered. It is important that subjective considerations should not influence us. The criterion of interpretation is what John intended to teach, not whether this coincides with our experience of holiness. We agree with Alford, therefore, that 'the plain words of the Apostle must be held fast' and must not 'be tamed down' to suit our convenience.

If, as we have argued in the commentary on these verses, John is not teaching that the Christian is impeccable, or that the condition of everyone who has been born of God is one of sinless perfection (*cf.* 1:8, 10; 2:1; 3:3), what does he mean when he asserts that the Christian does not and even 'cannot' sin? Seven answers appear to have been given to this question.

1. Some have tried to narrow the definition of 'sin' in this passage and to restrict the sins which the Christian 'cannot' do to notorious crimes, or offences against love (so Augustine, Bede and Luther, interpreting 'righteousness' as 'love' from v. 10), or 'moral' as opposed to 'venial' sins (Roman Catholic commentators). This is certainly special pleading. No such limitations are in John's mind. On the contrary, he begins by defining sin as 'lawlessness'. The references to 'sin' in this passage are general, not specific.

2. Others have attempted to argue that the Christian 'cannot' sin because what is sin in the life of an unbeliever is not so regarded by God in a believer. It is inconceivable that such a preposterous idea even occurred to John's mind. 'Sin is lawlessness', whoever commits it. Besides, this double standard or view of morality was just the kind of subtle argument which the heretics were using to justify their continuance in sin. John is clear that 'everyone who sins breaks the law' (3:4), whether he be Christian or non-Christian.

3. Others have drawn a distinction not between the believer and the unbeliever, but between the old and the new natures of the believer. The old nature may continue to sin; it is the new nature which 'cannot', they argue. 'It is literally true of the Divine nature imparted to the believer. That does not sin and cannot sin' (Plummer). But, apart from the fact that such an argument would play into the hands of the heretics John is opposing, it is very doubtful if we can find biblical warrant for thus isolating a man's 'natures' from his 'person'. Our two natures can be separated in their desires and promptings, but not in their activities. The 'desires' of the sinful nature and of the Spirit are contrasted in Galatians 5:16–17, and it is stated that they are 'in conflict with each other'; but when Paul goes on to catalogue 'the acts of the sinful nature' and 'the fruit of the Spirit', what he is envisaging is the activities not of two 'natures' but of one 'person', dominated now by the sinful nature and now by the Spirit. The practical relevance of this should be clear. We can distinguish between our different desires within ourselves, attributing some to the sinful nature and some to the Spirit. But we cannot ascribe an act to one of our two natures *in such a way as to distinguish ourselves from it*. We cannot say of a

sin: 'my old nature did it; I did not'. What either of my natures prompts me to do, *I* do, and I cannot relieve myself of the responsibility for it. It is true that in Romans 7:17 Paul says 'it is no longer I myself who do it, but it is sin living in me'. Nevertheless, his purpose in that context is not to deny that he is himself acting sinfully, but to explain why his behaviour conflicts with his will. So throughout this paragraph it is a person who sins or does not sin, not one of his natures. The subject of the verbs 'to sin' and 'not to sin' is in each case 'he', a person, not 'it', a nature. This is particularly clear in verse 9, where John does not write 'God's seed remains in him and *it* cannot go on sinning', but 'God's seed remains in him and *he* cannot go on sinning'. There can be no doubt that this is the correct translation, since John goes on 'because *he* has been born of God'. It is not the 'seed' which is born of God but the 'person', through the implantation of the seed; and it is, therefore, the 'person' in whom the seed remains who 'cannot go on sinning'.

4. A more popular interpretation of this paragraph has been the suggestion that what John is here describing is not a reality, but the ideal. Alford follows the German commentator Düsterdieck (on whom he depends a great deal in his exposition) in adopting this view. John speaks throughout the letter, he asserts, 'of the ideal reality of the life of God and the life of sin as absolutely excluding one another'. So too Westcott, 'the ideas of divine sonship and sin are mutually exclusive'. Dodd and Barclay both mention this view as a possibility, and, in support of it, quote the description of life in the new age from Enoch 5:8: 'they will all live and never again sin, either through heedlessness or through pride'. The argument is this: it was anticipated that sinlessness would be a characteristic of the age to come, and since John believed that the age to come had come (2:8), he naturally asserted the sinlessness of Christians. Marshall opts for this view, adding that John's statement of the eschatological ideal, 'though indicative and factual in terms of syntax, is logically an imperative or statement of obligation' (p. 184).

I find this interpretation attractive but unsatisfying. John was writing in a time of crisis. The situation he was addressing was one of harsh reality; it would do little good to resort only to 'ideas' and 'ideals'. The pre-Gnostic false teachers made concrete claims, and John was outspoken in contradicting their claims and calling them lies. In doing so, he also made counter-claims. Are we to imagine that these were 'ideals' which his opponents could have dismissed as untrue, unpractical and unattainable? Besides, John did not write as an idealist that, ideally speaking, the Christian 'should not' sin. His language was that of the realist. He stated categorically that the Christian does not, and indeed 'cannot' do so.

Law, who rejects the idealistic interpretation, nevertheless proposes a somewhat similar solution. He emphasizes that John was not writing with the calm of a theologian, but 'in view of a definite controversial situation and in a vehemently controversial strain'. He was opposing those who turned Christian liberty into licence. So he used absolute assertions, 'suffused with holy passion', 'unqualified contradictions of tenets of unqualified falsity'. In doing so his expressions were coloured by 'apparent exaggeration and over-emphasis' and are only 'theoretically . . . true'. But what is the difference between 'ideal' and 'theoretical' statements? We must insist that John sought to overthrow the false theories of the heretics not with alternative 'theories', however true, but with facts.

5. Those who hold that John was expressing an 'ideal' mostly go on to assert that it was nevertheless a relatively realistic ideal. Thus, Alford quotes Düsterdieck as writing, 'None . . . of all the expositors, who in any way has recognized the ideal character of St. John's view, has overlooked the fact, that even in the actual life of all that are born of God there is something which in full verity answers to the ideal words "they cannot sin" . . . they sin not, and they cannot sin, just in proportion as the new divine life, unconditionally opposed to all sin . . . is present and abides in them.' Commentators who pursue this explanation tend to concentrate on the expression in verse 6, 'no-one who lives in him'. They interpret this living in Christ, not as a description of all Christians, but as a condition which some Christians fulfil. The degree of the Christian's holiness then varies in proportion to his living in Christ. 'In quantum in ipso manet, in tantum non peccat' – 'To the extent that he remains in him, to that extent he does not sin' (Augustine, Bede). Hence the command 'continue in him' (2:28). If the command is disobeyed, the Christian sins: if

the command is obeyed, he does not sin.

This is quite true. It is clearly taught by our Lord in his allegory of the vine and the branches (Jn. 15:1ff.). The fruitfulness of the branches depends on their remaining in the vine. But this interpretation cannot be said to exhaust the meaning of this paragraph. It may be a legitimate exposition of verse 6; it is not of verse 9. There are two differences between the verses. First, in verse 6 it is stated that the Christian does not, in verse 9 that he cannot, sin. Secondly, the Christian's conquest of sin is attributed in verse 6 to his present living in Christ, but in verse 9 to his past birth of God, as a result of which, God's seed 'remains' in him. And the remaining of God's seed in us is as constant and invariable as our living or remaining in Christ may be inconstant and variable. In brief, the statement that he 'does not' practise sin (6) may be conditional on whether he is living in Christ; the statement that he 'cannot', however, is absolute, since it depends on the fact that he has been born of God (9).

6. Ebrard interprets the sin which a regenerate Christian 'cannot' do as wilful and deliberate sin. 'To the truly regenerate man', he writes, 'it is altogether impossible willingly and wilfully to do that which he knows to be forbidden by God.' He concedes that a Christian may be ensnared by sin, but sin 'is contrary to the bent of his will', 'he cannot love, and cherish, and entertain sin', or sin in such a way as 'knowingly and willingly to act contrary to the will of God'. From these quotations it will be seen that Ebrard emphasizes the Christian's knowledge (or conscience) and will, and affirms that the Christian does not and cannot violate either. As in Romans 7:20 'a Christian does not *do* sin, he suffers it' (Besser, quoted by Law). Calvin writes similarly, 'they are said not to sin because . . . they do not consent to sin, but in fact struggle and groan, so that they can truly testify with Paul that they do the evil they would not'. Indeed, they 'cannot consent to sin' (Tyndale).

It is probably within this sixth explanation that John Wesley's doctrine belongs. In his *A Plain Account of Christian Perfection*[1] there are clear echoes of John's first letter, both in the references to 'perfect love' (4:18) and in the conclusion that 'a Christian is

[1]1767 (Epworth Press, 1952).

so far perfect as not to comit sin' (p. 19, alluding to 1 Jn. 3:6, 9). By 'sin' Wesley says he meant 'sin properly so called (that is, a voluntary transgression of a known law)'. Involuntary transgressions, however, are improperly called 'sins', and 'there is no such perfection in this life as excludes these involuntary transgressions' (p. 45). In response to this, we have to ask whether a clear line can be drawn between voluntary and involuntary transgressions, and whether it is true that God's servants do not sin voluntarily. Candlish is right to ask 'was it true of David?' Indeed, are there not many examples of God's people in the Bible who have sinned knowingly and wilfully? Christian biographies would endorse this. 'I dare not persuade myself that I never sin voluntarily' (Candlish). More important, can it be shown that this is what John meant? I think not. All sin, he says, is 'lawlessness', a breach of the laws of God. He draws no distinction between voluntary and involuntary, knowing and unknowing, lawlessness.

7. The seventh interpretation is that the sin a Christian 'does not' and 'cannot' do is habitual and persistent sin. He may sin sometimes, even with the consent of the mind and the will, but he is overwhelmed by grief and repentance afterwards (Ps. 51). For the whole direction of his life is towards God and holiness. His mind is set on the Spirit (Rom. 8:6) and on the things above (Col. 3:2), not on earthly things (Phil. 3:19). His eyes are ever focused on the Lord (Ps. 25:15), whom he sets always before him (Ps. 16:8). His eyes are fixed upon all God's commands (Ps. 119:6, RSV); his heart is steadfast also (Ps. 57:7). 'Although the believer sometimes sins, yet not sin, but opposition to sin, is the ruling principle of his life' (Plummer). His whole life is one of 'truceless antagonism to sin' (Law). The 'seed' within the believer's spirit 'fills it with an irreconcilable hate against every sin, and urges it to an unceasing conflict against all unrighteousness' (Alford). It is not that Christians are 'wholly free from all vice' but that they 'heartily strive to form their lives in obedience to God' (Calvin). 'Sin does not reign in them', for the Spirit 'does not let it flourish' (Calvin).

That this is what John meant is evident from his use of tenses, as has been shown in the commentary on verse 9. This is surely not 'a grammatical subtlety' (Dodd, Alexander), but one which his readers will have readily grasped. It is confirmed by linguistic specialists today, *e.g.* 'The present tense in the Greek verb implied habit, continuity, unbroken sequence' (Blaiklock). Hence the NIV translation that no true believer 'keeps on sinning' (6) or 'continues to sin' (6, 9). On the contrary, 'he cannot go on sinning' (9).

Turning back to John's own words (1 Jn. 3:4-9), it may be helpful to summarize his argument. The paragraph is in two symmetrical sections (4-7, 8-9). Each begins with a statement of the gravity of sin (its nature 'lawlessness', 4; its origin diabolical, 8); continues with a reference to the purpose of Christ's appearing (to 'take away our sins', 5; 'to destroy the devil's work', 8); and concludes with a moral deduction, first concerning the incompatibility of habitual sin (does not 'keep on sinning', 6) and secondly concerning its impossibility ('cannot go on sinning', 9).

The argument is theological, based on the doctrine of Christ's saving work. His nature is without sin and his mission was against sin. 'You know' this, John says (5). Therefore, of course, everyone who lives in Christ does not keep sinning. For Christ and sin are incompatible. To continue in sin is to supply clear evidence that we have never seen or known Christ. Since he is the sinless taker away of sins, how could we tolerate sin in our lives and still claim to have seen and known him? In verse 8 the theme begins in the same way. Christ appeared to undo the devil's work; to sin is therefore to undo the Saviour's work. 'The whole passage is a keen, concise demonstration of the inadmissibility of sin' (Findlay).

But the Christian has not just 'seen and known' Christ as the sinless Saviour of sinners; he has been born of God. His theology (the doctrine of Christ) makes persistent sin incompatible; his experience (birth of God) makes it impossible. The divine nature within the regenerate believer asserts itself against all evil. It is impossible for him to make a practice of sin. 'We are children of God, and sin is abnormal and unnatural to us' (Dodd). 'The believer may fall into sin, but he will not walk in it' (Smith).

Additional Note: John's teaching about the devil (3:8, 10)

John assumes the existence of the devil, and writes of his origin, activity, power and overthrow.

1. *His origin*. John 8:44 describes him as 'not holding to the truth'. This seems to indicate a fall from the truth in which he once 'stood' (RV), in which case the following clause, 'for there is no truth in him', indicates not why he fell, but how we know that he fell. The explanation of his present lack of truth is that he fell from the truth long ago. For a similar use of *hoti* see Luke 7:47. Twice the expression 'from the beginning' (*ap' archēs*) is used of the devil (Jn. 8:44; 1 Jn. 3:8). If we are right to interpret the clause 'not holding to the truth' as referring to his fall from the condition in which he was created, then his murderous and evil activity must be dated from the 'beginning', not of his existence, but of his fallen career. 'He is the aboriginal sinner; and what he became he still is' (Law).

2. *His activity* is constantly malevolent because he is by nature 'the evil one'. This title was used by our Lord (*e.g.* Mt. 6:13) and six times by John (Jn. 17:15; 1 Jn. 2:13, 14; 3:12; 5:18, 19). The devil's evil work belongs particularly to three spheres, in which are seen his complete lack of righteousness, love and truth, and which correspond to the three tests which John applies in his first letter. First, he 'has been sinning from the beginning' (1 Jn. 3:8) and tempts others into sin (*cf.* Mt. 6:13). He is, in fact, so certainly the origin of all sin that it may be said: 'he who does what is sinful is of the devil' (1 Jn. 3:8). Secondly, he is 'a murderer' (Jn. 8:44). Thus Cain, in killing his brother Abel, gave evidence of his diabolical origin (1 Jn. 3:12). So did the Jews who sought to kill Jesus (Jn. 8:40–41). Foiled in his assault upon Jesus, the devil now persecutes the church (Rev. 12:4–6, 13–17). He is called 'the destroyer' (Rev. 9:11; *cf.* Heb. 2:14). Thirdly, the devil is 'a liar and the father of lies' (Jn. 8:44). This is due to the fact we have already noted that he fell from the truth and 'there is no truth in him'. Consequently, he both accuses the people of God (Rev. 12:10), being their adversary (the meaning of the Hebrew word *Satan*) and a slanderer (the meaning of the Greek word *diabolos*), and seeks to deceive them into error by the lies of false prophets (*cf.* 1 Jn. 2:21–22; 4:2).

3. *His power* is considerable, as is plain from his widespread, malicious activity. It is not just that he is able to insinuate evil thoughts and designs into the minds of human beings (Jn. 13:2; *cf.* Lk. 22:3; Mt. 8:33), and even enter into them himself personally (Jn. 13:27), but that 'the one who is in the world' (1 Jn. 4:4) is 'the prince (lit. "ruler", *archōn*) of this world' (Jn. 12:31; 14:30; 16:11; *cf.* 2 Cor. 4:4; Eph. 6:12). He rules from a 'throne' (Rev. 2:13), and his dominion is so extensive that 'the whole world is under the control of the evil one' (1 Jn. 5:19). Indeed, the unredeemed are said to be not only *under*, but *of*, the devil. He is their 'father' and they his 'children' (Jn. 8:44; 1 Jn. 3:10). Phrases such as these express the real and terrible influence which the evil one has over people's lives, so that they are motivated by and succumb to his desires (Jn. 8:44; *cf.* 2 Tim 2:26). Their will is to do his will.

4. *His overthrow* began with the arrival of the Son of God, whom the devil had 'no hold' on (Jn. 14:30). The express purpose of his appearing was to 'destroy the devil's work' (1 Jn. 3:8). This he accomplished supremely by his death and resurrection. The emphatic repetition of 'now' in relation to the judgment of this world and the driving out of its ruler (Jn. 12:31) refers in the context to the hour of the Son of Man's glorification (Jn. 12:23, 27). In anticipation of that hour Jesus could say both that the ruler of this world 'now stands condemned' (Jn. 16:11, translating *kekritai*, perfect tense) and that as a result he would draw all people to himself (Jn. 12:32). It may be to this preliminary downfall that the binding of Satan refers (Rev. 20:1ff.; *cf.* Mk. 3:27). So far, however, his overthrow has been a dethronement rather than a decisive destruction. His final defeat will not take place until the last day (Rev. 20:10). Meanwhile, it is possible for the Father to 'protect' his people from the evil one. So Jesus prayed (Jn. 17:15), and John affirms that, because those who are born of God are 'kept safe' (the verb is *tērein* again) by 'the one who was born of God', the evil one does not even 'touch' them (1 Jn. 5:18). It is, of course, by this power of Christ and by the Word of God that the young men can be said to 'have overcome the evil one' (1 Jn. 2:13–14; *cf.* 4:4).

B. AN ELABORATION OF THE SOCIAL TEST: LOVE (3:11–18)

The last phrase of the previous section has prepared us for the change of subject from righteousness to love. In 2:7–11 John has briefly outlined his social test of the true Christian, namely that to love is the new command (which is yet old) and belongs to the new age in which the true light is already shining. As he now fills in his preliminary sketch, he uses no colours but black and white. He continues the stark contrast he has already pointed in verse 10 between the children of God and the children of the devil, and writes of hatred and love, life and death, murder and self-sacrifice. After reminding his readers that the duty of reciprocal love is the original message they had heard (11), the first part of this paragraph concerns the hatred of Cain, the prototype of the world (12–13), while the second describes the love of Christ, which should also be seen in the church (14–18).

11. The heretics were boasting about their new teaching; John's appeal here, as in 1:5, is to the original, apostolic gospel, which was also public knowledge in contrast to the private and secret enlightenment which the false teachers claimed. His readers will be safe if they hold fast to *the message* which they *heard*, and that publicly and openly, *from the beginning*. This has been John's concern when treating the theological error of the followers of Cerinthus: *See that what you have heard from the beginning remains in you*, he wrote (2:24). Now he is expounding ethical rather than doctrinal truth, but his appeal is still the same. See also 2:7. The gospel does not change. The truth about the person of Jesus Christ and about Christian conduct is unalterable. In both doctrine and ethics we must go right back to *the beginning* and enquire what the apostles originally taught and their first converts both *had* (2:7, *eichete*, aorist) and *heard* (2:24 and 3:11, *ēkousate*, another aorist). An essential part of that *message* was that *we should love one another* (cf. 3:23; 4:7; 11–12; 2 Jn. 5; Jn. 13:34; 15:12, 17).

1. The hatred of Cain, and of the world (3:12–13)

With this mutual love which is commanded us, John immediately contrasts the behaviour of *Cain*. His hatred originated in the devil, *the evil one*, and issued in murder, indeed in an act of brutal slaughter (*esphaxen* is rendered by Law 'butchered'). It is not only sin in general which is 'of the devil' (8), but hatred and murder in particular, for as Jesus had said, 'the devil . . . was a murderer from the beginning' (Jn. 8:44). And what was the cause of Cain's murder of Abel? John asks. It was not because Abel was wicked, but the reverse: *because his own actions were evil and his brother's were righteous*. Jealousy lay behind his hatred, not the jealousy which covets another's greater gifts but that which resents another's greater righteousness, the 'envy' which made the Jewish priests demand the death of Jesus. Jealousy-hatred-murder is a natural and terrible sequence.[1]

13. Cain was the prototype of *the world*, which still manifests the ugly qualities he first displayed. The 'world' is Cain's posterity; so we are not to be surprised if the world hates us.[2] It is only to be expected that the wicked should continue to regard and treat the righteous as Cain regarded and treated his righteous brother Abel. Jesus warned us that it would be so (*e.g.* Jn. 15:18–19, 25; 16:1ff.; 17:14), and by its hatred the world is simply giving evidence of its true spiritual condition which is 'death' (14). A similar instruction not to be surprised by the opposition and persecution of the world is given in 1 Peter 4:12ff.

2. The love of Christ, and of the church (3:14–18)

It is a relief to turn from John's exposition of the world's hatred to his teaching about the love which should be manifest in the

[1]The Genesis story of Cain and Abel (Gn. 4:1–8) does not tell us explicitly why Abel's sacrifice of the firstlings of his flock was acceptable to God, while Cain's offering of the fruit of the soil was not. It is, however, implied that Cain had no ground for complaint (6); if he had done what was 'right', his sacrifice also would have been accepted (7). According to Heb. 11:4 it was 'by faith' that 'Abel offered God a better sacrifice than Cain did', and since faith is always a response to God's word of promise and command, we may assume that God had revealed his will to the two brothers. By faith Abel obeyed; indeed, his righteousness consisted of his believing obedience. Cain, on the other hand, was wilfully disobedient, as is indicated in Jude 11. His murder of Abel exemplified the violent antipathy which righteousness always provokes in the unrighteous (*cf.* Jn. 3:19–20).
[2]See the Additional Note, 'The meaning of "the world"', pp. 106–108.

church. He writes first of the evidence of love, what it proves, namely life (14–15), and then of the essence of love, what it is, namely self-sacrifice, whether in Christ or in his people (16–18).

14. This verse begins dramatically in the Greek with the pronoun *we* (*hēmeis*). Let the world hate; *we* do not hate, but *love*. Moreover, the fact that *we love our brothers* gives us a good ground for certainty that we possess eternal life. John associates himself with his readers in this glorious affirmation. *We know* (*oidamen*, 'we know as a fact') *that we have passed* (NEB 'crossed over') *from death to life*. Becoming a Christian is nothing less than a resurrection or quickening 'out of' (*ek*) spiritual death 'into' (*eis*) eternal life (*cf.* Jn. 5:24). Great stress is laid in the New Testament on love as the pre-eminent Christian virtue, the first-fruit of the Spirit (Gal. 5:22), the sign of the reality of faith (Gal. 5:6) and the greatest of the three abiding Christian graces, which never ends and without which we are 'nothing' (1 Cor. 13:2, 8, 13). Love is the surest test of having life, as it has already been shown to be the test of being in the light (2:10). The contrary is also true: *Anyone who does not love remains in death*, just as he is 'in darkness' (2:9, 11). In the vocabulary of John love, light and life belong together, as do hatred, darkness and death. It is noteworthy, however, that the precise proof of life which he gives is that *we love our brothers*, just as the people the world hates is 'you . . . my brothers' (13).

It is appropriate that John should depart from his normal custom of calling his readers 'beloved' or 'children' and should here, uniquely, address them as 'my brothers'. It is not just hatred, but hatred of Christian people, which reveals the world in its true colours, for in their persecution of the church their antagonism to Christ is concealed. 'Why do you persecute me?' Similarly, eternal life is evidenced not only in a general love for all humankind, but in a particular love for our brothers and sisters in Christ. The authentic followers of Jesus Christ, who have 'passed from death to life', hunger for Christian fellowship. They do not 'give up meeting together' (Heb. 10:25), but delight to worship and pray together, and to talk together on spiritual topics, while their personal relationships with each other are marked by unselfish and caring love.

15. John now proves his point, that lack of love is evidence of spiritual death. He is not necessarily denying the possibility of repentance and of forgiveness to a murderer (Jesus prayed that his murderers might be forgiven). He is rather stating as a general principle that to take life is to forfeit life and that *no murderer has eternal life in him* as a present and permanent possession. If this is so, and John accepts it as axiomatic, then clearly *anyone who hates his brother* does not possess eternal life either, because to hate is to be *a murderer*. This is a faithful echo of the teaching of Jesus in the Sermon on the Mount (see Mt. 5:21–22, and *cf.* Mt. 5:27–28). In equating the hater with the murderer, John is not exaggerating, 'for we wish him to perish whom we hate' (Calvin).

16. Having shown that love is the evidence of life, he explains that the essence of love is self-sacrifice, which has been perfectly manifested in Christ and should characterize the lives of his followers also. Hate is negative, seeks the other person's harm, and leads to activity *against* him, even to the point of murder ('Cain rose up *against* his brother Abel, and killed him', Gn. 4:8, RSV). Love is positive, seeks the other person's good, and leads to activity *for* him, even to the point of self-sacrifice (Christ 'laid down his life *for* us', 16). Indeed, it is precisely because 'he' (the emphatic *ekeinos* again, whom NIV rightly identifies as *Jesus Christ*) *laid down his life for us* that we *know* (*egnōkamen*, perfect, 'have come to know') *what love is*. The expression is peculiar to John (Jn. 10:11, 15, 17–18; 13:37–38; 15:13). It seems to imply not so much the laying down as the laying aside of something like clothes, the 'divesting oneself of a thing' (Westcott). It is, in fact, used in John 13:4 of Christ taking off his outer garment. As Cain has been given as the supreme example of hate, Christ is presented as the supreme example of love. A person's life is his most precious possession. Consequently, to rob him of it is the greatest sin we can commit against him, while to give one's own life on his behalf is the greatest possible expression of love for him (*cf.* Jn. 15:13; Rom. 5:6–10). This, then, is the ultimate contrast: Cain's hatred issued in murder, Christ's love in self-sacrifice. Indeed, true love, *agapē*, is self-sacrifice. 'Love is the giving impulse' (Law).

But the self-sacrifice of Christ is not just a revelation of love to be admired; it is an example to copy. *We ought* (*i.e.* we should be willing) *to lay down our lives for our brothers*; otherwise our profession to love them is an empty boast. We 'ought' to do this, as a definite Christian obligation, because we belong to Christ, just as we 'ought' to follow his example in all things and walk even as he walked (2:6), and just as, if God's love for us is so great, we 'ought' also to love one another (4:11). For the cross as an example of humility and forbearance see Philippians 2:5–8 and 1 Peter 2:19–23 respectively.

17. But true love is revealed not only in the supreme sacrifice; it is expressed in all lesser givings. Not many of us are called to lay down our lives in some deed of heroism, but we constantly have the much more prosaic opportunity to share our possessions with those in need (*cf.* Jas. 2:15–16). Love is 'the willingness to surrender that which has value for our own life, to enrich the life of another' (Dodd). The transition from the plural ('our brothers', 6) to the singular (*his brother*, 17) is deliberate and significant. 'It is easier to be enthusiastic about Humanity with a capital "H" than it is to love individual men and women, especially those who are uninteresting, exasperating, depraved, or otherwise unattractive. Loving everybody in general may be an excuse for loving nobody in particular' (Lewis). So John writes that *if anyone has material possessions* (Gk. *bion*) *and sees his brother in need,* he is in debt to him. Two factors place him, as they placed the Good Samaritan, in a position of inescapable responsibility. First, he must see a brother's need, 'not merely cast a passing glance, but see, long enough to appreciate and understand the circumstances of the case' (Brooke). Secondly, he must be in a position to meet his need.

If, on the other hand, instead of applying what he 'has' to what he 'sees', he 'has no pity' on his needy neighbour, this much is certain: he cannot claim to have *the love of God . . . in him.* As life does not dwell in the murderer (15), so love does not dwell in the miser (17). The genitive may be objective, 'love for God' (*cf.* 2:5, 15; 4:20); or it may be definitive and qualitative, describing a 'love like God's love', 'the divine love' (NEB). But it is probably subjective and should be translated simply 'God's love' (RSV). God's love was revealed historically in the death of Christ (16; *cf.* 4:9–10); but it dwells, or should do, in us. It is not to be understood merely as displayed once in Christ, but as continuously active in and through his followers. And the essence of such divine love, whether in Christ or in us, is costly self-giving, the giving of our *bios* (17), our possessions, if not of our physical *psychē* (16), life itself.

18. John's final plea in this section, addressed to himself as well as to his readers, whom he again fondly calls *dear children*, is a reminder that protestations of love are not enough. Actions speak louder than words. Essentially love is neither sentiment nor talk, but deeds. If our love is to be genuine (*in truth*), it will inevitably be positive and constructive (*with actions*).

It may be helpful to summarize the teaching in this passage about hatred and love. Hatred characterizes the world, whose prototype is Cain. It originates in the devil, issues in murder and is evidence of spiritual death. Love characterizes the church, whose prototype is Christ. It originates in God, issues in self-sacrifice, and is evidence of eternal life.

C. A DIGRESSION ABOUT ASSURANCE AND THE CONDEMNING HEART (3:19–24)

The link between this new paragraph and what has gone before seems to be the word 'truth'. John has urged upon his readers the necessity of loving 'in truth' (18) and immediately goes on to indicate that this is how we may *know that we belong to the truth* (19). Truth can only characterize the behaviour of those whose very character originates in the truth, so that it is by our loving others 'in truth', that we know that we ourselves belong to it. The same expression, to be *ek tēs alētheias*, occurs also in John 18:37.

This paragraph begins (19) and ends (24) with a sentence introduced by the words 'this is how we know' (although in v. 19 the verb is future, *gnōsometha*, while in v. 24 it is present, *ginōskomen*), and is concerned, as is the whole letter, with the doctrine of assurance.

1. The condemning heart, and how to reassure it (3:19–20)[1]

It is within the general context of the letter's teaching on assurance that this paragraph about the condemning heart must be read. However firmly grounded the Christian's assurance is, his heart may sometimes need reassurance. Indeed, if the NIV and RSV are correct in translating the first phrase of verse 20 'whenever our hearts condemn us', the suggestion seems to be that it may not be either an unusual or an infrequent experience for the Christian's serene assurance to be disturbed. Sometimes the accusations of our 'conscience' (as the NEB legitimately renders *heart*) will be true accusations, and sometimes they will be false, inspired by 'the accuser of our brothers' (Rev. 12:10). In either case, the inner voice is not to overcome us. We are rather to *set our hearts at rest in his presence*, that is, we must be able to do so in the sight of God (the words *in his presence* are emphatic).

It is implied that we shall be able to do this only if *we know that we belong to the truth*. It is the mind's knowledge by which the heart's doubts may be silenced. But how can we know this? What is the meaning of the *this is how* with which the verse begins? Usually in this letter the phrase looks on to what follows, but here (as in 4:6) it seems to refer back to the preceding paragraph about love. It is 'everyone who loves' who 'has been born of God and knows God' (4:7). Love is the final objective test of our Christian profession, for true love, in the sense of self-sacrifice, is not natural to human beings in their fallen state. Its existence in anyone is evidence of new birth and of the indwelling Spirit (3:24; 4:12–13), and it shows itself 'with actions'. 'There are actual things we can point to – not things we have professed or felt or imagined or intended, but things that we have done' (Law). If we thus love 'in truth' (18), we may indeed have full assurance in our hearts. 'The fruit of love is confidence' (Westcott).

20. It is not easy to determine the grammatical construction of this verse. See the Additional Note, 'The meaning of 1 John

[1]See the Additional Note, 'The meaning of 1 John 3:19–20', pp.150–152, for linguistic and grammatical points.

3:19–20', pp. 150–152. The NIV and RSV are probably correct that we can reassure our hearts *whenever our hearts condemn us. For God is greater than our hearts.* There are then three actors in this spiritual drama, three speakers in this inward debate. It is a kind of trial, with our heart as the accuser, ourselves as the defendant and God as the Judge (Law). *Whenever our hearts condemn us*, we ourselves, who are distinct from our heart, and stand, as it were, outside it, must set it at rest, or reassure and pacify its misgivings. But how? Partly, as we have already seen, by the fact that 'we know that we belong to the truth' (19). But partly also by the fact that *God is greater than our hearts*, and himself *knows everything.* Often our conscience accuses us justly. At such times 'only when it is overruled by the pardoning edict of God can its voice be properly hushed' (Bruce, p. 99). But our conscience is by no means infallible; its condemnation may often be unjust. We can, therefore, appeal from our conscience to God, who is greater and more knowledgeable. Indeed, he knows everything, including our secret motives and deepest resolves, and, it is implied, will be more merciful towards us than our own heart. His omniscience should relieve, not terrify, us (*cf.* Ps. 103:14; Jn. 21:17). So it is knowledge which alone can quieten the condemning heart, our own knowledge of our sincere love for others and supremely God's knowledge of our thoughts and motives. Stronger than any chemical tranquillizer is trust in our all-knowing God.

Additional Note: The meaning of 1 John 3:19–20

This passage is a *locus vexatissimus* (Law). Its general sense is clear, but it is grammatically confused, and from the earliest days commentators have had difficulty in interpreting it. The three chief problems are first the meaning of the verb 'to set at rest' (*peisomen*), secondly the two clauses in verse 20 beginning with *hoti*, and thirdly the statement that 'God is greater than our hearts'.

1. *Peithein* usually means to 'convince' or 'persuade' (RV mg.) and is followed by a clause defining the truth of which the person is to be convinced or persuaded. If this is the meaning here, some have suggested either supplying a clause, *e.g.* 'that

we belong to the truth' (so Plummer), which is forced, or using the second *hoti* clause, 'we shall convince our hearts in his presence . . . that God is greater than our hearts'. But this yields no satisfactory sense, although the NEB appears to adopt it. 'The consciousness of a sincere love of the brethren does not furnish the basis of the conviction of the sovereign greatness of God' (Westcott).

The second meaning of *peithein* is to 'pacify', although it is rare, occurring in the New Testament only in Matthew 28:14. *Cf.* 2 Maccabees 4:45. The RV ('assure'), RSV ('reassure'), and NIV ('set at rest') all take the verb in this sense. 'We shall still and tranquillize the fears and misgivings of our heart' (Westcott).

2. How are we to render the two *hoti* clauses? The second *hoti* must be translated 'because' rather than 'that'. God's greatness thus becomes not the truth of which we convince our hearts but the truth by which we pacify them.

The first *hoti* could also mean 'because'. In this case the words 'if our hearts condemn us' are a subordinate clause almost in parenthesis and the second *hoti* merely resumes the first. But this is clumsy, and the parenthetic clause is not really long enough to warrant a resumptive *hoti*. The AV recognizes this and does not translate the second *hoti*, which is indeed omitted in some MSS. The alternative is to accept as the true reading not *hoti* but *ho ti*, which two words, with *ean* added, become a construction meaning 'whenever' (RSV and NIV), 'whereinsoever' (RV, Westcott, Law) or 'in matters where' (NEB mg.). This is the solution adopted by most modern commentators. It preserves the antithesis between verse 20 ('whenever our hearts condemn us') and verse 21 ('if our hearts do not condemn'), and such opposites are not uncommon in the letter (*e.g.* 1:9–10; 2:10–11; 3:7–8; 4:2–3).

3. The third question concerns the description of God as 'greater than our hearts'. Is he so called 'because he is more merciful than our heart, or because he is more rigorous in his judgment upon us' (Ebrard)? Alford's interpretation may be taken as an example of the latter view, which was adopted by the early Greek commentators and the Reformers. He translates the second *hoti* 'because', but regards the clause as elliptical and supplies a verb before it: 'if our heart condemn us (it is) because

God is greater than our heart . . .' The greatness of God is thus viewed as a challenge not a comfort. It explains not why we can pacify our hearts but why they condemn us and why we therefore need to pacify them. 'Our conscience is but the faint echo of His voice who knoweth all things; if it condemn us, how much more He?' (Alford). *Cf.* 1 Corinthians 4:3–4. The main objection to this interpretation is that the emphatic purpose of the whole paragraph is to heal the wounded conscience, not to open its wound wider, 'to give assurance, and not to strike terror into their hearts' (Brooke).

2. *The uncondemning heart, and its blessings* (3:21–24)

John turns from the curse of a condemning heart, and how to reassure it, to the blessing of a heart which has been made tranquil or which does not condemn. This blessing is not only in itself, in the peace of an untroubled conscience, but in its result, namely a communion with God which is free and unrestricted (*parrēsian*) on the one hand, and actively sought and experienced (*pros ton theon, before God*) on the other. For *parrēsia* see commentary on 2:28. 'The thought here is of the boldness with which the Son appears before the Father, and not of that with which the accused appears before the Judge' (Westcott).

22. The second blessing of an uncondemning heart is now stated. We have confidence not only to enjoy access to him in prayer (*pros ton theon*), but to receive answers from him too (*ap' autou*). The same combination of confidence and granted petitions is found in 5:14–15. But John does not mean to imply that God hears and answers our prayers merely for the subjective reason that we have a clear conscience and an uncondemning heart. There is an objective, moral reason, namely *because we obey his commands and*, more generally, *do what pleases him*. Obedience is the indispensable condition, not the meritorious cause, of answered prayer. The statement that we *receive from him anything we ask* describes the Christian's habitual experience (the verbs are in the present tense), and Candlish is right to point to the incarnate Son as the supreme example of pleasing God and so being heard by God (Jn. 8:29; 11:41–42). It is an echo of our Lord's promise, where the same two verbs occur: 'Ask and it will be given to you . . . For everyone who asks receives' (Mt. 7:7–8).

This simple and unqualified promise must, of course, be interpreted in the light of further conditions upon which, in other parts of Scripture, God promises to grant his people's requests. If a prayer is to be answered it must be 'according to his will' (5:14; cf. Ps. 37:4; Jn. 15:7). Law is probably right that 'to obey his commands' is the condition of being heard, simply because such obedience is the evidence that 'our will is in inward harmony with God's'. We must also pray in Christ's name (Jn. 16:23–24), and for God's glory (Jas. 4:2–3), while the petitioner must be cleansed from his sins (Ps. 66:18; Pr. 15:29; Is. 59:1–2; Jas. 5:16), forgiven and himself forgiving others (Mk. 11:25), and believing God's promises (Mt. 21:22; Mk. 11:24; cf. Jas. 1:5–7) as well as obeying his commands. For the concept of pleasing God cf. Jn. 8:29; 2 Cor. 5:9; Eph. 5:10; Col. 1:10; 3:20; 1 Thes. 4:1; Heb. 13:21.

23. And what are the commands of God which we must obey if we are to receive our petitions? Fundamentally, there is only one *command* (the word is singular), embracing faith in Christ and love for one another. The faith that is commanded is variously expressed in these letters. It is simply to 'acknowledge Jesus' (4:3), to believe and acknowledge 'that Jesus is the Christ' (2:22; 5:1; cf. 2 Jn. 9) or 'the Son' (2:23); or, more elaborately, to believe 'that Jesus is the Son of God' (4:14; 5:5), and that 'Jesus Christ has come in the flesh' (4:2; 2 Jn. 7). But here the credal confession is given in full, namely, to *believe in* (although there is no preposition in the Greek as there is in 5:13; the simple dative is used) *the name*, the revealed person, *of his Son, Jesus Christ.* That is, Jesus of Nazareth, the historical person, is to be identified with the Christ, the Son of God. He is given his complete title also in 1:3 and 5:20.

The second part of the command is that we should *love one another as he commanded us, he* meaning perhaps 'Jesus Christ', and the command he gave, that of John 13:34 and 15:12, 17. Reciprocal love has already been mentioned as a command in 2:7–8 (cf. 2 Jn. 6) but here for the first time faith and love are brought together (*cf.* Gal. 5:6). Both are the will of God, and both are commanded by him. There is a significant difference in the tense of the two verbs, *believe* and *love*, faith in Christ being here regarded as a decisive act (accepting *pisteusōmen* as the correct reading), and love for the brothers as a continuous attitude. Both are tests of a true Christian. In 3:10 John linked the practice of righteousness with brotherly love. Here he links love with belief in Christ, and in the next verse completes the trio by adding a general obedience to the commands of God, of which he has also written in verse 22.

24. The concept of a mutual 'abiding' (RSV), mentioned here in the letter for the first time, *we in him and he in us*, is derived ultimately from our Lord's allegory of the vine and the branches (Jn. 15:1ff.). There it is Christ who dwells in his own, and they in him. Here, if we may judge from the use of '*him*', '*his*' and '*he*' in verses 22–23, it is 'God' who dwells in us, as in 4:12, and we in him. The difference would have been unimportant to John, however, for in John 17:21 Jesus prays that they 'may . . . be in *us*' (*cf.* Jn. 14:23, '*we* will come to him and make our home with him'). Both here and in John 15 (v. 10) the condition of continuous mutual indwelling is obedience; although obedience is also the issue and evidence of the indwelling. *Cf.* 2:3–6 for an exposition of the same truth.

With this verse John unites the various strands which he has been unfolding separately in these first three chapters of his letter. No-one may dare to claim that he lives in Christ and Christ in him unless he is obedient to the three fundamental commands which John has been expounding, which are belief in Christ, love for the brothers and moral righteousness. 'Living in Christ' is not a mystical experience which anyone may claim; its indispensable accompaniments are the confession of Jesus as the Son of God come in the flesh, and a consistent life of holiness and love. *And this is how we know*, he concludes, *that he lives in us: We know it by the Spirit he gave us* at the beginning of our Christian life. It may at first sight seem that this reference to the Holy Spirit within us introduces a subjective criterion of assurance (like Rom. 8:15–16) which is inconsistent with what has gone before. But this is not so. The Spirit whose presence is the test of Christ's living in us, manifests himself objectively in our life and conduct. It is he who inspires us to confess Jesus as the Christ come in the flesh, as John immediately proceeds to show (4:1ff.; *cf.* 2:20, 27). It is also he who empowers us to live righteously and to love our brothers and sisters (*cf.* 4:13; Gal. 5:16, 22). So if we would set our hearts at rest, when they accuse and condemn us, we must look for evidence of the Spirit's working, and particularly whether he is enabling us to believe in Christ, to obey God's commands and to love our brothers; for the condition of Christ dwelling in us and of our dwelling in him is this comprehensive obedience (24a), and the evidence of the indwelling is the gift of the Spirit (24b).

D. AN ELABORATION OF THE DOCTRINAL TEST: BELIEF (4:1–6)

The background of these verses, as of 1 Corinthians 12 and 14, is a situation in which 'prophecy' was prevalent. The present tense of the command *do not believe every spirit* (1) suggests that John's readers were tending to accept uncritically all teaching which claimed to be inspired. They needed to be shown that 'to identify the supernatural and the Divine is a perilous mistake' (Findlay). So John urges them to investigate the source of every pretension to inspired utterance. Was it *from God*? Or were the speakers *false prophets*? This need for the critical assessment of religious teachers has always been felt. The test given by Jesus was moral: 'by their fruit you will recognise them'. John also applied moral tests, both righteousness (3:10) and love (4:8). But there are theological tests as well (as in Dt. 13:1–5 and Je. 23:9ff.). In 3:23 John linked under a single divine command the duty to love one another, which had been his main theme during the latter part of that chapter, with the duty to believe in the name of God's Son Jesus Christ. Now he takes up and further develops this central Christian belief as a searching test of the true Christian and the true prophet. The test is applied in two ways, first with reference to the teachers and, secondly, with reference to the hearers. *This is how you can recognise* (2) true and false teachers, he says, and goes on to make the content of the teaching the decisive test. 'This is how we recognise' them

(6b), he says again at the end of the paragraph, and goes on to make the character of the audience an almost equally revealing test.

1. The content of the teaching (4:1–3)

God has given us his Spirit (3:24), but there are other spirits active in the world. It is important to observe that the command to believe in the name of God's Son Jesus Christ (3:23) is followed by the prohibition *do not believe every spirit*, much as the command to love our brothers and sisters (2:7–11) was followed by the prohibition 'do not love the world or anything in the world' (2:15). Neither Christian believing nor Christian loving is to be indiscriminate. In particular, Christian faith is not to be mistaken for credulity. True faith examines its object before reposing confidence in it. So John tells his readers to *test the spirits to see whether they are from God*. Every prophet is the mouthpiece or spokesman of some spirit, true prophets of 'the Spirit of God' (2), who in verse 6 is called 'the Spirit of truth', and *false prophets* of 'the spirit of falsehood' (6b) or 'the spirit of the antichrist' (3). So behind every prophet is a spirit, and behind each spirit either God or the devil. Before we can trust any spirits, we must test them. It is their origin that matters. We may note the similar command given by Paul in 1 Thessalonians 5:19–22. The apostles Paul and John assumed that even the humblest Christian possessed 'the right of private judgment', as the Reformers properly insisted, and both could and should apply the objective test John is about to give in the next verse.

The reason for this need to test the spirits is now given. The reference may be general, to false teachers setting forth on a missionary expedition, or, more particularly, to the 'many antichrists' described in 2:18–19 who had formerly been church members but had now gone out. Westcott thinks the allusion is to 'the great outbreak of the Gentile pseudo-Christianity which is vaguely spoken of as Gnosticism'. Jesus warned his disciples of false prophets (Mt. 7:15; Mk. 13:22–23). So did Paul (Acts 20:28–30) and Peter (2 Pet. 1:1). Still today there are many voices clamouring for our attention, and many cults gaining widespread popular support. Some of them claim a special revelation or inspiration to authenticate their particular doctrine. There is need for Christian discernment. For many are too gullible, and exhibit a naïve readiness to credit messages and teachings which purport to come from the spirit-world. There is such a thing, however, as a misguided tolerance of false doctrine. Unbelief (*do not believe every spirit*) can be as much a mark of spiritual maturity as belief. We should avoid both extremes, the superstition which believes everything and suspicion which believes nothing.

2. From the command and the need to test, John passes to the test itself: *This is how you can recognize the Spirit of God.*[1] The origin of the inspiring spirit may be discerned from the teaching of the prophet through whom it speaks. *Every spirit that acknowledges that Jesus Christ has come in the flesh is from God.* By this acknowledgment is meant not merely a recognition of his identity, but a profession of faith in him 'openly and boldly' (Westcott) as the incarnate Lord. Even evil or unclean spirits recognized the deity of Jesus during his ministry (*e.g.* Mk. 1:24; 3:11; 5:7–8; *cf.* Acts 19:15). But though they knew him, they did not acknowledge him. The Spirit of God, on the other hand, always honours the Son of God. Jesus taught that it is the Holy Spirit's particular ministry both to testify to, and to glorify, him (Jn. 15:26; 16:13–15; *cf.* also 1 Cor. 12:3). The precise words of the test formula should be carefully noted. Probably the phrase should read, 'Jesus is the Christ come in the flesh'.[2] The confession is that the man Jesus is himself none other than the incarnate Christ or Son, which is the doctrine Cerinthus and his disciples denied. The perfect tense *come* (*elēlythota*), compared with the present tense in 2 John 7 (*erchomenon*), seems to emphasize that the flesh assumed by the Son of God in the incarnation has become his permanent possession. Far from coming upon Jesus at the bap-

---

[1] The verb *you can recognize* (*ginōskete*) could be an imperative or an indicative. In favour of the imperative some commentators have argued that John is adding to the two commands of v. 1 not to believe every spirit but to test the spirits, the further instruction to recognize the Spirit of God. Since, however, every other occurrence in the letter of the phrase *This is how we know* or *recognize* (although in the first person, while here it is in the second) is followed by an indicative verb, the indicative seems preferable here also. John is making a statement, not issuing a command.

[2] See the Additional Note, 'The interpretation of 1 John 4:2', pp.158–159.

tism and leaving him before the cross, the Christ actually came in the flesh and has never laid it aside. Such a confession of faith is sufficient to show that the *spirit* inspiring it *is from God*. The fundamental Christian doctrine which can never be compromised concerns the eternal divine-human person of Jesus Christ, the Son of God.

3. The contrary is also true: *but every spirit that does not acknowledge Jesus is not from God*. To *acknowledge Jesus*, in the mind of John, can mean only one thing, namely to confess him as the Christ come in the flesh. To deny this, whatever claim to inspiration may accompany the denial, is to reveal the working of *the spirit of the antichrist*, which John's readers had *heard* (no doubt from himself in his previous teaching) was *coming* (*erchetai* as in 2:18). Not only does the antichrist ape the 'coming' of the true Christ, but his spirit *even now is already in the world*. John has said the same thing in 2:18, 22, although what he here calls *the spirit of the antichrist* is there yet more explicitly said to be embodied in *many antichrists*, *i.e.* false prophets, who have come. *Cf.* 2 Thessalonians 2:3–8 where, although 'the man of lawlessness' is still to be revealed, 'the secret power of lawlessness' is already at work, albeit under restraint.

Comparing the two passages, 2:18–23 and 4:1–3, it is instructive to observe the difference of emphasis. In chapter 2 our confession or denial of the Son determines whether we possess the Father or not, while in chapter 4 our confession or denial of the Son indicates whether we are inspired by the Spirit or not. The person of Christ is central. No system can be tolerated, however loud its claims or learned its adherents, which denies that Jesus is the Christ come in the flesh, in other words either his eternal deity or his historical humanity. Those who deny the Son have neither the Father nor the Spirit.

Additional Note: The interpretation of 1 John 4:2

Brooke points out that when the verb *homologein*, to acknowledge or confess, is followed by an accusative, the latter may be single or double. The single accusative occurs in 2:23 and 4:3, to acknowledge 'the Son' and to acknowledge 'Jesus', and the double in John 9:22, to acknowledge Jesus as 'the Christ'. Which is it here (and in 2 Jn. 7)? Brooke prefers to regard the expression 'Jesus Christ come in the flesh' as a single, comprehensive accusative and thinks this 'the simplest construction'. It seems better, with other commentators, to understand the object of the verb as a double accusative, either 'Jesus Christ' as 'come in the flesh', or 'Jesus' as 'Christ come in the flesh'. The former is unlikely. Although John does employ the combined name 'Jesus Christ' (1:3; 2:1; 3:23; 5:20), to speak of 'Jesus Christ' as having 'come in the flesh' would be a strange 'theological anachronism' (Findlay), since it was not until *after* the incarnation that he was called 'Jesus'. This being so, we should probably adopt the alternative double accusative, namely to acknowledge 'Jesus' as 'Christ come in the flesh', or 'the Christ incarnate' (Moffatt). This accords both with the use of the name 'Jesus' by itself in the best MSS of verse 3 ('acknowledge Jesus'), and with what is known of the heretics' views, that the Christ, a divine aeon, descended upon the man Jesus at his baptism, and withdrew from him before his death. John repudiates this doctrine. The truth is not that the Christ came 'into' the flesh of Jesus, but that Jesus was the Christ come 'in' the flesh. The two are to be identified. 'The statement, simple as it is, is of exquisite precision' (Law).

This interpretation is consistent also with the interesting variant reading of verse 3, which instead of *mē homologei* ('does not acknowledge') has the verb *lyei*. This could be translated 'destroys' (as in 3:8) or 'looses'. Its attestation, which is slight, is summarized in full by Brooke (pp. 111–114). It is found in the Vulgate as 'solvit', ('severs'), in other Latin versions, in Latin translations of Irenaeus and Origen, and in Tertullian and Augustine. It is preserved in the RV margin as 'annulleth'. Probably it was an early scribal gloss, and is not authentic; but it is significant as showing that 'not to acknowledge Jesus' was regarded as to 'loose' him, that is, to 'divide' Jesus from the Christ, instead of identifying them. Later the verb *lyein* came to be used almost technically for the Gnostic heresy which 'separated' Jesus from the Christ; and this variant reading was used in argument against the Nestorian heresy.

2. *The character of the audience* (4:4–6)

John now turns from a consideration of the teachers and their message to an examination of the audience which listens to them. In the Greek text, each of these three verses (4, 5, 6) begins with an emphatic personal pronoun (4, *hymeis*), referring to his Christian readers in general, *they* (5, *autoi*), referring to the false teachers, and *we* (6, *hēmeis*) referring to himself as representative of the authoritative apostles. See Introduction, pp. 32–33.

4. *You . . . are from God*, he says (as is 'every spirit that acknowledges that Jesus Christ has come in the flesh', 2), *and have overcome them, i.e.* 'these false prophets' (NEB). This 'overcoming' is not so much moral (as in 2:13–14, where the same word occurs) as intellectual. The false teachers have not succeeded in deceiving you. Not only have you tested them and found them wanting, but you have conquered them by decisively repudiating their teaching. You have not succumbed to their blandishments or believed their lies. Hence, no doubt, they 'had found themselves obliged to depart' (Ebrard), as 2:19 declares. And the cause of your victory is the superior strength of *the one who is in you*. This must be the 'Spirit of truth' (6), 'the anointing' which 'remains in you' (2:20, 27), while *the one who is in the world* is the devil, 'the spirit of falsehood' (6). Although (it is implied) the evil spirit is 'great', the Holy Spirit is *greater*, and by his illumination all false teaching may be overcome. Here, as in 2:18–27, protection against falsehood and victory over it are ascribed both to an objective standard of doctrine and to the indwelling Spirit who illumines our minds to grasp and apply it, for 'unless the Spirit of wisdom is present, there is little or no profit in having God's Word in our hands' (Calvin).

5–6. These two verses are complementary. In them John contrasts in striking fashion not only the false prophets and the true apostles (*they* and *we*), but the different audiences who listen to them, namely *the world* and *whoever knows God*. The world recognizes its own people and listens to their message, which originates in its own circle and reflects its own perspectives. This explains their popularity. *We,* on the other hand, *are from God.* This is not the same as 'you are from God' in verse 4. There he declares the divine origin of his Christian readers; here he is particularizing. The *we* of this verse is in direct antithesis to the *they* of the previous verse. So, if *they* means the false teachers, *we* must mean the true teachers, namely the apostles. But how can it be known that *we are from God* and are teaching the truth? You can tell that our message is God's message, John explains, because God's people listen to it and receive it. This statement sounds the height of arrogance. So it would be if uttered by an individual Christian. No private believer could presume to say: 'whoever knows God agrees with me; only those who are not from God disagree with me'. But this is what John says. For he is writing in the name neither of himself nor of the church but of Christ, as one of his chosen apostles. He is carrying a stage further the argument of the first three verses. There the test of doctrine was whether it acknowledged the divine-human person of Jesus Christ; here the test is whether it is accepted by Christians and rejected by non-Christians. There is a certain affinity between God's Word and God's people. Jesus had taught that his sheep hear his voice (Jn. 10: 4–5, 8, 16, 26–27), that everyone who is on the side of truth listens to his witness to the truth (Jn. 18:37), and that 'he who belongs to God hears what God says' (Jn. 8:47). In the same way John asserts that since *we are from God* (6) and 'you . . . are from God' (4), you listen to us. There is a correspondence between message and hearers. The Spirit who is in you (4) enables you to discern his own voice speaking through us (2). Still today we can recognize God's Word because God's people listen to it, just as we can recognize God's people because they listen to God's Word. Those who do not listen to apostolic teaching, but prefer to absorb the teaching of the world, not only pass judgment on themselves but thereby also on the message to which they do give attention.

All this is consistent with John's repeated emphasis that safety from error is to be found in loyalty to that which his readers 'had' or 'heard' 'from the beginning' (2:7, 24; 3:11; 2 Jn. 5; *cf.* 2 Jn. 9). The identity of the 'us' in the phrase *whoever knows God listens to us* (6) cannot be understood as the church, or as the papacy (as some Roman Catholic commentators have claimed), without doing violence to John's insistence in this letter upon primitive apostolic doctrine, quite apart from the historical question whether the consensus of Christian opinion has been a reliable criterion of truth. Dodd is right to say that prophets, representing spontaneity and freedom, were (and still are) always 'subordinate to apostles' and their authority (pp. 103–106).

This is how we recognize the Spirit of truth and the spirit of falsehood, John concludes. We can test the spirits, and 'get to know' which is which (*ginōskomen*, present tense), by examining both the message they proclaim through their human instruments and the character of the audience which listens to them.

V. THIRD APPLICATION OF THE TESTS (4:7–5:5)

A. A FURTHER ELABORATION OF THE SOCIAL TEST: LOVE (4:7–12)

In 3:23 John summarized God's commands in terms of believing in Christ and loving one another. He has unfolded in 4:1–6 some of the implications of believing in Christ; he now turns abruptly to the subject of mutual love. In Tyndale's words, 'John singeth his old song again.' For it is the third time in the letter that he takes up and applies the supreme test of love. (See also 2:7–11 and 3:11–18.) Each time the test is more searching. In this third treatment John is concerned to relate the love which should be in us not to the true light which is already shining (2:8, 10), nor to the eternal life of which it is the evidence (3:14–15) but to God's very nature of love and to his loving activity in Christ and in us. 'Here the epistle rises to the summit of all revelation' (Law).

The refrain of the paragraph is the reflexive *love one another*. It occurs three times – as an exhortation (7, 'let us love one another'), as a statement of duty (11, 'we also ought to love one another'; *cf.* 2:6; 3:16), and as a hypothesis (12, 'if we love each other . . .'). What John is at pains to demonstrate is the ground of this imperative obligation. Why is reciprocal love the plain duty of Christians? It is, as he began to say in 3:16, that God has revealed himself to us in Jesus Christ as self-sacrificial love. God is love in himself (8, 16); God has loved us in Christ (10–11); and God continues to love in and through us (12–13); these are the reasons why we must love each other.

7–8. The Greek sentence in verse 7 opens with a striking assonance: *agapētoi agapōmen* ('Beloved, let us love', RSV). Here and in v. 11 (*cf.* 2:7) the author practises what he preaches. In urging them to love each other, he begins by assuring them of his own love for them. He then continues by developing his first argument for brotherly love, which is based on God's eternal nature. He states it twice, first, *for love comes from God* (7) and secondly, *because God is love* (8). Since God is the source and origin (*ek*) of love and all true love derives from him, it stands to reason that *everyone who loves*, that is, loves either God or neighbour with that selfless devotion which alone is true love according to John's teaching, *has been born of God and knows God* (7). Not only is God the source of all true love; he is love in his inmost being. There are three other statements in the New Testament concerning what God is in substance and nature: he is 'spirit' (Jn. 4:24), 'light' (1 Jn. 1:5) and 'a consuming fire' (Heb. 12:29 from Dt. 4:24). The Gnostics believed that God is immaterial spirit and light, but they never taught that God is love. It is the most comprehensive and sublime of all biblical affirmations about God's being, and is repeated here twice (8, 16). Nevertheless, it is important to hold the biblical assertions about God together. It is true that the words *God is love* mean not that loving is 'only one of God's many activities' (Alexander) but rather that 'all his activity is loving activity' and that, therefore, 'if He judges, He judges in love' (Dodd). Yet, if his judging is in love, his loving is also in justice. He who is love is light and fire as well. Far from condoning sin, his love has found a way to expose it (because he is light) and to consume it (because he is fire) without destroying the sinner, but rather saving him.

From the truth that *God is love* John draws a further deduction, not now positive and inclusive like that of verse 7, but negative and exclusive: *whoever does not love does not know God*. The argument is plain and compelling. For the loveless Christian to profess to know God and to have been born of God is like claiming to be intimate with a foreigner whose language we cannot speak, or to have been born of parents whom we do not in any way resemble. It is to fail to manifest the nature of him whom we claim as our Father (*born of God*) and our Friend (*knows God*). Love is as much a sign of Christian authenticity as is righteousness (2:29).

If John grounds his first argument for mutual love on God's eternal nature, he bases his second (9–11) on his historical gift. The God who is love (8) 'loved us' (10) and expressed his love by sending his Son to earth. While the origin of love is in the being of God, the manifestation of love is in the coming of Christ. And, John writes, 'since God so loved us, we also ought to love one another' (11). This time the duty of reciprocal love is enforced not merely by the abstract truth that God is love, but by the concrete fact that he 'showed his love among us' by sending 'his one and only Son into the world' for us (9). It should be added that the concept of God 'sending' his Son (9–10, 14) 'involves the doctrine of Christ's pre-existence and divinity' (Ebrard) in addition to the doctrine of the love of God. John is already hinting at the organic relation between his doctrinal and social tests which he elaborates later.

9–10. There have been and are many manifestations of the love of God. It is no doubt constantly manifest in heaven (though not to human eyes) in the mysterious relations between the persons of the Godhead. 'Among us', however, God's love, which had already been displayed in his choice, redemption and protection of Israel, has been pre-eminently made known in the gift of his Son. This is stated with emphasis twice in this paragraph (*cf.* also vv. 14, 16). The sending of God's Son was both the revelation of his love (*This is how God showed his love . . .* 9) and, indeed, the very essence of love itself (*this is love . . .* 10). It is not our love that is primary, but God's (10), free, uncaused and spontaneous, and all our love is but a reflection of his and a response to it.

The coming of Christ is, therefore, a concrete, historical revelation of God's love, for love (*agapē*) is self-sacrifice, the seeking of another's positive good at one's own cost, and a greater self-giving than God's gift of his Son there has never been, nor could be. The way in which John sees this emerges from the similar pattern in which the three statements of verses 9–10 and 14 are made.

1. Each says that God sent his Son, called now 'the Son' (14, literally), *his Son* (10) and his *monogenēs*, 'only begotten Son' (9, AV; 'one and only', NIV). *Monogenēs* is used both of Abraham's only son Isaac (Heb. 11:17) and of the only son of the widow of Nain (Lk. 7:12). In John's letters it occurs here alone, but four times in his Gospel (1:14, 18; 3:16, 18). In the LXX it sometimes translates the Hebrew word 'well beloved' (*cf.* Mk. 1:11; 9:7; 12:6). Applied to Jesus Christ, it indicates his uniqueness; he is 'the Son' in an absolute sense. No greater gift of God is conceivable because no greater gift was possible. This was God's indescribable gift' (2 Cor. 9:15). *Cf.* John 3:16; Romans 8:32.

2. It is further implied that the Father sent his Son to die for us. Not the incarnation but the atonement is the pre-eminent manifestation of love (*cf.* 3:16). It is true that no explicit reference is made in these verses to the Son's death, but that it was in John's mind is certain from his theology of salvation. In order to be *the Saviour of the world* (14), the Lamb of God took away the sin of the world (Jn. 1:29; *cf.* 1 Jn. 3:5). In order *that we might live through him* (9), he died (Jn. 3:14–15; 11:49–52; 12:24). In order to be *an atoning sacrifice for our sins* (10), he shed his blood (1:7; 2:2, where see commentary; *cf.* Rom. 3:25).

3. The greatness of God's love, manifest in the nature of his gift and its purpose, is seen also in its beneficiaries, for God gave his Son to die for us undeserving sinners. The degraded condition to which our sins had brought us is clearly implied. If we need a *Saviour* (14), it is because we are sinners, unable to save ourselves. Since Christ came *that we might live through him* (9) and *as an atoning sacrifice for our sins* (10), it is clear that apart from him we are 'dead in transgressions and sins' (Eph. 2:1; *cf.* 3:14) and under the holy wrath and judgment of God. In the ancient world outside Christianity, it was thought appropriate to love only those who were regarded as worthy of being loved. But God loves sinners who are unworthy of his love, and indeed subject to his wrath. He loved us and sent his Son to rescue us, not because we are lovable, but because he is

love. So the greatness of his love is seen in the costliness of his self-sacrifice for the wholly undeserving (*cf.* Rom. 5:7–8). A clearer manifestation of God's love could not be imagined.

11. The historical manifestation of God's love in Christ not only assures us of his love for us, but lays upon us the obligation to love one another. No-one who has been to the cross and seen God's immeasurable and unmerited love displayed there can go back to a life of selfishness. Indeed, the implication seems to be that our love should resemble his love: *since God so loved us, we also ought* – in like manner and to a like degree of self-sacrifice – *to love one another.* Cf. 3:16, where the duty of Christian self-sacrifice is deduced from the self-sacrifice of Christ.

12. We are not to think of love only as constituting God's eternal being and as historically manifested in the sending of his Son into the world. For God who is love and has loved still loves, and today his love is seen in and through our love. So John's third argument for reciprocal love is based on God's present and continuous activity of love. His opening statement about the invisibility of God is indisputable. God is spirit (Jn. 4:24) and in himself invisible (1 Tim. 1:17; 6:16). Even if he were visible, no human being could see him and live (Ex. 33:20). In fact, nobody has seen him (*cf.* v. 20). The Old Testament theophanies were revelations either of God's glory or of God-in-disguise ('the angel of the Lord' appearing as a man); they were not visions of God as he is in himself (*theon* without the article). The vision of God lies still in the future when Christ appears (3:2).

It is significant that this is not the only occurrence in the Johannine literature of the phrase *No-one has ever seen God*. It comes also (in almost identical words) at the end of the Prologue to the Gospel (1:18). How then can he be known? In the Prologue to the Gospel John continues that 'God the only Son, who is at the Father's side, has made him known' (*cf.* Col. 1:15). But here, to our astonishment and confusion, John goes on to say that *if we love each other, God lives in us and his love is made complete in us.* That is, the unseen God, who once revealed himself in his Son, now reveals himself in his people if and when they love one another. God's love is seen in their love because their love is his love imparted to them by his Spirit (*cf.* v. 13). The words do not mean that when we begin to love, God comes to dwell in us, but the reverse. Our love for one another is evidence of God's indwelling presence. See 3:17 for another reference to God's love living in us.

John goes further still. Reciprocal Christian love means not only that God *lives* in us but also that *his love is made complete in us*. It would be hard to exaggerate the greatness of this conception. It is so daring that many commentators have been reluctant to accept it and have suggested that the genitive in *his love* is not subjective ('God's love') but objective ('our love for God'; *cf.* 2:5) or definitive ('Godlike love'). But the whole paragraph is concerned with God's love and we must not stagger at the majesty of this conclusion. God's love, which originates in himself (7–8) and was manifested in his Son (9–10), is made complete in his people (12). It is 'brought to perfection within us' (NEB). God's love *for* us is perfected only when it is reproduced *in* us or (as it may mean) 'among us' in the Christian fellowship. It is these three truths about the love of God which John uses as inducements to brotherly love. We are to love each other, first because God is love (8–9), secondly because God loved us (10–11), and thirdly because, if we do love one another, God lives in us and his love is made complete in us (12).

B. A COMBINATION OF THE DOCTRINAL AND SOCIAL TESTS (4:13–21)

The two statements with which the previous paragraph concluded, namely that 'God lives in us' and 'his love is made complete in us', are now taken up and elaborated – God's indwelling in verses 13–16, and completed or perfect love in verses 17–21.

1. God's indwelling (4:13–16)

The new paragraph is introduced by the familiar formula, *We know that* (NEB, 'Here is the proof that . . .'). The previous two sections have been exhortations – a warning not to believe every spirit (1–6) and an appeal to love one another (7–12). These two tests of belief and love are now applied more personally, no longer in exhortation but in affirmation. The belief and love, which John has been urging upon his readers, are now assumed, and deductions are drawn from them. Moreover, their relation to each other is for the first time indicated. This passage 'is the high-watermark of the thought of the epistle' (Dodd). That 'the Father has sent his Son' is not only the chief test of doctrinal orthodoxy but also the supreme evidence of God's love and inspiration of ours. The divine-human person of Jesus Christ, God's love for us, and our love for God and neighbour cannot be separated. The theology which robs Christ of his Godhead, thereby robs God of the glory of his love, and robs us of the one belief that can generate a mature love within us. 'To weaken faith is to deaden love' (Findlay). Further, the ability to believe and the ability to love are alike attributable to the Holy Spirit. Thus belief and love are seen to be related both in the mission of the Son and in the indwelling of the Spirit.

13. God's indwelling is mentioned three times in this paragraph, and what in verse 12 was single ('God lives in us') is now each time reciprocal (13, *we live in him and he in us*; 15, 'God lives in him and he in God'; 16, 'Whoever lives in love lives in God, and God in him'). Moreover, each time the reciprocal indwelling is described, evidence of it is supplied as follows: verse 13, *because he has given us of his Spirit*; verse 15, 'if anyone acknowledges that Jesus is the Son of God'; verse 16, 'whoever lives in love'.

Of these three tests of the indwelling of God, the last two are developments of the first. It is by the Spirit that we come to acknowledge the incarnation of the Son (*cf.* 4:1–3 and 1 Cor. 12:3), and by the same Spirit that we are enabled to love (12–13; *cf.* 3:23–24). In our fallen and unredeemed state we are both blind (unable to believe) and selfish (unable to love). It is only by the grace of the Holy Spirit, who is the Spirit of truth and whose first-fruit is love (Gal. 5:22), that we ever come to believe in Christ and to love others. Emphasis on the Holy Spirit is, in fact, 'the *predominant idea* of this section' (Ebrard). This, then, is the sequence of thought: we know that we live in God and God in us 'because he has given us of his Spirit' (13), and we know he has given us of his Spirit because we have come to 'acknowledge that Jesus is the Son of God' (15), and to live 'in love' (16).

Some commentators make the mistake of seeing in this paragraph the conditions of our living in God and of his living in us. Belief and love are not the conditions of the indwelling, however, but the tests and evidences of it. John writes not 'by this we live in him', but 'by this we know that we live in him'. The theme of this section, as of the whole letter, is 'the grounds of assurance' (Dodd).

14. From the truth that God has given us his Spirit (13), John moves to the fact that God has sent his Son (14). The trinitarian reference is plain, since it is the Father who sent his Son into the world as Saviour, who also sent his Spirit into our hearts as witness (*cf.* Gal. 4:4–6). Christian certainty rests on this combination of the objective and subjective, the historical and experiential, the Son's mission and the Spirit's testimony. As for the Father's sending of his Son, this (John writes) *we have seen*. The verb is the same as in verse 12. God in himself 'no-one has ever seen', but 'we have seen' the Son whom he sent. Who is this 'we' who have seen him? 'The word must here refer to the actual eyewitnesses of the life of Jesus on earth' (Brooke). In other words, John is referring in this verse to himself and his fellow apostles. It is they who were the primary witnesses, uniquely qualified to testify because of what they had seen. *Cf.* Introduction, pp. 30ff. Thus God has provided a twofold testimony to Christ, that of the apostles, who witnessed to the historic Jesus whom they had seen and heard (14), and that of the Holy Spirit, who confirms their witness in the hearts of believers (13). For this double witness see John 15:26–27 and Acts 5:32.

Much Christian truth is contained in the straightforward affirmation of verse 14. Here is the essence of the gospel. *The world* means sinful society, estranged from God and under the dominion of the evil one (*cf.* 5:19). Its urgent need was to be rescued from sin and Satan. And *the Father* 'so loved the world' (Jn. 3:16) that he *sent his Son*, his dear and only Son, to be its *Saviour*. The perfect tense of the verb (*apestalken*, 'has sent') points not just to the historical event of the sending, but to the purpose and result of it, namely the salvation of the world. Further, within this statement of the gospel all three of the apostle's tests are implicitly contained, the doctrinal (it was *his Son* himself whom the Father sent), the social (God's love seen in the sending of his Son, 9–10, 16, obliges us to love each other), and the ethical (if Christ came to be our *Saviour*, we must forsake the sins from which he came to save us). It is clear, then, that John's tests are not arbitrary. He has not made a random selection. They arise inexorably from the central Christian revelation. The mission of Christ manifests his divine-human person, God's great love and our moral duty. Once grasp the truth of verse 14, and we shall acknowledge Christ, obey his commands, and love one another.

15. Of the three tests it is the doctrinal one on which John now lays emphasis (*cf.* 2:23; 4:2). The aorist tense (*homologēsē*) cannot be rendered precisely in English. John is referring neither to a future confession ('shall confess', AV, RV), nor to a present and continuing confession ('confesses', RSV; 'acknowledges', NIV), but to a single and decisive public confession, the time of which is unspecified. But how do people come thus to acknowledge the divine-human person of Jesus? The apostolic testimony is necessary (14), but it does not compel assent. It is only by the Spirit of God that anybody ever confesses that Jesus is the Christ come in the flesh (4:2). Or, as he puts the same truth here, *if anyone acknowledges that Jesus is the Son of God*, he thereby gives evidence of the fact that *God lives in him and he in God*. Again, the witness of the apostles must be supplemented by the witness of the Spirit.

16. The historical mission of Jesus is evidence as much of the Father's love as of the Son's deity. It tells us not only that God loved, but that *God is love.* It is one thing, however, to know and believe *the love God has for us* and that *God is love*; it is another to 'live in love' ourselves. Yet this we must do, for (as John has unfolded at great length in vv. 7–12) the love that is eternally in God and was historically manifested in Christ is to come to fruition in us. The only way to love, as the only way to believe (15), is by living in God and God in us. For it is the divine indwelling which alone makes possible both belief and love. They are its fruit, and therefore its evidence: 'he who dwells in love is [*i.e.* is thereby seen to be] dwelling in God' (NEB).

There is, then, in these verses a double interweaving of themes, first of believing and loving (the doctrinal and social tests), and secondly of the mission of the Son and the witness of the Spirit through which both are possible. There is objective historical evidence in the sending of the Son both of his unique person (which 'we have seen', 14) and of the Father's love (which *we know and rely on*, 16). But even this is insufficient. Without the Holy Spirit our minds are dark and our hearts cold. Only the Holy Spirit can enlighten our minds to believe in Jesus and warm our hearts to love God and each other. So believing and loving are evidence that his Spirit is at work within us.

2. *Perfect love* (4:17–21)

In verse 12 John declared that if we love each other, God lives in us and his love is made complete in us. In verses 13–16 he has enlarged on the divine indwelling; in verses 17–21 he reverts to the theme of complete love, although now he is concerned with the completion not of God's love in us but of our love for God. John is not suggesting that any Christian's love could in this life be flawlessly perfect, but rather developed and mature, set fixedly upon God. He describes two marks of such 'perfect love', namely confidence before God and love of our brothers and sisters.

17. *Parrēsia* is a word John has already used to portray both the unshrinking confidence we should have at Christ's coming (2:28) and the bold assurance we should enjoy as we approach God in prayer (3:21–22; *cf.* 5:14–15). Here he reverts to the future, to *the day of judgment* which will follow the Lord's return. There is no evidence that John has jettisoned belief either in the parousia or in the judgment day. That day will be one of shame and terror for the wicked, but not for the redeemed people of God. Our confidence (like our obedience in 2:5) is a sign that our love has been *made complete*. It is grounded upon the fact that *in this world we are like him* (*sc.* Christ). To be sure, we are not yet like him in our character or in our bodies (3:2), although to some extent we do resemble him in our conduct (2:6; 3:3), but in our standing before God, even while remaining *in this world*, we are

171

already like him. We are sons in and through the Son, begotten or born of God as he was (5:18), the objects of God's love and favour like him (cf. Eph. 1:6). Therefore if Jesus called and calls God 'Father', so may we. We can share the confidence before God which he enjoys.

18. The same truth is now stated negatively. The love that spells confidence banishes fear. *There is no fear (i.e.* no servile fear) *in love.* That is, 'there is no room for fear in love' (NEB). The two are as incompatible as oil and water. We can love and reverence God simultaneously (cf. Heb. 5:7), but we cannot approach him in love and hide from him in fear at the same time (cf. Rom. 8:14–15; 2 Tim. 1:7). Indeed, it is by love for God that a false cringing fear of God is overcome. It 'flings it out of doors' (Law). The reason why perfect love cannot coexist with fear is now given: *fear has to do with punishment* (the word *kolasis* occurs elsewhere in the New Testament only in Mt. 25:46). That is to say, fear introduces the category of punishment, which is quite alien to God's forgiven children who love him. Or the phrase may signify rather that fear 'includes, brings with it' (Westcott, *cf.* NEB) the very punishment it fears. In other words, 'fear has in itself something of the nature of punishment' (Brooke, Law); to fear is to begin to suffer punishment already. Once assured that we are 'like him' (17) God's beloved children, we cease to be afraid of him. It is evident, therefore, that *the one who fears is not made perfect in love.*

19. So we are not afraid of God. Instead, *we love* (*agapōmen,* which is here surely an indicative statement and not an exhortation in the subjunctive as it is in v. 7). The weight of MS evidence is against the addition of an object to the verb, whether 'God' or 'him'. Instead, John makes a general affirmation about God's people. Our great characteristic, he says, is not that we fear, but that we love. And the reason is that *he first loved us.* God's love was primary; all true love is a response to his initiative. John repeats the truth he has asserted in verse 10. Fear lives within us by nature, and needs to be driven out (18). *Agapē,* godlike love, on the other hand, does not reside in our fallen nature; 'our very capacity to love, whether the object of our love be God or our neighbour' (Dodd) is due entirely to his prior love for us and in us.

20. Love for God expresses itself not only in a confident attitude towards him, devoid of fear, but in a loving concern for our brothers and sisters (*cf.* 3:14). The perfect love that drives out fear, drives out hatred also. If God's love for us is made complete when we love one another (12), so is our love for God. John does not mince his words. If how a person behaves contradicts what he says, *he is a liar*. To claim to know God and have fellowship with God while we walk in the darkness of disobedience is to lie (1:6; 2:4). To claim to possess the Father while denying the deity of the Son is to lie (2:22-23). To claim to love God while hating our brothers is also to lie. These are the three black lies of the letter: moral, doctrinal and social. We may insist that we are Christian, but habitual sin, denial of Christ or selfish hatred would expose us as liars. Only holiness, faith and love can prove the truth of our claim to know, possess and love God.

That it is ludicrous for a person to say he loves God while he hates his brother should be clear from the fact that he can see his brother but cannot see God. Indeed, the verb indicates not only that he 'can' see his brother, but that he *has seen* him (*heōraken*); he has him 'continually before his eyes' (Plummer), with ample opportunity to serve him in love. It is obviously easier to love and serve a visible human being than an invisible God, and if we fail in the easier task, it is absurd to claim success in the harder. 'It is a false boast when anyone says that he loves God but neglects His image which is before his eyes' (Calvin). As Dodd points out, this 'cannot' expresses not so much the person's incapacity to love God, as the proof that he does not. It is easy to deceive ourselves. The truth, however, is plain. Every claim to love God is a delusion if it is not accompanied by unselfish and practical love for our brothers and sisters (3:17-18).

21. The folly of the liar's position is seen not only in its inherent inconsistency, but in the fact that love for God and love for our brother form one single command (*cf.* 3:23). Jesus himself taught this. It was he who united Deuteronomy 6:4 and

Leviticus 19:18, and then declared that all the Law and the Prophets hung upon them (Mt. 22:37–40). We may not separate what Jesus has joined. Besides, if we love God we shall keep his commands (2:5; 5:3), and his command is to love our neighbour as ourselves.

C. A COMBINATION OF THE THREE TESTS (5:1–5)

We have by now become familiar with the three tests which John applies, with repeated but varied emphasis, to the professing Christian. In chapter 2 he describes all three tests in order, obedience (3–6), love (7–11) and belief (18–27). In chapter 3 he treats only obedience (2:28–3:10) and love (11–18), while in chapter 4 only belief (1–6) and love (7–12). In 4:13–21 he has combined the doctrinal and social tests. Now, however, in the brief opening paragraph of chapter 5, we meet the three together again. The words 'believe' and 'faith' occur in verses 1, 4 and 5, 'love' in verses 1, 2 and 3, and the need to obey or carry out 'his commands' in verses 2 and 3. What John is at pains to show is the essential unity of his threefold thesis. He has not chosen three tests arbitrarily or at random and stuck them together artificially. On the contrary, he shows that they are so closely woven together into a single, coherent fabric that it is difficult to unpick and disentangle the threads.

The previous paragraph, at the end of chapter 4, ended with a statement of our duty, if we love God, to love our brother also. John now elaborates the essential connection between these two loves, and between them and both belief and obedience. We cannot believe in Jesus Christ without loving the Father and his children (1–2a); we cannot love the Father without obeying his commands and overcoming the world (2b–4a); and we cannot overcome the world without believing in Jesus Christ (4b–5). So this compressed paragraph begins and ends with belief, but between these two termini is concerned with love and obedience. The real link between the three tests is seen to be the new birth. Faith, love and obedience are all the natural growth which follows a birth from above, just as in 4:13–16 faith and love were shown to be evidences of the mutual indwelling of God and his people.

1. Neither *is born of God* (NIV), nor 'is a child of God' (RSV, NEB) is a very satisfactory translation of *ek tou theou gegennētai*, whose perfect tense means literally 'has been born [begotten, RV] of God'. The combination of present tense (*ho pisteuōn, believes*) and perfect is important. It shows clearly that believing is the consequence, not the cause, of the new birth. Our present, continuing activity of believing is the result, and therefore the evidence, of our past experience of new birth by which we became and remain God's children. Moreover, belief in Christ is congruous with birth of God just because Christ is Son of God (*cf.* vv. 1, 5). Clearly the sons of God will manifest the fact that they have been 'begotten' of God by recognizing and believing in God's eternal, 'only begotten' or unique Son.

This new birth, which brings us into believing recognition of the eternal Son, also involves us in a loving relationship with the Father and his other children. Whoever has been begotten of God naturally loves him who begat him (this is to be understood in the sentence), and *everyone who loves the father loves his child as well*. Here is a universal, self-evident principle, and John implies that 'what is true of the human family is also true of the Divine Society' (Brooke). The AV is clumsier: 'every one that loveth him that begat loveth him also that is begotten of him'. But at least it retains more obviously the truth that it is the 'begetting' and the experience of being 'begotten' which establish an affinity and therefore an affection not only between parent and child but between children and children. The expression 'him that is begotten of him' can hardly in this context be made to refer to the only begotten Son (as Augustine thought), but rather to every child of God.

2-3. Indeed, so surely and unavoidably does love for the heavenly Parent carry with it love for his children on earth that John can continue: *This is how we know that we love the children of God: by loving God*. It is as impossible to love the children of God (as such) without loving God as it is to love God without loving his children (4:20-21). A family relationship unites the two loves. Love for God has a second inescapable consequence, namely obedience. If we truly love God, we not only love his children, but also find ourselves *carrying out his commands*. In verse 3

John goes further. So inexorable is the connection between the two that love for God, which in one sense issues in obedience, in another sense may be identified with it. Love for God is not an emotional experience so much as a moral commitment. Indeed, whether shown to God or human beings, *agapē* is always practical and active. Love for our brothers and sisters expresses itself 'with actions and in truth', and especially in sacrificial service (3:17–18); love for God in carrying out his commands. Jesus said the same thing about the meaning of love for himself (Jn. 14:15, 21).

Nor should we find it difficult to express our love by our obedience, because *his commands are not burdensome* or 'irksome' (Moffatt). The pernickety regulations of the scribes and Pharisees were 'heavy burdens, hard to bear' (Mt. 23:4, RSV; *cf.* Lk. 11:46), but the yoke of Jesus is easy and his burden light (Mt. 11:30). God's will is 'good, pleasing and perfect' (Rom. 12:2). It is the will of an all-wise, all-loving Father who seeks our highest welfare.

4a. The reason why we do not find the commands of God burdensome lies not, however, only in their character. It lies also in ourselves, namely that we have been given the possibility of keeping them. The commands of God today, whether found in the Old Testament or the New, appear intolerably burdensome to the world. But to the children of God they are not, because *everyone* born of God overcomes the world. By his use of the neuter *to gegennēmenon*, translated 'whatever' in RSV but *everyone* in NIV, John states the principle in its most general and abstract form. He does so to emphasize not 'the victorious *person*' but 'the victorious *power*' (Plummer). 'It is not the man, but his birth from God, which conquers' (*ibid.*). The new birth is a supernatural event which takes us out of the sphere of the world, where Satan rules, into the family of God. We have been rescued from the dominion of darkness and transferred into the kingdom of God's dear Son (Col. 1:13). The spell of the old life has been broken. The fascination of the world has lost its appeal.

4b–5. Three times in three successive sentences, as if to hammer the truth home, John repeats the phrase *overcome the world*. First, he declares that 'everyone born of God overcomes the world' (4a). He goes on to ascribe the Christian's conquest not to his birth but to his *faith* (4b). He then proceeds to enlarge on this fact in the form of a question which he immediately answers: *Who is it that overcomes the world? Only he who believes that Jesus is the Son of God.*

It is noteworthy that in the second of these three references to overcoming the verb is an aorist participle (*hē nikēsasa*). It 'naturally points to a definite act, or fact' (Brooke), not to the victory which Christ claimed to have won in John 16:33 (Westcott), but either to the conversion of the readers, or, more probably, to their decisive rejection of the false teaching and the withdrawal of the false teachers from the church. This was the victory mentioned in 4:4 (*nenikēkate*, perfect). However, the other two occurrences of the verb here are in the present tense (*nika*, 4, and *ho nikōn*, 5) and describe the continuous victory which the Christian should enjoy. What is this victory? It is won over *the world*, by which word John 'gathers up the sum of all the limited, transitory powers opposed to God which make obedience difficult' (Westcott). Sometimes these are moral pressures – the outlook, standards and preoccupations of a godless, secular society, 'the cravings of sinful man, the lust of his eyes and the boasting of what he has and does' (2:16). Sometimes they are intellectual (heresy) and sometimes physical (persecution). But, whatever form the world's assault on the church may take, the victory is ours. The unshakeable conviction that the Jesus of history is 'the Christ' (5:1), in the sense in which the false teachers denied it (2:22), the pre-existent *Son of God* (5:5), who became human in order to bring us salvation and life (4:14, 9), enables us to triumph over the world. Confidence in the divine-human person of Jesus is the one weapon against which neither the error, nor the evil, nor the force of the world can prevail. Blaiklock, who entitled his devotional studies in this letter *Faith is the Victory*, rightly pointed out the daring of this first-century claim that the victory belongs not to Rome, then reigning supreme, but to Christ and to the humble believer in Christ.

With this final sentence, affirming belief in Jesus, we are back where we started, and the argument has come full circle. Let us summarize it: Christian believers are God's children, born from above. God's children are loved by all who love God. Those who love God also keep his commands. They keep his commands because they overcome the world, and they overcome the world because they are Christian believers, born from above.

One way of unravelling this argument is to regard it not as a circle but as a long line and to make obedience the centre of it. The two extremities are identical, namely birth of God leading to belief in Christ. Moving forwards from the beginning, the believing child of God reaches obedience by way of love for God and for the children of God. Moving backwards from the end, the road from belief to obedience is by way of the conquest of the world. In both cases belief and obedience are coupled, whether the link is loving God or overcoming the world. The new birth has the double result of detaching us from the world and attaching us to God. The result in each case is keeping the commands.

Another way is to regard the centre of the sentence as 'this is love for God' (3). Certainly the word *love* occurs five times in this paragraph and is strongly emphasized. Certainly, too, faith and love are as indissoluble as faith and obedience. Indeed, as Paul put it, 'the only thing that counts is faith expressing itself through love' (Gal. 5:6). Thus, if we love God, on the one hand we love the children of God because we are born of God and believe in Christ, and on the other hand we keep the commands of God and overcome the world because we are born of God and believe in Christ. Here love for God and faith in Jesus are chained to each other by the links of brotherly love and obedience.

Whichever is the best way of seeking to follow John's closely-knit argument, what is plain is that his three tests belong together and cannot be separated. The true Christian, born from above, believes in the Son of God, loves God and the children of God, and keeps the commands of God. Each involves the others. Belief, love and obedience are marks of the new birth. The new birth brings us willynilly into a certain relation to Christ, to God, to the church and to the world which we cannot repudiate and which marks us out as Christians.

VI. THE THREE WITNESSES AND OUR CONSEQUENT ASSURANCE (5:6–17)

We have already noted that the previous paragraph begins and ends with a reference to faith, *viz.* believing that the human Jesus is (*i.e.* is the same person as) the Christ (1), or the Son of God (5). Both statements are compressions of John's full formula of Christian faith, namely that Jesus is 'the Christ come in the flesh' (4:2; 2 Jn. 7).

But how can people come to faith in the divine-human person of Jesus? John's answer here, as in the Gospel, is that faith depends on testimony, and that the reasonableness of believing in Jesus is grounded upon the validity of the testimony which is borne to him. Verses 6–9 describe the nature of the testimony (by the 'three witnesses', 8, RSV) and verses 10–12 its results; while in verses 13–17 the Christian's consequent assurance is unfolded.

A. THE THREE WITNESSES (5:6–12)

6. Jesus, who has been called 'the Christ' (5:1) and 'the Son of God' (5:5), is now further and more fully described, particularly with regard to his mission on earth. *This is the one who came by water and blood – Jesus Christ. He did not come by water only, but by water and blood.* Various interpretations have been given to these phrases, which Plummer calls the 'most perplexing' in the letter. There can be little doubt that John was using phraseology which was already familiar to his readers, either through his own teaching or through that of the false teachers, and which is not so readily understood by us. There have been three principal suggestions about the meaning of *water and blood*.

First, some commentators (including Luther and Calvin) have seen in them a reference to the two sacraments of the gospel. This is extremely doubtful, at least as the primary thought. If *water* stands for baptism, *blood* would be an unprecedented symbol for the Lord's Supper. It would also be an unnatural symbol, both because blood is one of the things signified, not one of the signs, and because no reference is made to the body of Christ. Further, although it might be possible to describe Jesus as 'coming' through the sacraments, it is difficult to see how it could be said that he came (aorist, *ho elthōn*) through them. The verb clearly indicates not some present activity of Jesus but his past historical coming.

The second interpretation (adopted by Augustine and other ancient commentators) links the passage with the spear thrust and the issue of blood and water from the side of Jesus recorded in John 19:34–35. Certainly, both passages are Johannine, and both are associated with testimony, and the flow of blood and water was a past, historical event. Even so, it would be forced to say that in this incident Jesus *came by* (that is, 'through') *water and blood*, when in fact they came out of him. Moreover, the link between blood, water and testimony, which we have observed in both passages, is not identical. In the Gospel it is the evangelist who bears witness to them; here it is they which bear witness to Christ. Again, if in the Gospel they are taken as bearing any witness, it must be to the reality of Christ's death, and perhaps to the saving efficacy of it; but here in the letter they bear witness to Christ's divine-human person.

We need therefore to find an interpretation of the phrase which makes *water and blood* both historical experiences 'through' which he passed and witnesses in some sense to his divine-human person. The third and most satisfactory interpretation, first given by Tertullian, does this. It takes *water* as referring to the baptism of Jesus, at which he was declared the Son and commissioned and empowered for his work, and *blood* to his death, in which his work was finished. True, 'water' and 'blood' remain strange and surprising word symbols, and we can only guess that they were thus used in the theological controversy which had engulfed the Ephesian church. At least this meaning of the expression tallies with what Irenaeus disclosed of the heretical teaching of Cerinthus and his followers. They distinguished between 'Jesus' and 'the Christ'. They held that Jesus was a mere man, born of Joseph and Mary in natural wedlock, upon whom the Christ descended at the baptism and from whom the Christ departed before the cross. According to this theory of the false teachers, Jesus was united with the Christ at the baptism, but became separated again before the cross. It was to refute this fundamental error that John, knowing that Jesus was the Christ before and during the baptism and during and after the cross, described him as 'the one who came through water and blood'. Neither word has the definite article. The author is stressing the unity of the earthly career of Jesus Christ. He who came (from heaven, that is) is the same as he who passed 'through' water and blood. For further emphasis he adds (using the definite article this time before each noun, and changing the preposition from *dia*, 'through', to *en*, 'in'), 'not with the water only', since the heretics agreed that at least he was the Christ at his baptism, 'but with the water and (with) the blood' (RV, RSV). 'The statement is as precise as grammar can make it' (Brooke), and it is disappointing that neither the NEB nor the NIV expresses this precision. For full measure, in opposition to the heretics' differentiation between Jesus and the Christ, John adds that the one who so came was *Jesus Christ*, one person who was simultaneously from his birth to his death and for evermore (*this is the one*, present tense) both the man Jesus and the Christ of God. See commentary on 4:3.

The false teachers whom John was opposing are dead, and their particular creed has no adherents today. Yet all who deny the incarnation, whether or not they believe that the person of Jesus underwent a change at the baptism to fit him for his public ministry, deny that he *came by water and blood*. This is no trivial error. It undermines the foundations of the Christian faith and robs us of the salvation of Christ. If the Son of God did not take to himself our nature in his birth and our sins in his death, he cannot reconcile us to God. So John emphasizes not just that he *came*, but especially that he came by water *and* blood, since it is his blood which cleanses from sin (1:7).

Having accepted that the primary reference of this verse is to the historical events of the baptism and crucifixion of Jesus, it is not impossible that it also contains secondary allusions, since the past events remain present witnesses (8). 'Water and blood', which occur together in some of the Levitical rituals, are intelligible symbols of 'purification and redemption' (Plummer). Candlish, who insists much on this interpretation, draws the distinction between 'precious blood to atone for all guilt' and 'pure water to cleanse from all pollution', and refers the symbols to the blessings of justification and sanctification available through the gospel. To these aspects of salvation Jesus himself had referred in the discourses which John recorded in chapter 3, 4 and 7 ('water') and 6 ('blood') of his Gospel. Perhaps John also saw them set forth once in the issue of blood and water from the side of the Crucified, and even regularly in the two sacraments.

And it is the Spirit who testifies. This is undoubtedly a reference to the Holy Spirit. The form of the Greek construction indicates that it is as characteristic of the Spirit that he *testifies*, as it is of Christ that he *came* (at the beginning of the verse). The fact that the Spirit is said to bear witness gives evidence, 'the more striking because involuntary' (Smith), of his personality, since testifying is an activity of persons. Of what his testimony consists is not explictly stated, but both the context and the teaching of this letter and of the Gospel suggest that he testifies to Christ (*e.g.* 4:2). He is competent to do so, Jesus said, because he is 'the Spirit of truth' (Jn. 15:26; 16:13; *cf.* 1 Jn. 4:6). John goes further and writes *because the Spirit is the truth* (contrast Jn. 14:6) – conveying either that he is 'essentially fitted' to bear witness, or that he is 'constrained' to do so (Westcott). The truth cannot be hidden. But how does the Spirit testify? John appears to be referring to the inward witness of the Holy Spirit, who opens our eyes to see the truth as it is in Jesus (*cf.* 1 Cor. 12:3, *etc.*). Certainly he has written twice already of how the Spirit has been 'given to us' as an indwelling possession (3:24; 4:13), and has twice ascribed our acknowledgment of Christ as the divine-human Lord to the 'anointing' or enlightenment of the Spirit (2:20, 27 and 4:1–6). We have then here, as in 4:13–14, two kinds of corroborative testimony, objective and subjective, historical and experimental, *water and blood* on the one hand and *the Spirit* on the other. 'He it is who seals in our hearts the testimony of the water and the blood' (Calvin).

7. In AV, verses 7–8a read: 'For there are three that bear record [*i.e.* witness] in heaven, the Father, the Word, and the Holy Ghost: and these three are one. And there are three that bear witness in earth . . .' But this whole passage must be regarded as a gloss. The words occur in no Greek MS before the fourteenth century (except one eleventh-century and one twelfth-century MS, in which they have been added in the margin by a much later hand); in no quotation by the early Greek fathers, who, if

they had known the text, would surely have quoted it in their trinitarian debates; and in none of the ancient versions (translations), even the early editions of the Vulgate. They first appeared in a fourth-century Latin treatise, after which some Latin fathers began to quote them. They found their way into the AV because Erasmus reluctantly included them in the third edition of his text. Plummer calls the reading 'quite indefensible' and gives a very thorough survey of the evidence in an Appendix (pp. 163–172), and so does Brooke (pp. 154–165). Metzger writes: 'That these words are spurious and have no right to stand in the New Testament is certain' (p. 715). They are rightly absent even from the margin of the RV and RSV, although the NIV mentions them in a marginal note. Some tidy-minded scribe, impressed by the threefold witness of verse 8, must have been made to think of the Trinity and so suggested that there was a threefold witness in heaven also. Actually, his gloss is not a very happy one, as the threefold testimony of verse 8 is to Christ; and the biblical teaching about testimony is not that Father, Son and Holy Spirit bear witness together to the Son, but that the Father bears witness to the Son through the Spirit.

8. Having written independently of 'the water and the blood' (6, RSV), and of the Spirit, without stating that the former were in any sense a 'testimony', John now brings the three together and declares that they all *testify*. Moreover, *the three are in agreement*. The false witnesses at the trial of Jesus, seeking to discredit him, did not agree (Mk. 14:56, 59); the true witnesses, however, the Spirit, the water and the blood, seeking to accredit him, are in perfect agreement. The significance of the 'three that testify' (7) is that according to the law no charge could be preferred against an accused person in court unless it could be confirmed by the evidence of two or three witnesses (Dt. 19:15; *cf.* Jn. 8:17–18). In contrast to verse 6, where the Spirit is placed last, he is now made the first witness, partly because 'the Spirit is, of the three, the only living and active witness', and partly because 'the water and the blood are no witnesses without him; whereas He is independent of them, testifying both in them and out of them' (Alford).

9. The importance of this verse is that it declares explicitly what has so far only been hinted, namely that God is the subject and Christ the object of the threefold testimony. The Spirit, the water and the blood all testify to Christ, and the reason why they agree is that God himself is behind them. The three witnesses form, in fact, a single divine testimony to Jesus Christ, which God *has given*. The perfect tense indicates the continuing validity (in itself and through the Spirit) of God's historical testimony to Christ. It is God who testified to his Son in history, in the water and the blood, and it is God who testifies to him today through his Spirit in our hearts. Moreover, it is *because* (*hoti*) the witness is divine, that we ought humbly to receive it. For *we accept man's testimony*, when it consists of the evidence of two or three; how much more, then, should we accept *the testimony of God* which is itself threefold and which, because it is God's, *is greater* than any man's?

10. Having described the nature of the testimony (the threefold divine witness to the Son through the Spirit, the water and the blood), John proceeds to unfold its results (10–12). The purpose of testimony to Christ is to evoke faith in Christ (*e.g.* Jn. 1:7; 20:31). Receiving the testimony leads naturally to believing in the one to whom the testimony is borne. Indeed, to 'accept . . . the testimony of God' (9) and to 'believe in the Son of God' (10) are virtually synonymous expressions. Further, so identical in meaning are the two phrases, that at the end of verse 10 John can use the preposition *eis* with *the testimony God has given about his Son*, thus making the object of our personal confidence not the Son himself but God's testimony to his Son. The results of belief and disbelief are starkly contrasted. The believer *has this testimony in his heart*. That is, he is given a yet deeper assurance by the inward testimony of the Spirit that he was right to trust in Christ, a striking example of the spiritual principle that 'everyone who has will be given more' (Mt. 25:29; Lk. 19:26; *cf.* Mk. 4:25). So testimony is both the cause and the consequence of belief, and belief is a stepping-stone between God's first and further testimony. The unbeliever, on the other hand, who 'has not believed' (RSV, the perfect tense indicating a past 'crisis of choice' – Westcott), forfeits the possibility of receiving any further testimony from God because he has rejected the first and in so doing *has made him out to be a liar*. Unbelief is not a misfortune to be pitied; it is a sin to be deplored. Its sinfulness lies in the fact that it contradicts the word of the one true God and thus attributes falsehood to him. Another example of 'making God a liar' is to be found in 1:10.

11–12. John now forgets the unbeliever and summarizes the blessing granted to the believer who receives and responds to the testimony of God. *This is the testimony* is the same expression as that in the middle of verse 9, which the NIV translates 'it is the testimony [of God]'. There it looks back to what I have called the 'first' testimony, that of the water, the blood and the Spirit. Here it seems to include also the 'further' testimony which, according to v. 10, the believer receives 'in his heart'. This becomes more plain when we consider how the testimony is here described, namely that *God has given* (RSV, rightly, 'gave') *us eternal life, and this life is in his Son*. To what event does this gift of life refer? Some commentators refer it to the historical career of Jesus (*cf.* 1:2 and Jn. 10:10, 28; 17:2), and others to our conversion, at which we personally appropriated, or received, the life that is in Christ (*cf.* 3:14). Perhaps both are true, and both are part of the 'testimony', historical and experimental, which God has given concerning his Son. Historically, God's testimony concerning (*peri*, vv. 9, 10) Jesus is not only that he is the divine-human Christ but that he is also the life-giver, 'the Saviour of the world' (4:14); not only that he is the Son, but that in him is life. *Eternal life* is emphatic in the sentence; *i.e.* the testimony is that it is eternal life which God gave us in giving his Son. But the testimony is not only objective to Christ as the life-giver but subjective in the gift of life itself. Eternal life is a free gift which God gives to those who believe in his Son, and the gift of life, the experience of fellowship with God through Christ which is eternal life (*cf.* Jn. 17:3), is God's final testimony to his Son (*cf.* v. 20). John has previously written: 'anyone who believes in the Son of God has this testimony in his heart' (10). He now puts the same truth in these words: *He who has the Son* (*cf.* 2:23 for another use of the verb *echein* to describe our personal possession of the Father through confessing the Son) *has life; he who*

does not have the Son of God does not have life (literally, both times,
'the life', RV). The alternative is clear and uncompromising. We
cannot escape its logic. Eternal life is in God's Son and may be
found nowhere else. It is as impossible to have life without
having Christ as it is to have Christ without thereby having life
also. This is because the Son is the life (1:2; Jn. 11:25; 14:6).

Three important truths are taught in these verses about eternal life. First, it is not a prize which we have earned or could
earn but an undeserved gift. Secondly, it is found in Christ, so
that, in order to give us life, God both gave and gives us his Son.
Thirdly, this gift of life in Christ is a present possession. True, it
is further described as *eternal, aiōnios,* which means literally
'belonging to the age', *i.e.* the age to come. But since the age to
come has broken into this present age, the life of the age to
come, namely 'eternal life', can be received and enjoyed here
and now.

In this paragraph (6–12) John has been elaborating that he has
stated briefly in one verse of the Gospel: 'But these are written
that you may believe that Jesus is the Christ, the Son of God,
and that by believing you may have life in his name' (Jn. 20:31).
The Gospel, recording the words and works of Jesus, was John's
testimony to him as 'the Christ, the Son of God'. The purpose of
this testimony was 'that you may believe', and the result of faith
is 'that by believing you may have life in his name'. The way to
life is faith, and the way to faith is testimony. The sequence of
thought is the same here. God has borne witness to his Son, in
order that we may believe in him and so 'have' him, and having
him may have life.

B. OUR CONSEQUENT ASSURANCE (5:13–17)

13. Although the RV, RSV, NEB and NIV all begin a new paragraph
with this verse, it surely belongs essentially to the previous
section. It forms a fitting conclusion to what the author has there
written both about the three witnesses and about having eternal
life in the Son. For here he tells his readers the ostensible
purpose of his letter, now drawing to a close. (And it is natural
to contrast it with the purpose of his Gospel in 20:31, to which

we have just referred.) The letter was written *that you may know that you have eternal life*. The Gospel was written for unbelievers, that they might read the testimony of God to his Son, believe in him to whom the testimony pointed, and thus receive life through faith. This letter, on the other hand, was written for believers. John's desire for them is not that they may believe and receive, but that having believed, they may know that they have received, and therefore continue to *have* (present), *eternal life*. *That you may know* (*eidēte*) means, both in word and tense, not that they may gradually grow in assurance, but that they may possess here and now a present certainty of the life they have received in Christ. They had been unsettled by the false teachers and become unsure of their spiritual state. Throughout the letter John has been giving them criteria (doctrinal, moral, social) by which to test themselves and others. His purpose is to establish their assurance. 'This letter is to assure you that you have eternal life' (NEB).

Putting together the purposes of Gospel and letter, John's purpose is in four stages, namely that his readers may hear, hearing may believe, believing may live, and living may know. His emphasis is important because it is common today to dismiss any claim to assurance of salvation as presumptuous, and to affirm that no certainty is possible on this side of death. But certainty and humility do not exclude one another. If God's revealed purpose is not only that we should hear, believe and live, but also that we should know, presumptuousness lies in doubting his word, not in trusting it.

14–15. In verses 14–17 John moves to a second *confidence* enjoyed by the believing Christian, not now of eternal life, but of answered prayer. This assurance is not so much a 'knowledge' (as in verse 13, although it results in one, 15) as a 'freedom of speech', as *parrēsia* means literally, or boldness *in approaching God*. See commentary on 2:28. The reference is to that access to God and fellowship with him which constitute the eternal life of which John has been writing (11–13). Christian confidence belongs not just to the future, to the parousia (2:28) and the judgment day (4:17), but to the here and now. It describes both the manner of our approach to God, free and bold (3:21), and our expectation of its outcome, namely *that . . . he hears us*. The qualification, however, is *if we ask anything according to his will*. In 3:22 the condition of answered prayer is whether our behaviour accords with God's commands; here whether our requests accord with his will. Prayer is not a convenient device for imposing our will upon God, or for bending his will to ours, but the prescribed way of subordinating our will to his. It is by prayer that we seek God's will, embrace it and align ourselves with it. Every true prayer is a variation on the theme 'your will be done'. Our Master taught us to say this in the pattern prayer he gave us, and added the supreme example of it in Gethsemane. In such prayers, and only in such, *he hears us*. That is, he takes note of our petitions and, in addition, he listens favourably to us (as in Jn. 9:31; 11:41–42). The Christian assurance is tantamount to a double certainty (*oidamen . . . oidamen*), which is in reality one. To say *we know that he hears us* is the same as saying *we know that we have what we asked of him*. The present tense *we have, echomen* ('we have obtained', RSV) is striking, and reminiscent of Mark 11:24 where we are told to believe we did receive (*elabete*) what we request, and so it shall be (*estai*). 'Our petitions are granted at once: the results of the granting are perceived in the future' (Plummer).

16. Having written generally of answered prayer (14–15), John now gives a specific illustration and a limitation (16–17). It is not now a case of petition, but of intercession. The assurance of eternal life which the Christian should enjoy (13) ought not to lead him into a preoccupation with himself to the neglect of others. On the contrary, he will recognize his duty in love to care for his brother or sister in need, whether the need which he 'sees' be material (as in 3:17–18) or, as here, spiritual: *if anyone sees his brother commit a sin*. He cannot say 'Am I my brother's keeper?' and do nothing. The verb translated *he should pray* is in the future tense, and is correctly rendered by RSV 'he will ask'. It expresses not the writer's command but the Christian's inevitable and spontaneous reaction. The way to deal with sin in the congregation is to pray. And God hears such prayer. The Greek sentence reads literally 'he will ask and he will give him life'. Since God is the giver of life (*cf.* vv. 11, 20), and since usually 'asking is man's part and giving God's' (Plummer), some have suggested a change of subject in the middle of this sentence, so that the second 'he' refers to God and not to the intercessor. So RV, RSV and NIV. On the other hand, the verbs are so simply and closely coupled in the Greek (*aitēsei kai dōsei*), that a different subject would appear forced. It is better to accept the ascription of real efficacy to prayer (as in v. 15), so that, under God, he who asks life for a brother may be said not just to gain it for him but actually to 'give' it to him. In either case the *him* to whom life is given is the sinner, not the intercessor. *Cf.* James 5:15, 20, where the prayer of faith for a sick man and the one who brings back a sinner are both said to 'save' him.

Not every sinner can be given life in answer to prayer, however. John draws a distinction between *a sin that does not lead to death* and *a sin that leads to death*. For those who commit the former the Christian will pray, and by prayer will give them life. For the latter John does not enjoin prayer; *I am not saying that he should pray about that*, that is, for one who is recognized as committing it. True, he does not explicitly forbid prayer, as God forbade Jeremiah to pray for the people of Judah (Je. 7:16; 11:14; 14:11; *cf.* 1 Sa. 2:25); but he does not advise it, for he clearly doubts its efficacy in this case.

What, then, is the *sin that leads to death*? John's readers were no doubt familiar with the expression, but commentators since the sub-apostolic fathers have debated its meaning. It can hardly refer to a sin punishable by physical death, as in some Old Testament situations and in Acts 5:1–11 and 1 Corinthians 5:5; 11:30, since the life with which it is contrasted is spiritual or eternal life.[1] In one sense all sin 'leads to death' spiritually, for death is the penalty for sin (Rom. 5:12; 6:23; Jas. 1:15); but here John distinguishes between sin which leads to death and sin

---

[1] Some students do, however, believe that the death and life John is alluding to are physical. They think the situation envisaged is one of serious sickness, whose outcome may or may not be death, according both to the gravity of the sin to which the sickness would be due and to the efficacy of the church's prayers. By means of intercession the sick person would be brought to repentance and given life, much as in James 5:14–15. The objections to this reconstruction seem to me (1) that sickness is not mentioned, (2) that all the references to life and death throughout the letter, including this context, are spiritual, not physical, and (3) that no guidance is given how to discern between serious illnesses which are, and are not, fatal.

which does not. We may divide the possible interpretations into three.

1. *A specific sin.* In the Mosaic law certain sins were listed as capital offences, punishable by death (*e.g.* Lv. 20:1–27; Nu. 18:22; *cf.* Rom. 1:32). Further, in the Old Testament generally a distinction was drawn between sins of ignorance, committed unwittingly, which could be cleansed through sacrifice, and wanton or 'presumptuous' sins (Ps. 19:13), committed 'with a high hand', for which there was no forgiveness. The same distinction was 'common among Rabbinic writers' (Westcott), and certain early Christian fathers carried it over into the gospel age. Clement of Alexandria and Origen both accepted that a line could be drawn between forgivable and unforgivable sins, but declined to classify them. Tertullian went a stage further and listed the grosser sins (including murder, adultery, blasphemy and idolatry) as beyond pardon, while minor offences could be forgiven. This developed into the familiar, casuistical differentiation between 'mortal' and 'venial' sins and the specification of the 'seven deadly sins'. But there is no New Testament warrant for such an arbitrary classification of sins, and certainly 'it would be an anachronism to try to apply it here' (Dodd). Indeed, although the rendering is 'a mortal sin' in RSV and 'a deadly sin' in NEB, it is doubtful whether John is referring to specific 'sins' at all, as opposed to 'sin' (as in 1:8), that is, 'a state or habit of sin wilfully chosen and persisted in' (Plummer).

2. *Apostasy.* The second suggestion, favoured among modern commentators by Brooke, Law and Dodd, is that the *sin that leads to death* is neither a specific sin, nor even a 'backsliding', but a total apostasy, the denial of Christ and the renunciation of the faith. Those who hold this view usually link these verses with such passages as Hebrews 6:4–6; 10:26ff. and 12:16–17, and apply them to the false teachers who had, in fact, so clearly repudiated the truth as to withdraw from the church (2:19).

But can a Christian, who has been born of God, apostatize? Surely John has taught clearly in this letter that the true Christian cannot sin, that is, persist in sin (3:9), let alone fall away altogether. He is about to repeat it: 'we know that anyone born of God does not continue to sin; the one who was born of God keeps him safe, and the evil one cannot harm him' (18). Can he who 'does not continue to sin' (18) commit *a sin that leads to death* (16)? Moreover, John has just written of having life (12) and knowing it (13). Can someone who has received a life which is eternal lose it and 'sin unto death' (AV?) It seems clear, unless John's theology is divided against itself, that he who sins unto death is not a Christian. If so, the sin cannot be apostasy. We are left with the third alternative.

3. *The blasphemy against the Holy Spirit.* This sin, committed by the Pharisees, was a deliberate, open-eyed rejection of known truth. They ascribed the mighty works of Jesus, evidently done 'by the Spirit of God' (Mt. 12:28), to the agency of Beelzebub. Such sin, Jesus said, would never be forgiven either in this age or in the age to come. He who commits it 'is guilty of an eternal sin' (Mk. 3:29; *cf.* Mt. 12:22–32). It leads him inexorably into a state of incorrigible moral and spiritual obtuseness, because he has wilfully sinned against his own conscience. In John's own language he has 'loved darkness instead of light' (Jn. 3:18–21), and in consequence he will 'die in his sins' (Jn. 8:24). His sin in fact, *leads to death.* That is, the outcome of his sin will be spiritual ruin, the final separation of the soul from God, which is 'the second death', reserved for those whose names are not 'written in the book of life' (Rev. 20:15; 21:8).

But, it may be objected, if the 'sin leading to death' is the blasphemy against the Holy Spirit committed by a hardened unbeliever, how can John call him a *brother*? To be exact, he does not. It is the one whose sin *does not lead to death* who is termed a brother; he whose sin *lead to death* is neither named nor described. Nevertheless, supposing John thinks of each as a brother, we must still assert that neither can be regarded as a child of God. The reasons for denying that he who sins 'unto death' is a Christian have already been given; what can be said about him *whose sin does not lead to death*? An important point, to which commentators surprisingly give no attention, is that he is given *life* in answer to prayer. This means that, although his sin *does not lead to death*, he is in fact dead, since he needs to be given life. For how can you give life to one who is already alive? This person is not a Christian, therefore, for Christians have received life, and do not fall into death when they fall into sin. True, 'life' to John means communion with God, and the sinning Christian cannot enjoy fellowship with God (1:5–6), but John would certainly not have said that when the Christian sins he dies and needs to receive eternal life again. The Christian has 'passed from death to life' (3:14; *cf.* Jn. 5:24). Death and judgment are behind him; he 'has life' (12) as a present and abiding possession. When he stumbles into sin, which he may (2:1), he has a heavenly Advocate (2:2). He needs to be forgiven and cleansed (1:10), but John never says he needs to be 'quickened' 'made alive', or 'given life' all over again.

If this is so, then neither he whose sin *leads to death* nor he whose sin *does not lead to death* is a Christian, possessing eternal life. Both are 'dead in transgressions and sins' (Eph. 2:1). Each 'remains in death' (3:14). The difference between them is that one may receive life through a Christian's intercession, while the other will die the second death. Spiritually dead already, he will die eternally. Only such a serious state as this would lead John to say that he does not advise his readers to pray for such.

The question remains: How can someone who (if the above interpretation be correct) is not a Christian be termed a brother? The only answer is that John must here be using the word in a broader sense either of a 'neighbour' or of a nominal Christian, a church member who professes to be a 'brother'. Certainly in 2:9, 11 the word 'brother' is not used strictly, for he who hates him is not a Christian at all but 'in the darkness'. In 3:16–17 also the word seems to have this wider connotation, where we are bidden to lay down our lives 'for our brothers' and to supply the material necessities of a 'brother in need'. Since Christ died for the ungodly and for his enemies, we can scarcely suppose that we are to limit our self-sacrifice and service exclusively to our Christian brothers and sisters, and to have compassion only upon them. Such a wider connotation of the word *brother*, implied also in the teaching of Jesus (Mt. 5:22–24; 7:3–5), 'arises not so much out of the character and standing of him whom you call your brother, as out of the nature of the affection with which you regard him' (Candlish). This suggestion is supported by the somewhat similar passage in the letter of James (5:19–20).

We have a further confirmation of the interpretation argued above if under the description of the *sin that leads to death* John is alluding, as many commentators believe, to the false teachers.

In John's view they were not apostates; they were counterfeits. They were not true 'brothers' who had received eternal life and subsequently forfeited it. They were 'antichrists'. Denying the Son, they did not possess the Father (2:22–23; 2 Jn. 9). They were children of the devil, not children of God (3:10). True, they had once been members of the visible congregation and had then no doubt passed as 'brothers'. But they went out, and by their withdrawal it was made evident that they 'did not really belong to us' (2:19). Since they rejected the Son, they forfeited life (5:12). Their sin did indeed lead to death.

17. *All wrongdoing is sin.* Sin is injustice, *adikia* (*cf.* 1:9), just as previously John has defined it as 'lawlessness', *anomia* (3:4). Both words imply that there is an objective moral standard, the will of God, whether expressed in 'law' or in 'justice', and that sin is to be understood as a violation of both. John adds these words because he does not want to be misunderstood. In distinguishing between *sin that leads to death* and *sin that does not lead to death*, he is not meaning to minimize the gravity of sin. Nor does he mean to discourage his readers from praying, for although he cannot advise them to pray for those whose sin leads to death, *there is sin that does not lead to death*, and such sinners may receive life in answer to believing prayer.

VII. THREE AFFIRMATIONS AND A CONCLUDING EXHORTATION (5:18–21)

The letter ends characteristically. It has been concerned throughout with the proper grounds, moral, doctrinal and social, of Christian assurance. So the author takes up the theme of what we should know (13) and do know (15) and concludes with the statement of three clear and candid certainties, each introduced by *oidamen, we know*. Here are no tentative, hesitant suggestions, but bold, dogmatic, Christian affirmations which are beyond all dispute and which neatly summarize truths already introduced in earlier parts of the letter.

18. The first assertion concerns every child of God. It is expressed as a generalization which admits of no exception: *anyone born of God does not continue to sin*. The Christian is again described as one who, literally, 'has been begotten (*gegennēmenos*, *cf*. 5:1, 4) of God'. The perfect participle indicates that the new birth, far from being a transient phase of religious experience, has a continuing result. He who has been begotten (or born) of God remains his child with permanent privileges and obligations. One of these obligations is expressed in the phrase that he *does not continue to sin*. The previous two verses (16–17), concerning sin, whether or not it 'leads to death', applied to unbelievers. Very different is the case of him who has been born of God. As in 3:4–10 (where see commentary) the tense of the verb is present and 'implies continuity, habit, permanence' (Blaiklock). It expresses the truth, not that he can never slip into acts of sin, but rather that he does not persist in it habitually or 'live in sin' (Dodd). The new birth results in new behaviour. Sin and the child of God are incompatible. They may occasionally meet; they cannot live together in harmony.

The apostle now proceeds to give the reason for his assurance that the Christian does not continue to sin, and introduces it with a strong adversative 'but' (RSV), which the NIV inadequately represents by a mere semi-colon. What is the antithesis? The AV, following the Codex Sinaiticus and most of the Greek manuscripts, reads 'he that is begotten of God keepeth himself'. For the concept of 'keeping oneself' see 1 Timothy 5:22; James 1:27; Jude 21, and also 3:3. The very important Alexandrine and Vatican Codices, however, which are followed by the Vulgate, have not *himself* (*heauton*) but *him* (*auton*). So the NIV. If, as seems probable, the latter is the correct reading, then the subject of the verb (*viz*. 'he that is begotten of God' or *the one who was born of God*) is Christ, not the Christian, and the truth here taught is not that the Christian keeps himself but that Christ keeps him. In adopting this interpretation, the RSV eliminates ambiguity by printing 'He' with a capital letter: 'but He who was born of God keeps him'. So too the NEB: 'it is the Son of God who keeps him safe'. If this is correct, we need to note that John deliberately uses almost identical expressions to portray Christ and the Christian, at the beginning and end of verse 18. Both are said to be *born of God*; only the tense of the verb is different. It is

appropriate that *the one who was born of God* should keep safe
anyone born of God. Note too that the power for deliverance from
sin, which is here attributed to the Son, is in 3:9 attributed to
God's 'seed' which remains in the Christian.

The Christian can only hope to 'keep' the commands of God
(3:24; 5:3) if the Son of God 'keeps' him. *Cf.* Jude 24; 1 Peter 1:5.
But why does he need to be 'kept'? If he has been born of God, is
he not immune to temptation? No. The devil, *the evil one,* is
maliciously active. Strong and subtle, he is more than a match
for him. But the Son of God came to destroy the devil's work
(3:8), and if he *keeps . . . safe (tērei)* the Christian, the devil will
not be able to *harm* him. 'Touch' (RSV) is too weak a rendering of
haptetai, as may be seen from John 2:17, the only other occurrence of the verb in the Johannine writings. It is here perhaps an
echo of Psalm 105:15 (LXX), 'Do not touch my anointed ones',
which means (as the parallel expression shows) 'do them no
harm'. Observe that the three verbs are all in the present tense.
They indicate abiding truths. The devil does not touch the
Christian because the Son keeps him, and so, because the Son
keeps him, the Christian does not persist in sin. This is that
'deliverance from the evil one' for which we pray at the end of
the Lord's Prayer. For Christ's promise and power to keep, *cf.*
John 10:28; 17:12, 15.

19. The second affirmation is couched not in the third person
singular, but in the first person plural and thus supplies a
personal and particular application of the generalization of verse
18. *We know that we* (the apostle associates himself with his
readers and thus with all Christian people) *are children of God.*
Having been 'born of God' (18), God remains the source of our
spiritual life and being. But, in dreadful contrast, *the whole world
is under the control of the evil one,* taking *en tō ponērō* as masculine
not neuter, just as in the previous verse and in 2:13–14 and 3:12.
The world according to John here is not 'of' the evil one, as we
are (literally) *of God,* although he has already stated this in 3:8,
10, 12, and *cf.* John 8:44, 47, but rather 'in' him, in his grip and
under his control. Moreover (again literally) it 'lies' there. It is
not pictured as struggling vigorously to be free but as quietly
lying, perhaps even unconsciously asleep, in the embrace of

Satan. The evil one does not 'touch' the Christian, but the world is helplessly in his grasp. 'On the child of God the evil one does not so much as lay his hand; the world lies in his arms' (Smith). For the devil's sway over the world, see his title 'the prince of this world' in John 12:31; 14:30; 16:11 and Paul's teaching in Ephesians 2:2 and 6:12.

John wastes no words and blurs no issue. The uncompromising alternative is stated baldly. Everyone belongs either to 'us' or to 'the world'. Everyone is therefore either *of God* or *under the control of the evil one*. There is no third category. Nowadays, when the line of demarcation between church and world is confused, it is important to learn again that all but those who have had a heavenly birth are under the authority and rule of 'the powers of this dark world' (Eph. 6:12) and of their chief, the god and prince of this world. We need to remember, however, that although the whole world lies in the power of the evil one, it is for the sins of the whole world (the only other occurrence of the expression in the letter) that Jesus Christ is the propitiation (2:2).

20. The third affirmation is the most fundamental of the three. It undermines the whole structure of the heretics' theology. It concerns the Son of God, through whom alone we can be rescued from the evil one and delivered from the world. Both revelation and redemption are his gracious work. Without him we could neither know God nor overcome sin. These are possible to us today only because *the Son of God has come*, and, having come, *has given us understanding*. The verbs must be viewed together. The Christian gospel is not concerned merely with the truth that Christ *has given us* certain things, but that he *has come*. It is another example in the letter of John's emphasis that the Christian religion is both historical and experimental, and not one without the other. Moreover, both verbs are in the perfect tense. The benefit of his coming remains. His gift he will not take away (*cf.* Rom. 11:29).

What he has given us is *understanding, dianoia*, 'the power or capacity of knowing' (Ebrard), *so that we may know him who is true*. God is here described not as 'true', (NIV), *alēthes*, but as 'real' (NEB), *alēthinos*. This is a favourite Johannine adjective. Just as Jesus called himself the 'true' or 'real' bread and vine (Jn. 6:32;

15:1), as opposed to the baker's bread and the farmer's vine, which are the shadows of which he is the substance (and not vice versa), so God is the ultimate reality ('the only true God', Jn. 17:3) as opposed to idols (21). This real God Christ has given us understanding to *know* (*ginōskomen* in contrast to *oidamen* at the beginning of the verse). We might paraphrase 'we know as a fact that the Son of God has . . . given us understanding to come to perceive and know in experience him who is real . . .' The present tense of *ginōskomen* implies 'a continuous and progressive apprehension' (Westcott).

Not only do we know him; we are also *in him*. Unlike the world which is 'under the control of the evil one', we are in God, sharing his very life, as well as being 'of God' (19), having derived our spiritual being from him. We are also *in his Son Jesus Christ*. The NIV, by inserting the word *even* before this phrase, places it in apposition to the preceding phrase, as if to say that being 'in him who is real' and *in his Son Jesus Christ* were equivalent expressions. But the possessive *his* would make this very awkward. It is more probable that the words of the second phrase 'supply a needed explanation' (Brooke) of the first. It is by being *in his Son Jesus Christ* that we are *in him who is true*. In this way the first two sentences of verse 20 teach the necessity of the mediation of Jesus for both the knowledge of God and communion with God. We know him who is true only because the Son of God has come and has given us understanding; we are in him who is true only because ('since', NEB) we are in his Son Jesus Christ. We cannot be in the Father without being in the Son, nor in the Son without being in the Father (*cf.* 2:22–23 and, *e.g.*, 1 Thes. 1:1). Our Lord is here at the end of the letter significantly given his full title as he was at the beginning (1:3). He is *Jesus* the man, *Christ* the Messiah, and God's eternal *Son*.

The final sentence of verse 20 runs: *He is the true God and eternal life*. To whom does *he* refer? Grammatically speaking, it would normally refer to the nearest preceding subject, namely *his Son Jesus Christ*. If so, this would be the most unequivocal statement of the deity of Jesus Christ in the New Testament, which the champions of orthodoxy were quick to exploit against the heresy of Arius. Luther and Calvin adopted this view. Certainly it is by no means an impossible interpretation. Nevertheless, 'the most natural reference' (Westcott) is to *him who is true*. In this way the three references to 'the true' are to the same person, the Father, and the additional points made in the apparent final repetition are that it is this one, namely the God made known by Jesus Christ, who is both *the true God* and *eternal life*. As he is both light and love (1:5; 4:8), so he is also life, himself the only source of life (Jn. 5:26) and the giver of life in Jesus Christ (11). The whole verse is strongly reminiscent of John 17:3, for there as here eternal life is defined in terms of knowing God, both Father and Son.

21. In his last sentence, in place of any formal farewell, John uses again his tender and affectionate address, *dear children*, which has not occurred since 3:8. His final exhortation is based on the three great assurances he has just uttered. The charge, *keep yourselves from idols*, arises naturally from the condition and character of the true Christian which he has been expounding. The Son of God will keep him (18), but this does not relieve him of the responsibility to keep himself. For these two keepings, his and ours, see Jude 21, 24. Actually, the verb here is not *tērein* (as in v. 18) but *phylassein*. It means properly to 'guard' (so RV), and Smith points out that it is used of guarding 'a flock (Lk. 2:8), a deposit or trust (1 Tim. 6:20; 2 Tim. 1:12, 14), a prisoner (Acts 12:4)'.

What the *idols* were to which John is referring we can only guess. He may have been uttering only a general warning that knowledge of, and communion with, *the true God* is inconsistent with the worship of idols. Or he may have been using the word 'idols', as Plato did, of the illusions of sense in opposition to ultimate reality. In this case John is saying: 'Do not abandon the real for the illusory' (Blaiklock). But the addition of the definite article (*apo tōn eidōlōn*, 'from the idols' or 'from your idols') suggests that he had some more particular danger in mind. Perhaps he was thinking of the pagan idolatries with which Ephesus at that time was filled (so Barclay). It is more likely, however, that the allusion is to 'the untrue mental images fashioned by the false teachers' (Brooke), which, because of their false view of the Son and therefore of the Father, constituted a monstrous idolatry. This may explain the 'peremptory aorist imperative' (Brooke, *phylaxate*). John was writing in a time of crisis. 'The Cerinthian heresy was a desperate assault demanding a decisive repulse' (Smith). What is certain is that all 'God-substitutes' (Dodd), all alternatives to the true God who has revealed himself in Jesus Christ, are properly 'idols', and that from them the Christian must vigilantly guard himself.

The worship of idols, unreal and dead, is inconsistent and incompatible with that knowledge of the true God, which is eternal life, just as sin and selfishness are incompatible with the knowledge of God who is light and love. It is this incompatibility, this incongruity, of sin, lovelessness and error with the true Christian, which is the underlying theme of the letter. Let Christians once recognize who they are, what they have become – 'born of God', 'belonging to God', knowing God', 'in God', the possessors of 'eternal life' in Christ (all these characteristic expressions occur in these final verses) – and they will surely live a life which is consistent with, and worthy of, their Christian status.

2 JOHN:
ANALYSIS

2 JOHN:
COMMENTARY

The second and third letters of John are the shortest documents of the New Testament – shorter even than the letter to Philemon and the letter of Jude, which are the only other New Testament letters consisting of but one chapter. Each of John's second and third letters contains less than 300 Greek words and was no doubt written on a single sheet of papyrus. The same themes which the author has elaborated in his first letter recur in brief in his second and third, but the form of what he writes is now less a treatise than a letter, and the particular subject treated is hospitality to travelling missionaries.

The establishment and consolidation of the Roman Empire made travel throughout the inhabited world much easier and safer than it had ever been before. It was facilitated by the great roads which the Romans built and by the *pax Romana* which their legions maintained, as well as by a commonly understood language. The rapid spread of the gospel in the first century AD owed much to these advantages.

But where should travelling Christians stay when they came to some city on a business journey or, more important still, on a missionary journey? 'The comforts of the modern hotel, or even of the village inn, were then unknown' (Findlay). Besides, according to W. M. Ramsay[1] 'the ancient inns . . . were little removed from houses of ill-fame . . . The profession of inn-keeper was dishonourable, and their infamous character is often noted in Roman laws'. 'Inns were notoriously dirty and flea-infested', while 'innkeepers were notoriously rapacious' (Bar-

---

[1] Article 'Roads and Travel (New Testament)' in Hastings' *Dictionary of the Bible*.

clay). As a result, it was natural that Christian people on their travels should be given hospitality by members of local churches. There are many traces in the New Testament of this custom. For example, Paul was entertained by Lydia in Philippi, Jason in Thessalonica, Gaius in Corinth, Philip the evangelist in Caesarea and the Cypriot Mnason in Jerusalem (Acts 16:15; 17:7; Rom. 16:23; Acts 21:8, 16).

Such hospitality was open to easy abuse, however. There was the false teacher, on the one hand, who yet posed as a Christian: should hospitality be extended to him? And there was the more obvious mountebank, the false prophet with false credentials, who was motivated less by creed than by greed, namely the material profit and free board and lodging he hoped to receive. It is against this background that we must read the second and third letters of John, for in them 'the elder' issues instructions concerning whom to welcome and whom to refuse, and why. Genuine Christian missionaries, he writes, may be recognized both by the message they bring and by the motive which inspires them. If they faithfully proclaim the doctrine of Christ (*cf.* 2 Jn. 7), and if they have set out not for gain but for the sake of the Name (3 Jn. 7), then they should be both received and helped forward on their journey 'in a manner worthy of God' (3 Jn. 6).

Rather similar instructions may be found in *The Didachē*, a manual of church order which is thought to date from the end of the first century AD and to offer guidance to the rural churches of Syria.[1] It is assumed that travelling Christians will visit the churches. Each must be examined, so that the genuine may be discerned from the false (11:7, 11; 12:1). The tests given concern his doctrine (11:1–2), his motives, and especially his attitude to money, board and lodging (11:5–6, 9, 12; 12:2–5) and his moral conduct (11:8, 10).

We may divide 2 John into three sections – the introduction (1–3), the message (4–11) and the conclusion (12–13).

---

[1] So Cyril C. Richardson, from whose translation of *The Didachē* the extracts quoted here are taken (*Early Christian Fathers*, Vol. 1 of *The Library of Christian Classics*, SCM Press, 1953, pp. 161–179).

I. THE INTRODUCTION (1–3)

1. The introduction consists of both an address (1–2) and a greeting (3). In accordance with Greek epistolary custom, the author begins his letter by announcing himself. He uses, however, not his personal name (as, *e.g.*, in the letters of Paul) but his title, *the elder* (*cf.* 3 Jn. 1). 'It described not age simply, but official position' (Westcott). It is evident that he was thus known to his readers. He had no doubt that they would immediately identify him by this title, which bears witness to his recognized authority. See Introduction, pp. 39ff.

His letter is addressed to *the chosen lady* (*eklektē kyria*). Commentators differ as to whether these words describe an individual person or are the personification of a church. Those who believe her to have been a person, have vied with one another in ingenious guesses about her identity. Some (beginning with Clement of Alexandria) have thought that her name was 'Electa'. J. Rendel Harris in *The Expositor* (March 1901) argued from papyri parallels that *kyria* was a term of endearment, and that 2 John was virtually a love-letter, written to a certain Electa who was far from being what he called 'a prehistoric Countess of Huntingdon'! But, if the lady's name was Electa, we should have to believe, according to verse 13, that she had a sister called Electa also. Others think, more reasonably, that she was called 'Kyria', a name vouched for in the papyri, and that John addresses her as *chosen* ('chosen by God', NEB) or 'elect'; but in this case the adjective would probably have been preceded by the definite article, as in 3 John 1 ('the beloved', RSV), verse 13 and Romans 16:13. A third group has even hazarded that both words are proper names and that she was called 'Electa Kyria'. These suggestions are all improbable. If the recipient was an individual, she was no doubt an anonymous *chosen lady*. The absence of the definite article confirms this, and 'the combination of terms is a natural expression of Christian courtesy' (Brooke). All attempts to identify her as Mary, the mother of our Lord (because of Jn. 19:27 and her traditional residence in Asia), or Martha (which is Aramaic for 'lady' or 'mistress') are pure conjecture.

The phrase is, however, more likely to be a personification

than a person – not the church at large but some local church over which the elder's jurisdiction was recognized, *her children* (1, *cf.* 4,13) being the church's individual members. John's language is not appropriate to a real person, either in his statement of love (1–2) or in his exhortation to love (5). The elder could hardly refer to his personal love for a lady and her children as a 'command' which 'we have had from the beginning' (see v. 5). The situation envisaged is no more suggestive of an individual than is the language, unless we are to imagine that she was a widow with a large family of children, only some of whom (4) were following the truth, while others had fallen into error, although none is named. The message of verses 7–11 about the treatment of itinerant false teachers may be applicable to every Christian home, but is more likely to have been addressed to a Christian community than to a single home in it. There are no obviously personal references in this letter, as there are in the third, *viz.* to Gaius, Diotrephes and Demetrius (vv. 1, 9, 12). Moreover, the unconscious transition from the second person singular to the second personal plural (marked in AV by the changes from 'thy' and 'thee' in vv. 4 and 5 to 'ye', 'yourselves' and 'you' in vv. 6, 8 and 10, and again from 'you' in v. 12 back to 'thy' and 'thee' in v. 13) seems to betray the fact that the author is thinking of a community rather than an individual. In the third letter, which is addressed to an individual called Gaius, the second person singular is employed consistently throughout. The contrast between the conclusions to the two letters is also striking.

Apart from these internal considerations of language and message, 'the personification of cities, countries and provinces in female form was a well-established convention' (Dodd), like our 'Britannia', and there is good biblical precedent for the use of a female personification to indicate the church, whether universal (Eph. 5:22–23; Rev. 21:9) or local. In the Old Testament Israel was now a virgin, the 'daughter of Zion' (Is. 52:2; *cf.* Is. 47:1ff.; Ezk. 16:7), now married (Is. 62:4–5; Je. 2:2) and a mother (Is. 54:1ff.; *cf.* Gal. 4:26), now a widow (Is. 54:4; La. 1:1). The Corinthian church had been betrothed to Christ as a bride to her husband (2 Cor. 11:2), and another church is described by Peter as 'she who is in Babylon, chosen together with you' (1 Pet. 5:13, *syneklektē*). This 'Babylon' is probably Rome. In the light of this evidence, it seems almost certain that *the chosen lady* was one of the churches of Asia, *her children* its individual members, her 'chosen sister' (13) the neighbouring church from which John was writing, and her sister's 'children' (13) its members. Indeed, John's letter to this church may be the one mentioned in 3 John 9, since both letters are concerned with the question of hospitality.

If it be asked why the apostle should have written thus to a local church, using the expression *chosen lady* as 'a disguise for a community', we can only guess the reason. It may have been for 'prudential reasons' in days when the world's persecuting hatred of the church was overt; or his device may have been 'little more than a "conceit", conforming to the taste of the period' (Dodd).

John describes his relationship to the church in the words *whom* (plural) *I love in the truth*. 'I' is emphatic (*egō*). Perhaps he is casting a side glance at the heretics. Not only had they compromised the truth, but they were a proud and loveless lot. John's declaration is in complete contrast. The Greek phrase translated *in the truth* (as in v. 3 and in 3 Jn. 1) lacks the article. It could therefore be an adverbial expression rendered 'whom I love in truth' (RV, NEB; *cf.* 1 Jn. 3:18), or 'truly', that is, 'in all Christian sincerity' (Plummer). But the context, with two subsequent references to *the truth*, with the article (1–2), surely justifies the RSV and NIV translation *whom I love in the truth*. It was *the truth* which bound John in love to this church, especially the truth about Christ in opposition to the 'lie' of the heretics (1 Jn. 2:21–23). Nor was he alone in his love for them, for *also all who know the truth* (literally 'have come to know' it, perfect, *egnōkotes*) shared his love. 'The communion of love is as wide as the communion of faith' (Alford).

2. Why did John and all other Christians love the members of this church? *Because of the truth, which lives in us and will be with us for ever.* If we are Christians, we are to love our neighbours and even our enemies; but we are bound to our fellow Christians by the special bond of truth. Truth is the ground of reciprocal Christian love. John stresses this fact by his four references to *the truth* in these three opening verses. We love each other not because we are temperamentally compatible, or because we are naturally drawn to one another, but because of the truth which we share. Not only have we come to know it objectively (1); but it lives in us (2) as a present indwelling force, and *with us* (emphatic) it will stay *for ever*. Heretics may leave us and go out into the world (7, *cf.* 1 Jn. 2:19), but in the Christian society the truth will remain secure. So long as the truth endures, in us and with us, so long shall our reciprocal love also endure. Moreover, since Christian love is founded upon Christian truth, we shall not increase the love which exists between us by diminishing the truth which we hold in common. In contemporary movements towards church unity we must never compromise the very truth on which alone true love and unity depend.

3. It is well known that letters written by friends to each other in the Greek language in the first century AD conformed to an accepted pattern with a stylized beginning and end. Usually the letter opened with the writer's name and the identity of the recipients, followed by the single word *chairein*, 'greeting'. This form may be found at the beginning of the letter of James and in Acts 15:23. Other authors of New Testament letters, while retaining the announcement of writer and readers, Christianized the greeting, replacing *chairein* by *charis*, 'grace'. Paul's customary formula, though he departed from it sometimes, was: 'Grace to you and peace from God our Father and the Lord Jesus Christ.' In 2 John 3 four deviations from this may be noted. First, the salutation is neither a prayer, nor a wish, but a confident affirmation. None of Paul's greetings contains a main verb. We have to understand a word like *eiē*, 'be', or Peter's *plēthyntheiē*, 'be yours in abundance' (1 Pet. 1:2; 2 Pet. 1:2; *cf.* Jude 2). John, on the other hand, places first in the sentence an emphatic *estai*, which should be translated not as a prayer, 'be with you' (AV), but as a declaration (RSV, NEB, NIV) 'shall/will be with us' or 'you'. In the second place, *mercy* is added between *grace* and *peace*, as in the three Pastoral Epistles. Grace and mercy are both expressions of God's love, grace to the guilty and undeserving, mercy to the needy and helpless. Peace is that restoration of harmony with God, others and self which we call 'salvation'. Put together, peace indicates the character of salvation, mercy our need of it and grace God's free provision of it in Christ. Thirdly, the words *from God the Father and from Jesus Christ* are almost identical with Paul's usage. John, however, adds a further designation of Christ as *the Father's Son*. This is his familiar theological emphasis. The man *Jesus* is not only the Messiah *Christ*, but the only Son of the Father. Also John repeats the preposition *from (para)*, which Paul never does with *apo* in his salutations, as if to emphasize the equality of the Son with the Father as the fount of all blessing.

The fourth Johannine deviation from Paul's normal epistolary greeting is the addition of *in truth and love*. This may mean either that we shall experience grace, mercy and peace from Father and Son only if we remain in truth and love, or that grace, mercy and peace from Father and Son will express themselves, work themselves out, in truth and love. Whether truth and love are the conditions or the consequences, or merely the accompaniments, of our receiving grace, mercy and peace, they are clearly essential marks of the Christian life. They have already occurred in combination in verse 1, 'whom I love in the truth'. Contrast Ephesians 4:15. The fellowship of the local church is created by truth and exhibited in love. Each qualifies the other. On the one hand, our love is not to be so blind as to ignore the views and conduct of others. Truth should make our love discriminating. John sees nothing inconsistent in adding to his command to love one another (5) a clear instruction about the refusal of fellowship to false teachers, who are deceivers and antichrists (7–11). Our love for others is not to undermine our loyalty to the truth. On the other hand, we must never champion the truth in a harsh or bitter spirit. Those who are 'walking in the truth' (4) need to be exhorted to 'love one another' (5). So the Christian fellowship should be marked equally by love and truth, and we are to avoid extremism which pursues either at the expense of the other. Our love grows soft if it is not strengthened by truth, and our truth hard if it is not softened by love. Scripture commands us both to love each other in the truth and to hold the truth in love.

II. THE MESSAGE (4–11)

The practical purpose of the letter now emerges. This concerns both the inner life of the local fellowship (4–6) and the doctrinal danger which threatens it from without (7–11). The two are related. John commends the faithful inner nucleus ('some of your children') who are 'walking in the truth' and begs them to keep God's other commands, especially that of mutual love. His reason for wanting to see the church thus strengthened in truth and love is that many deceivers have gone out into the world to spread their wicked lies (7). He rejoices greatly over the loyal church members (4), but warns them to look to themselves (8) lest they should either succumb to the false teachers or give them any encouragement in the dissemination of their errors. Here then, in this central section of the letter, is a succinct summary of those contrasts between truth and lies, the church and the world, Christ and antichrist, the commands of God and the deceptions of the devil, with which we have become familiar in the first letter.

4. John begins his message, much as Paul began eight of his thirteen letters, with an expression of thanksgiving. There is much in the local fellowship to give him cause for rejoicing. Yet he knew that not all the church members were living consistently. He could say no more than: *It has given me great joy to find* (either on a recent visit to them or, as in 3 Jn. 3, from news which had reached him) *some of your children walking in the truth* (*cf.* 3 Jn. 4). To 'walk in the truth' ('following the truth', RSV; 'living by the truth', NEB) includes both believing it, especially the central truth of the incarnation, and obeying it, seeking to conform our lives to it. It lives in us (2); we also walk in it. The truth seems thus to be likened to a path along which we walk, by which we keep course, and from which we should not deviate. Indeed, to go astray from revealed truth (whether in doctrine or in morals) is not just an unfortunate error, but an active disobedience, for we are to walk in the truth *just as the Father commanded us*. God has not revealed his truth in such a way as to leave us free at our pleasure to believe or disbelieve it, to obey or disobey it. Revelation carries with it responsibility, and the clearer the revelation, the greater the responsibility to believe and obey it (*cf.* Am. 3:2).

5. The command to walk in the truth is not the Father's only command; the word occurs three times more in verses 5 and 6. To the command to believe is added the command to love, as in the first letter. To be a Christian is to believe in Christ and to love one another (1 Jn. 3:23; *cf.* Col. 1:4; 2 Thes. 1:3). If we deny the Son and do not love, we neither have nor know God (1 Jn. 2:23; 4:8). Faith and love are signs of new birth (1 Jn. 5:1; 4:7). They are also commands. Some people object that faith and love are not amenable to discipline and are beyond the reach of any command. How can you tell me, they ask, to believe what I do not believe or love whom I do not love? The answer to this question lies in the nature of Christian faith and love. It is when faith is regarded as an intuition and love as an emotion that they appear to lie beyond the sphere of duty. But Christian faith is an obedient response to God's self-revelation in Christ. This revelation has a moral content. If people hate the light, it is because their deeds are evil (Jn. 3:19–21). They do not 'believe' in the Son because they are resolved not to 'obey' him (the significant contrast in Jn. 3:36). This is why unbelief is sin and the unbeliever condemned already (Jn. 16:8–9; 3:18). Similarly, Christian love belongs rather to the sphere of action than of emotion. It is not an involuntary, uncontrollable passion, but unselfish service undertaken by deliberate choice. So faith and love are both commanded (here and in 1 Jn. 3:23). Moreover, observe the pronouns: *I ask that we love one another.* John does not issue to the church a command from which he is himself exempt. Indeed, he gives no command at all. Brooke well says: 'The Elder who has the right to command merely grounds a personal request, as between equals, on the old command laid on both alike by the Master.' *I am not writing you a new command*, he insists, *but one we have had from the beginning.* It was not new when John was writing; it was as old as the gospel. It was not even new to his readers; they had known it from the first days of their Christian life (*cf.* 1 Jn. 2:7–8; 3:11, 23b; 4:21, with commentary *ad loc.*, and v. 6 'as you have heard from the beginning').

6. The mention of the command to love leads John to state in epigrammatic form the reciprocal relation between love and obedience. He explains each in terms of the other. First, *this is love: that we walk in obedience to his commands*, and secondly *his command is that you walk in love* (the Greek sentence ends *en autē*, 'in it', but RSV and NIV are surely right to interpret the words as meaning 'in love'). It is plain that love is expressed in obedience. If we love God or Christ, we shall show it by keeping his commands (Jn. 14:15, 21; 15:10; 1 Jn. 5:2–3). If we love our neighbour, we shall do the same, for 'he who loves his neighbour has fulfilled the law' (Rom 13:8, RSV). But what is the law? It is to love God with all our heart, mind, soul and strength, and to love our neighbour as ourselves. 'All the Law and the Prophets hang on these two commandments' (Mt. 22:40). So law and love are not incompatible; on the contrary, each involves the other.

The Christian life is here viewed from the standpoint of commands. It is the word *command* which, occurring four times in three verses, gives cohesion to the paragraph. We are to *walk in obedience to his commands* (6a) and therefore to walk in truth (4) and to walk in love (6b), because these are his commands. This then is the threefold Christian 'walk'. Unselfconsciously John alludes again to the three tests (truth, love and obedience) which he has been applying throughout his first letter. In addition, Christian liberty is not inconsistent with law any more than love is. True, Christians are not 'under law' in that our salvation does not depend on obedience to the law. Yet this does not relieve us of the obligation to keep the law (Mt. 5:17–20; Rom. 8:4; 13:10). The freedom with which Christ has made us free is not freedom to break the law, but freedom to keep it. 'I will walk about in freedom, for I have sought your precepts' (Ps. 119:45).

7–11. John now comes to the second part of his message. He turns from the true believers to the false teachers, from the wheat to the tares. Although he is thankful that 'some' (4) are walking in the truth, he is deeply disturbed that 'many' deceivers have gone out into the world (7). Indeed, his entreaty to the church, contained in verses 4–6, is founded upon the dangerous activity of these false teachers. Their error is to deny the incarnation; their character is to be both a deceiver and an antichrist. On this factual situation John bases a double warning to his readers, first not to be deceived themselves lest they lose their full reward (8–9), and secondly, not to give any encouragement to the deceivers (10–11).

7. Jesus himself warned the apostles of the rise of 'false Christs and false prophets' who would attempt to deceive even the elect, and of whom they were to take heed (Mk. 13:22–23). The Lord's prophecy was fulfilled. John wrote in his first letter of the 'many false prophets' who were abroad (4:1) and here he calls them *many deceivers*. In both passages, although there the tense is perfect and here aorist, he describes them as having *gone out into the world*. The verb *exēlthon* may refer to their having left the church, for the same verb occurs in the same tense in 1 John 2:19. But it seems more likely that the language is deliberately reminiscent of the mission of Christ and of his apostles. Christ was being aped by antichrist. The Son had 'gone out' from the Father into the world (Jn. 7:29; 8:42; 13:3), and had sent forth the apostles into the world (Jn. 17:18; 20:21; *cf.* Mt. 28:19; Mk. 16:15 and 3 Jn.7 which also has *exēlthon*). Perhaps the implication is that as the apostles were sent forth into the world to preach the truth, so these false teachers had gone forth to teach lies, as emissaries of the devil, the father of lies. At all events, we are to think of them as itinerant false prophets, travelling along the great Roman roads of Asia Minor, seeking to insinuate their error into the churches they visited. 'From their own point of view, they were Christian missionaries. From the standpoint of the Presbyter they were impostors' (Dodd).

The heresy of these teachers was that they *do not acknowledge Jesus Christ as coming in the flesh*. We are not told that they categorically denied the incarnation, but that they did not confess it. Perhaps they were subtle enough to counterfeit rather than contradict it. Nevertheless, their teaching was tantamount to a contradiction. The central Christian affirmation about Jesus is variously phrased in the Johannine letters. Sometimes it is simply 'that Jesus is the Christ' (1 Jn. 2:22; 5:1), which is taken as being equivalent to an acknowledgment of him as the Son (1 Jn. 2:23; 5:5). The full confession, however, is that he 'has come in the flesh' (1 Jn. 4:2), where the perfect participle *elēlythota* is used. Compare the use of the aorist participle in 1 John 5:6, *ho elthōn*, 'the one who came'. But here the participle is present, *erchomenon, coming in the flesh*. In strict grammar this should refer to a future coming, and some have wondered if a reference to the parousia, mentioned twice specifically in the first letter (2:28; 3:2), is intended. However, since we know of no early controversy as to whether Jesus Christ would come again in the flesh, whereas these letters are concerned to assert that his first coming was in the flesh, the latter is almost certainly in mind here. In this case the present tense is 'altogether timeless' (Alford). 'The Incarnation is not only an event in history. It is an abiding truth' (Brooke). Jesus did not become the Christ or the Son at his baptism, or cease to be the Christ or the Son before his death; Jesus was 'the Christ come in the flesh'. The two natures, manhood and Godhead, were united already at his birth, never to be divided. The combination of the perfect and the present tenses (in 1 Jn. 4:2 and here) emphasizes this permanent union of natures in the one person.

Whoever denies the incarnation is not just 'a' deceiver or 'an' antichrist, one of many, but *the deceiver and the antichrist*, that is, 'the arch-deceiver' (NEB). There is in this heresy a double affront: it opposes Christ and it deceives people. The false teachers were referred to in different verses of the first letter as purposing to 'deceive' (2:26, RSV) and as 'antichrists' (2:18, 22); now the two ideas are brought together.

8. Having described the fact and indicated the danger of the itinerant false teachers, John now issues his first warning: *Watch out*. The verb is the same as in Mark 13:23, where Jesus' warning against false Christs and false prophets is recorded. Their error was subtle and insidious. Church members could not afford to relax their vigilance. The importance of such watchfulness is given both negatively (*that you do not lose what you have worked for*) and positively (*but that you may be rewarded fully*). In each of the three verbs in this double sentence the MSS vary between the first and second person plural, 'we' and 'you'. The NIV, RSV and NEB are very probably right in the first and last, *i.e. that you do not lose . . . but that you may be rewarded fully*. The middle verb may be either. Westcott and Brooke think the AV 'which we have wrought' is 'almost certainly the true text'. On the other hand the RSV and NIV give the better sense, *what you have worked for*. In this case John is not so much concerned lest his own work for them should prove vain (though *cf.* Gal. 4:11; Phil. 2:16), as that they should win and not lose the full reward of their Christian labour. The thought is not of their winning or losing their salvation (which is a free gift), but rather their reward for faithful service. The metaphor seems to be taken from the payment of labour, since *reward* (*misthos*) is a workman's wage (as in Mt. 20:8; Jn. 4:36; Jas. 5:4). John may be thinking of himself and them as 'fellow labourers in the Lord's vineyard', in which case he is anxious that they should not slack and so receive 'less than a full day's pay' (Smith).

9. John's warning to his readers is not exaggerated. He grounds it on a careful evaluation of the extreme seriousness of the false teaching. *Anyone who runs ahead and does not continue in the teaching of Christ does not have God*. In describing the false teacher as one who *runs ahead, proagōn* ('runs ahead too far', NEB), John is almost certainly borrowing from the vocabulary of the heretics. They claimed to have 'go-ahead' views, a superior *gnōsis*, which had enabled them to advance beyond the rudiments of the faith in which the common herd were content to 'continue'. John refers sarcastically to their claim. They had indeed 'run ahead'. They had advanced so far that they had even left God behind them! For anyone who denies Christ thereby forfeits God. He cannot reject Christ and retain God, or *have God* in the sense of enjoying fellowship with him. By contrast, *whoever continues in the teaching has both the Father and the Son*. This is a repetition of 1 John 2:22–23. In both passages 'the Christ' and 'the Son' are equivalent expressions. No-one can have the Father without acknowledging the Son. For the Son is both the revelation of the Father (*e.g.* Jn. 1:18; 14:7, 9; 1 Jn. 5:20; *cf.* Mt. 11:27) and the way to the Father (Jn. 14:6; *cf.* 1 Tim. 2:5), combining the functions of prophet and priest. Therefore to acknowledge the Son is to possess the Father; to deny the Son is to lose the Father.

This is as true today of all non-Christian religions as it was of Cerinthian Gnosticism in the first century. Many today want

God without Jesus Christ. They believe in God, they say, but see no necessity for Jesus. Or they regard other religions, whether ancient or modern, as alternative roads to God. Such claims must be strenuously resisted. In this the Christian is conservative, not progressive, seeking to 'continue' in the doctrine of Christ, not to 'advance' beyond it. Dodd thinks John incautious and adds that he may appear 'to condemn Christian theology to lasting sterility'. This is exaggerated. Brooke rightly draws attention to 'the non-repetition of the article *ho* before *mē menōn*', and adds: 'all "progress" is not condemned, but only such progress as does not fulfil the added condition of "abiding in the teaching"'. Christian faith is rooted in the historical events of the incarnation and the atonement, the revelation and redemption which were finished in Christ. To 'advance' beyond Christ is 'not progress but apostasy' (Plummer), not enlightenment but darkness. More than that: the Christian seeks to continue not only in Christ but in 'the doctrine of Christ' (AV). At first sight this phrase, literally 'the doctrine of the Christ' (NEB), might be taken as meaning 'the teaching which recognizes Jesus as the Christ' (Smith), and this would suit the context well. But the 'usage of the N.T.' (Westcott, Brooke) requires that the genitive be interpreted not as objective, 'the teaching about Christ', but as subjective, 'Christ's teaching'. This no doubt includes what Christ continued to teach through the apostles (*cf.* Acts 1:1; Col. 3:16; Heb. 2:3). Such authoritative apostolic doctrine is equivalent to what in his first letter John called 'what you have heard from the beginning' (2:24; *cf.* 2:7; 3:11; Jn. 8:31; 2 Tim. 3:14 and 2 Jn. 5–6). The necessary development of Christian people into maturity is not 'progress' beyond Christ's teaching, whether as recorded in the Gospels, or as given through the apostles in their letters, but a progressive understanding of it.

10. John now introduces his second warning. So grave is the consequence of the deceivers' error (causing its adherents to lose the Father as well as the Son) that he not only exhorts them to take heed to themselves but instructs them how to treat a false prophet who, having 'gone out into the world' (7), now *comes to you*. Their duty is clear and definite: *do not take him into your house or welcome him*. This uncompromising order to Christians who are normally to be 'given to hospitality' (*e.g.* Rom 12:13; 1 Tim. 3:2; 5:3–10; Tit. 1:8; Heb. 13:2; 1 Pet. 4:8–10), and who are generously to entertain true missionaries (3 Jn. 5–8), has proved unacceptable to many. Dodd suggests that these are 'emergency regulations' relating to 'a situation of extreme danger to the Church', but that 'this fierce intolerance' was neither necessary nor right. He therefore declines 'to accept the Presbyter's ruling here as a sufficient guide to Christian conduct' and declares it 'incompatible with the general purport of the teaching of the New Testament and not really consistent with the teaching of these epistles themselves'. But are we to suppose that John was divided against himself? This instruction is given by the apostle of love immediately following an exhortation to love (6). Did John first insist on the command of love and then immediately break it himself? Besides, we are not 'at liberty to set aside direct ethical injunctions of the Lord's Apostles in this manner' (Alford).

What John writes is relevant both to those who are so tolerant that they will condemn nobody's views and to those who are so intolerant that they condemn everybody's views which diverge from their own. But neither compromise nor separation can find support in this text. For a balanced interpretation of it, the following three facts need to be borne in mind.

First, John is referring to teachers of false doctrine, not merely to believers in it. The person who is not to be received is one who *comes to you*, not as a casual visitor but as an official teacher, and who is said not just to believe, but to *bring*, a message other than *this teaching* (of Christ), as a merchant 'brings' with him wares for sale. Christians may surely welcome and entertain someone who holds false views, and will seek to bring him to a better mind. It is those who are engaged in the systematic dissemination of lies, dedicated missionaries of error, to whom we may give no encouragement. Dodd does not seem to appreciate this difference. Although he writes of 'missionaries', he seems to be thinking of individual heretics. We must 'find a way', he writes, 'of living with those whose convictions differ from our own upon the most fundamental matters'. But of course! In the case of a private individual who denies Jesus Christ, it is enough to watch out (8) lest we embrace his error, and to seek to win him to the truth. But in the case of someone officially commissioned to teach his error to others, we must reject not only it but him.

Secondly, John's instruction may well relate not only to an 'official' visit of false teachers but to the extending to them of an 'official' welcome, rather than merely private hospitality. Two details suggest this. First, this letter was addressed, as we have seen, to a church, not to an individual, and the phrase *if anyone comes to you* (plural, *hymas*) describes the anticipated visit of a false teacher (or a group of them, v. 7) to the church in question. They had left the church where John was (*cf.* v. 7 *exēlthon* with 1 Jn. 2:19 *exēlthan*), but they had evidently not yet arrived where the recipients of the second letter were. 'A widespread movement of heretical propaganda is afoot, and may at any time reach their city' (Dodd). The second detail is John's order not to *take him into your house*, which is literally 'into the house' (RSV). Which house? Of course he may mean that every Christian house was to be closed to the false prophets. But may it not be that John was primarily referring to 'the house' (in days before church buildings existed) in which the church met for worship (*cf.* Rom. 16:5; 1 Cor. 16:19; Col. 4:15; Phm. 2)? Perhaps, therefore, it is not private hospitality which John is forbidding so much as an official welcome into the congregation, with the opportunity this would afford to the false teacher to propagate his errors. 'He is to be treated as excommunicate' (Dodd). But Bruce justly comments: 'It does not mean that (say) one of Jehovah's Witnesses should not be invited into the house for a cup of tea in order to be shown the way of God more perfectly in the sitting-room than would be convenient on the doorstep' (p. 142).

In the third place, John is referring to teachers of false doctrine about the incarnation, and not to every false teacher. This verse gives us no warrant to refuse fellowship to those, even teachers, who do not agree with our interpretation of apostolic doctrine in every particular. It is inaccurate to write about ostracizing 'people whose opinions we dislike' (Dodd). It is the entertainment of antichrist which is forbidden us, the arch-deceiver who in his teaching denies the essential deity and humanity of Jesus. If John's instruction still seems harsh, it is probably because his concern for the glory of the Son and the good of human souls is greater than ours, and because 'the tolerance on which we pride ourselves' is in reality an 'indifference to truth' (Alexander). The false teacher whom John forbids the church to entertain, is 'the deceiver' and 'the antichrist' (7). His teaching is derogatory to Christ and dangerous to the church. How then can we make him welcome in our home or church or wish him well on his journey? If we were to do so in the name of love, we would not be acting in the best interests either of the false teachers or of those they would pervert. 'Charity has its limits: it must not be shewn to one man in such a way as to do grievous harm to others' (Plummer).

11. The reason for John's instruction is now given. False teaching which denies Christ and so robs people of the Father is not just an unfortunate error; it is a 'wicked work'. It may send souls to eternal ruin. If, then, we do not wish to further such evil work (to become 'an accomplice in his wicked deeds', NEB), we must give no encouragement to the worker.

III. THE CONCLUSION (12–13)

12. The conclusions of the second and third letters are strikingly similar. With this verse compare 3 John 13–14. The elder has come to the end of his sheet of papyrus. The ink, 'commonly made of soot and water thickened with gum' (Alford), was still wet. He has yet *much to write to you* (*cf.* Jn. 16:12)), he says, but he prefers to speak than to write. Talking *face to face* (literally 'mouth to mouth' as in Nu. 12:8; Je. 32:4) is a more satisfactory method of communication between persons than writing. Spoken words are less easily misunderstood than written words, because it is not only by language that the speaker conveys his meaning, but by the tone of his voice and the expression on his face. So John tells them of his hope that he will be able to visit them. And his coming to them as their true teacher will be very different from the coming of the false teachers. He assumes that they will welcome him. Speaking to them will make possible a personal communion with them, which the writer and the readers of a letter can scarcely enjoy. The purpose of this fellowship is *so that our joy may be complete.* Complete joy is the result of fellowship. The New Testament knows nothing of perfect joy outside fellowship with each other through fellowship with the Father and the Son (*cf.* 1 Jn. 1:3–4 and commentary *ad loc.*).

13. The letter concludes with a message of greeting from *the children of your chosen sister,* namely 'the members of your sister-congregation' (Alexander), the church from which John is writing. See commentary on verse 1.

3 JOHN:
ANALYSIS

3 JOHN:
COMMENTARY

Like the second letter, the third is brief enough to have been
written on a single sheet of papyrus. A similar problem lies
behind both letters, namely the visits of itinerant teachers and
what treatment is to be given to them. Both letters are therefore
concerned with Christian truth and love and with their relation
to hospitality. There are differences, however. In the second
letter 'the elder' writes to a local church, personified as 'the
chosen lady and her children', whereas in the third letter he
addresses by name one of the leading members of a local
church, and refers to two others. This mention of Gaius (1),
Diotrephes (9) and Demetrius (12) makes the third letter more
vivid than the second and gives us a clearer glimpse into the
inner life of a first-century church. The message differs also. In
the second letter the church is warned not to extend hospitality
to false teachers who deny the doctrine of the incarnation, while
in the third 'the elder' commends Gaius for the hospitality he
has shown to teachers of the truth, urges him to continue it, and
sharply rebukes Diotrephes for his refusal to welcome them and
for his opposition to those who wished to. In this way the
positive instruction of the third letter is complementary to the
more negative instruction of the second. The two letters must be
read together if we are to gain a balanced understanding of the
duties and limits of Christian hospitality.

The Didachē, the first-century church manual to which reference was made in the introductory comments on the second
letter, shows that early Christian hospitality was sometimes
abused. Instructions are given that an 'apostle' may not stay
beyond one day or, 'in case of necessity', two. 'If he stays three

days, he is a false prophet' (11:5). On departing, he may receive enough food to last him his journey. But 'if he asks for money, he is a false prophet' (11:6). Again, if a prophet, apparently speaking under the inspiration of the Spirit, says 'give me money, or something else', he is not to be heeded unless the money is 'for others in need' (11:12). It is recognized that true prophets have a right to stay and be supported (13), but an ordinary Christian traveller must not be entertained free for more than two or three days (12:2). If he wants to settle, 'he must work for his living . . . If he refuses to do this, he is trading on Christ' (12:3–5).

The third letter contains messages to or concerning Gaius (1–8), Diotrephes (9–10), and Demetrius (11–12), with a conclusion and greeting (13–14).

I. THE MESSAGE TO GAIUS (1–8)

1. The writer again announces himself not by his personal name but by the title by which his readers evidently knew him, *the elder*. See commentary on 2 John 1. The recipient of the letter is called *Gaius*. Several men named Gaius appear in the pages of the New Testament – Gaius of Corinth, who after his baptism by Paul became host to the apostle and to 'the whole church' (1 Cor. 1:14; Rom. 16:23), and who, according to Origen, was traditionally thought to have been the first Bishop of Thessalonica; Gaius of Macedonia, linked with Aristarchus of Thessalonica as one of Paul's companions, who suffered in the riot at Ephesus (Acts 19:29); and Gaius of Derbe, who travelled with Paul on his last journey from Greece through Macedonia at least as far as Troas and was probably his church's delegate for the transmission of the collection for the poor in Judea (Acts 20:4). According to the fourth-century so-called 'Apostolical Constitutions' (7.46.9), it was this last Gaius of Derbe to whom the third letter of John was sent and whom John appointed the first Bishop of Pergamum. This latter suggestion has attracted some commentators. Indeed 'there is nothing unlikely about it, but the document is late and there is no early support for its statement' (Dodd).

Since 'Gaius' was 'perhaps the most common of all names in the Roman Empire' (Plummer), it is safer to resist the attempt to identify the Gaius of this letter. We do not know who he was. It is clear, however, from the terms in which John writes, that he occupied a position of responsibility and leadership in the local church. Visiting evangelists seem to have stayed with him rather than with others, and the elder would hardly have written so outspokenly of Diotrephes to any but a church leader. Although we can only guess his identity and his position, John leaves us in no doubt of his personal affection for him. He calls him his *dear friend* (1), and three times addresses him directly by the same term *agapēte*, 'beloved' (RSV) or 'my dear friend' (NEB). See verses 2, 5 and 11. John's love for him was *in the truth*. As in 2 John 1 there is no definite article in this phrase. Dodd quotes two letters from an Egyptian farmer in AD 110 in which he sends greetings to 'all who love you (or us) truly'. Nevertheless, the RSV and NIV are certainly right to translate the expression here not 'in truth' (RV), or 'sincerely', but *in the truth*, the truth being the sphere in which their mutual love existed and flourished. Perhaps their relationship to each other was more personal even than this and the reference to 'my children' (4) hints that Gaius owed his conversion to John.

2. Three of the first eleven Greek words with which the letter opens refer to love. The love of 'the elder' for Gaius is genuine and now expresses itself in a 'wish' (AV) or prayer (*I pray*) for his material well-being. The verb translated *that all may go well with you* (*euodousthai*) means literally 'to have a good journey' (Dodd), and metaphorically to 'succeed' or 'prosper' (Rom. 1:10; 1 Cor. 16:2). The other verb rendered *enjoy good health* (*hygiainein*) is used by Luke the physician to describe those who are 'fit and well' or 'safe and sound' (*e.g.* Lk. 5:31; 7:10; 15:27). Taking the words together, 'the elements of progress and vigour are combined' (Westcott). Both verbs belonged to the everyday language of letter writing. 'So regular was this sort of thing in Latin letters', comments Bruce (p. 147), 'that it was customarily expressed by the use of initials SVBEEV (*si uales, bene est; ego ualeo*, "if you are well, that is good; I am well").' John's wish for Gaius' body and estate, however, although expressed in conventional terms, is doubtless a sincere one. There is no need for him to express a similar desire for Gaius' spiritual well-being, because he says he knows that his *soul is getting along well*. There is biblical warrant here for desiring the physical as well as the spiritual welfare of our Christian friends.

At the same time, those who have recently developed the so-called 'prosperity gospel' (*viz.* that God means all his children to enjoy health and wealth in abundance) can find in this text only the flimsiest foundation for their position. Consider these points: (1) they depend almost entirely on Old Testament promises of prosperity, which were spoken to the nation Israel and were not repeated in the New Testament to either Christian individuals or the Christian community; (2) they are insensitive to the poverty and hunger of many believers in developing nations, to whom the prosperity gospel evidently does not apply; and (3) they overlook the New Testament emphasis on adversity rather than prosperity as the chief mark of the followers of the Suffering Servant.

3. The evidence of Gaius' spiritual well-being, which had caused John *great joy*, had been brought to him by certain *brothers*. They are mentioned in this verse and in verse 5. They had visited the church in which Gaius held a responsible position and had seen certain things about him which enabled them, on their return to 'the elder', to bring him a good report. Two characteristics of Gaius' spiritual prosperity are mentioned, namely *your faithfulness to the truth* (3), literally 'your truth' (RV), and 'your love (6). To both the travelling brothers had 'borne witness' (3 and 6). Gaius was a balanced Christian. He held the truth in love (*cf.* Eph. 4:15). He also loved in truth. For the relation between these two qualities see commentary on 2 John 1 and 3. Since testimony can be borne only to what has been seen (see commentary on 1 Jn. 1:2), it is clear that Gaius was a transparent, open Christian who was letting his light shine and not hiding it. His truth and love were known to all. Even 'strangers' (5) could see his sterling worth and bear witness to it. For the meaning of *your faithfulness to the truth*, see commentary on the next verse.

4. 'The elder' regarded Gaius as his child, much as all those to whom he addressed his first letter were his 'dear children'. He had a fatherly affection for them (*cf.* 1 Cor. 4:14–16; 1 Thes. 2:11) and his joy as a parent was bound up in their welfare (*cf.* 1 Thes. 3:1–10). In particular he rejoiced if his children were continuing to *walk in the truth* (*cf.* the similar statement in 2 Jn. 4). This expression, which has the definite article (*en tē alētheia*), explains the meaning of the two earlier phrases in the previous verse, 'your truth' ('the truth of your life', RV, RSV; 'your faithfulness to the truth', NIV) and 'how you continue to walk in the truth' (which has no definite article). To *walk in* ('follow', RSV) *the truth* is more than to give assent to it. It means to apply it to one's behaviour. Whoever 'walks in the truth' is an integrated believer in whom there is no dichotomy between profession and practice. On the contrary, there is in him an exact correspondence between creed and conduct. Such conformity of life to the truth on the part of his children brought John *greater joy* than anything else. To him truth mattered. The alternative reading of *charin*, 'favour' (meaning 'no greater favour from God'), for *charan* (*joy*), followed by the Vulgate, and adopted by Westcott and Hort perhaps because it is found in the Codex Vaticanus, is almost certainly a copyist's error. 'Joy' is much more strongly supported.

5–6a. 'The elder' again addresses Gaius as *dear friend* and proceeds to write not now of his truth but of his love. He was 'given to hospitality', as all Christians (Rom. 12:13; Heb. 13:2; 1 Pet. 4:9) and particularly widows (1 Tim. 5:10) and presbyter-bishops (1 Tim. 3:2; Tit. 1:8) are commanded to be. In each of these verses the Greek word is either the noun *philoxenia* or the adjective *philoxenos*, which indicate literally a love for strangers. In welcoming such, we may not only entertain angels without knowing it (Heb. 13:2), but will be receiving the Lord Jesus himself (Mt. 10:40–42; 25:35, 38; *cf. Didachē* 11:2, 4, 'welcome him as the Lord'). This love for strangers is just what Gaius possessed, for his ministry had been exercised towards *the brothers, even though they were strangers* to him. 'The brethren and the strangers are not two classes, but one and the same' (Plummer). Gaius' *philadelphia* (love of the brothers) and *philoxenia* (love of strangers) were combined. *Cf.* Hebrews 13:12, where these words occur together. He must have received them into his house and entertained them at his own expense. He was *faithful*, 'the elder' comments, in what he was doing. This may signify that John recognized in the hospitable practice of Gaius a token of his loyalty to himself and his principles. He could 'still be counted on' (Dodd); *cf.* RSV, 'it is a loyal thing you do' and NEB, 'you show a fine loyalty'. Or, as Westcott suggests, the phrase should perhaps be rendered: 'thou makest sure . . .' *i.e.* 'such an act . . . will not fail of its due issue and reward'. But it is noteworthy that what Gaius is said to be *faithful in . . . doing* is his 'work' (*ergasē*). His work was the outcome of his faith; it was 'a faithful work' (RV). The word 'faithful' seems to link together the truth and the love of Gaius. His practical ministry to strangers was true to his profession. His love was consistent with the truth which he believed. The verb *they have told* is an aorist (*emartyrēsan*, 'have testified', RSV) and must refer to some particular occasion when before the assembled congregation, of which John was leader, the returned travellers had spoken appreciatively of the love Gaius had shown them, and of his truth (3).

6b. 'The elder' now turns from the past to the future, from 'what you are doing' (5) to what *you will do* (6). John is perhaps anxious lest the vociferous Diotrephes (9–10) should succeed in persuading Gaius to change his policy of keeping open house. So he urges him to continue to entertain travelling teachers. The implication of extending hospitality to itinerant missionaries is now clear. They are not just to be received when they arrive, but to be so refreshed and provided for (no doubt with supplies of food and money) as to be sent forward on the next stage of their journey *in a manner worthy of God* (*cf.* Col. 1:10; 1 Thes. 2:12). They are the servants of God and represent him. They must be treated accordingly. Such thoughtful sending forth of missionaries on their journey is not only 'a loyal thing' (5, RSV), but a 'beautiful' thing (*kalōs poiēseis, you will do well*). *Cf.* Mark 14:6 for another deed of love which is recognized as 'a beautiful thing' (RSV).

Dodd suggests that the verb translated *send them on their way* (*propempsas*) was 'something like a technical term of early Christian missions', implying 'the assumption of financial responsibility for the journey' of departing missionaries. This is probably the case for, although in Acts 20:38 and 21:5 it seems to mean no more than to 'accompany' or 'escort', in other places, as here, it indicates to receive and entertain travellers in preparation for the next stage of their journey (Rom. 15:24; 1 Cor. 16:6, 11; 2 Cor. 1:16) and possibly to supply them with provisions when they leave (as in Tit. 3:13 and possibly Acts 15:3). *Cf.* verse 8 here.

7. The reasons for such special hospitality are now given. 'The brothers' and 'strangers' of verse 5 are not ordinary Christians who happen to be travelling from one city to another, but missionaries. John writes of them that *they went out*. The verb (*exēlthon*) is the same as that used of the false teachers (1 Jn. 2:19; 4:1; 2 Jn. 7). It depicts a deliberate setting out on a mission, as when Paul embarked on his second missionary journey (Acts 15:40). Their motive is described as being *for the sake of the Name*. The AV had 'for his name's sake' and the RSV 'for his sake', but the possessive adjective is not there in the Greek sentence. There is no need for John to specify whose name is in his mind. For there is only one Name, exalted above all others (Phil. 2:9). Moreover, the 'name' of Jesus is the revelation of his divine-human person and saving work, and 'jealousy' for his name (zeal that it should receive the honour due to it) is the most compelling of all missionary motives (*cf.* Rom. 1:5 and, for suffering for the Name, Acts 5:40–41). *The pagans* (*hoi ethnikoi*) refers here not to non-Jews, but to 'the heathen' (RSV) in contrast to Christian believers. The phrase *receiving no help* need not be pressed into meaning that these Christian missionaries would refuse to accept gifts voluntarily offered to them by the unconverted. There is no prohibition here of taking money from non-Christians who may be well disposed to the Christian cause. Jesus himself asked for and accepted a glass of water from a sinful Samaritan woman. What is here said is that these itinerant evangelists would not (as a matter of policy) seek their support from unbelievers and did not (as a matter of fact) receive their support from them. Christian missionaries were not like many wandering non-Christian teachers of those days (or even the begging friars of the Middle Ages), who made a living out of their vagrancy. Dodd writes: 'Devotees of various religions tramped the roads, extolling the virtues of the deity of their choice, and collecting subscriptions from the public. Thus, a "slave" of the Syrian Goddess has put on record (in an inscription cited by Deissmann, *Light from the Ancient East*, pp. 108 *et seq.*) how he travelled in the service of his "Lady", and "at each journey brought back seventy bags" (that is, of money).' By contrast, Jesus told the Twelve and the Seventy to take with them 'no bag' (Mk. 6:8; Lk. 10:4), and Paul condemned those who 'peddle the word of God for profit' (2 Cor. 2:17; *cf.* 1 Thes. 2:5–9). Christian ministers and teachers certainly have the right to be supported by those who benefit from their service, as Paul several times insisted (especially 1 Cor. 9:1–18; Gal. 6:6; 1 Tim. 5:17–18). But a Christian congregation supporting its minister is one thing; missionaries begging money from unbelievers is another.

8. This verse complements verse 7. It is because the itinerant evangelists were not supported by the pagans that *we ought therefore to show hospitality to such men. We* is strongly emphatic in the Greek sentence, which also contains a pun, namely that we ought to 'support' (the RSV and NEB rendering of *hypolambanein*) those who 'receive' (*lambanontes*) no help from the unbelievers. If the first reason for entertaining travelling missionaries is that they are brothers whom we should honour for setting out for the sake of the Name, the second is the much more practical one that they have no other means of support. *We* must do for them what others will not do. An important principle lies buried here, namely that we Christians should finance Christian enterprises which the world will not, or should not be expected to, support. Indeed, we have an obligation (*ought*) to do so. There are many good causes which we *may* support; but we *must* support our brothers and sisters whom the world does not support. This is a good guiding principle in Christian giving. The third reason for entertaining and providing for travelling missionaries is that by so doing we *work together for the truth*. This may mean that we become 'fellow workers in the truth' (RSV), implying that we are co-operating with the missionaries and 'so play our part in spreading the truth' (NEB). Or the phrase could be translated 'fellow-workers with the truth' (RV), 'allies of the Truth' (Moffatt), the truth itself being personified and regarded as the one with whom we collaborate. For this construction see James 2:22. Such a personification of the truth, the gospel or the word, is not without precedent in the New Testament (see, *e.g.*, v. 12; 2 Cor. 13:8; Phil. 1:27; 1 Thes. 2:13). These itinerant evangelists are not 'deceivers' (2 Jn. 7), bringing with them the lie that Jesus is not the Christ, the Son of God. On the contrary, they bring with them *the truth*. To receive one of the former is to 'share in his wicked work' (2 Jn. 11); to receive the latter is to be a fellow worker with the truth. The Christian missionaries co-operate with the truth by proclaiming it; we co-operate with it by entertaining them. The Christian missionary enterprise is, therefore, not undertaken by evangelists only, but also by those who entertain and support them.

II. THE MESSAGE CONCERNING DIOTREPHES (9–10)

9. 'The elder' now introduces the problem created by Diotrephes. In character and behaviour he is entirely different from Gaius. Gaius is portrayed as walking in the truth, loving the brothers, entertaining strangers. Diotrephes, on the other hand, is seen as loving himself more than others and refusing to welcome the travelling evangelists, or to let others do so. Yet Gaius and Diotrephes were probably members of the same congregation, for 'in the visible Church the evil be ever mingled with the good' (Article 26 of the Thirty-Nine Articles), although Dodd thinks they were members of neighbouring churches. Matters had now come to a head, John says. *I wrote to the church, but Diotrephes . . . will have nothing to do with us.* What this letter was is not clear. It cannot be the letter he is now writing because, although the verb might grammatically be an epistolary aorist, the words *Diotrephes . . . will have nothing to do with us* seem to describe the response which the letter in question has already (in the past) received. So it must be some other letter, not a private message to Gaius, but an official directive addressed to *the church.* It can hardly be either the first or second letter of

John, since neither recommends the entertainment of travelling missionaries, which evidently was the subject of the letter mentioned in this verse. The letter in question must, therefore, have been lost, possibly because Diotrephes destroyed it.

Whether or not Diotrephes destroyed the letter, or declined to read it to the church, he certainly rejected the elder's written instruction (*ti*, 'something', RSV). It is noteworthy that in verses 9 and 10 John slips from the singular ('I wrote') to the plural (he 'will have nothing to do with *us*'), then reverts to the singular ('If *I* come, *I* will call attention to what he is doing'), but ends with the plural again ('gossiping maliciously about *us*'). It is difficult to resist the conclusion that his 'we' is the plural of authority, that by it he is referring to himself, and that the RSV is correct to translate the end of verse 9 that Diotrephes 'does not acknowledge *my* authority'. John was conscious of possessing a generally accepted authority in the church. He issued orders and expected them to be obeyed (*cf.* 2 Thes. 3 for apostolic commands requiring obedience). Diotrephes was the exception. He was not going to be dictated to by John. He evidently claimed an authority of his own, even to the point of excommunicating church members who disobeyed him (10).

What were the motives which prompted Diotrephes thus to assert himself against John? Several attempts have been made to reconstruct the situation. There is no evidence that their disagreement was theological. If the truth of the gospel were at stake, 'the elder' would surely not have hesitated to expose the error in the same uncompromising language which he had used in the first and second letters. Not doctrinal heresy but personal ambition was the cause of the trouble. Findlay points out that the name Diotrephes was as rare as Gaius was common. Since, literally translated, it means 'Zeus-reared, nursling of Zeus' and was only to be found 'in noble and ancient families', he goes on to make the ingenious conjecture that this Diotrephes 'belonged to the Greek aristocracy of the old royal city' (of Pergamum, to which Findlay believes this letter was addressed). In this case it was social prestige which lay behind his disgraceful behaviour. Other writers have tried to trace the rivalry between John and Diotrephes to the changing pattern of church order at the end of the first century AD. The age of the apostles was drawing to a close. Indeed, according to those who deny that the elder John was the apostle, it had already closed. It is known that by about AD 115, when Bishop Ignatius of Antioch wrote his letters to the Asian churches, 'monarchical episcopacy' (the acceptance of a single bishop with authority over a group of presbyters) was established among them. So this letter was written at the end of the apostolic era, or between it and the universal acceptance of episcopacy – a period of transition and tension which Dodd likens to the handing over of responsibility by foreign missionaries to the indigenous church.

Some commentators believe that the monarchical episcopate was already being introduced, and that Diotrephes, as the lawful bishop of the church, was chafing under the apostolic, or (if Dodd is right about 'the elder'; see Introduction, pp. 40f.) 'sub-apostolic', authority of John. Others think Diotrephes was rather aspiring to this office, while Gaius was the rival candidate favoured by John. Barclay suggests that the letter reflects the tension between the universal ministry of apostles and prophets and the local ministry of elders. He thinks Diotrephes may have been an elder who was determined to champion the autonomy of the local church and therefore resented both the 'remote control' of John and 'the interference of wandering strangers'. Precisely what his position was depends on whether his excommunication of church members (10) rested on any proper authority or was arrogantly presumptuous. Dodd is prepared to consider the former a possibility, and that Diotrephes may have been understandably rebelling against the old order represented by John. It is clear, however, that John himself held a different view of Diotrephes and, if we recognize his authority as a biblical writer, we must of course accept his standpoint.

To John the motives governing the conduct of Diotrephes were neither theological, nor social, nor ecclesiastical, but moral. The root of the problem was sin. *Diotrephes . . . loves to be first* or (RSV) 'likes to put himself first' (*philoprōteuōn*). He did not share the Father's purpose that in all things Christ should have the supremacy (Col. 1:18, *prōteuōn*). Nor would he kowtow to 'the elder'. He wanted the supremacy himself. He was 'greedy of place and power' (Findlay). He had not heeded the warnings of Jesus against ambition and the desire to rule (*e.g.* Mk. 10:42–

45; *cf.* 1 Pet. 5:3). His secret self-love erupted in the antisocial behaviour described in the next verse. Smith comments that '*proagein* (2 Jn. 9) and *philoprōteuein* denote two tempers which disturbed the Christian life of Asia Minor – intellectual arrogance and personal aggrandisement'.

10. John declares that if he comes in person to the church in question, he *will call attention to* (or 'will bring up', RSV, NEB, that is in public reproof) what Diotrephes has been saying and doing. He cannot overlook this challenge to his apostolic authority. He will be obliged to take some kind of disciplinary action. The seriousness of Diotrephes' behaviour is now exposed in three phrases. First, he is *gossiping maliciously about us*. The word for gossiping (*phlyarōn*) means in classical Greek to 'talk nonsense'. 'It conveys the idea that the words were not only wicked, but senseless' (Plummer). The noun *phlyaroi* in 1 Timothy 5:13 is translated 'tattlers' in AV and 'gossips' in NIV. The NEB renders the phrase: 'He lays baseless and spiteful charges against us.' Diotrephes evidently regarded John as a dangerous rival to his own assumed authority in the church and sought to undermine his position by slanderous gossip. It was not only against John's person and position, however, that Diotrephes was working, but against his instruction regarding the entertainment of the missionaries. He was *not satisfied* with a campaign of malicious gossip about John, but went further and deliberately defied 'the elder': *He refuses to welcome the brothers.* Thirdly, *he also stops those who want to do so and puts them out of the church.* For some reason Diotrephes resented the intrusion of the itinerant teachers. He did not honour them for setting out 'for the sake of the Name'; he was more concerned for the glory of his own name. Perhaps he had no better reason for refusing to welcome these strangers than that John had commanded it. He would not have them in his home or help them, and those who wanted to obey John and welcome them he first prevented from carrying out their desire and then excommunicated. Self-love vitiates all relationships. Diotrephes slandered John, cold-shouldered the missionaries and excommunicated the loyal believers – all because he loved himself and wanted to have the pre-eminence. Personal vanity still lies at the root of most dissensions in every local church today.

III. THE MESSAGE CONCERNING DEMETRIUS (11-12)

11. John turns from his description of the mischief being done by Diotrephes to give a word of personal counsel to Gaius, followed by a commendation of Demetrius. Perhaps he is anxious lest even Gaius should be influenced by Diotrephes. So he writes: *Dear friend, do not imitate what is evil but what is good.* Everybody is an imitator. It is natural for us to look up to other people as our model and to copy them. This is all right, 'the elder' seems to be saying, but Gaius must choose his model carefully. Diotrephes will not do, for instance. Gaius must 'not imitate evil but imitate good' (RSV), and John adds the reason. It is not just because of the effect which our copying others has on our behaviour, but because of the evidence which everybody's behaviour supplies of their spiritual condition. *Anyone who does what is good is from God. Anyone who does what is evil has not seen God.* This is the moral test which is often applied in the first letter (*e.g.* 2:3-6, 28-29; 3:4-10; 5:18). Indeed an illustration of each of the three tests is given in this letter – truth (vv. 3-4), love (6) and now goodness (11). The true Christian may be described both as being *from God* (*cf.* 1 Jn. 4:4, 6) and as having *seen God* (*cf.* 1 Jn. 3:6). Birth of God and the vision of God are to some extent equivalent. He who has been born of God has come, with the inner eye of faith, to see God. And this vision of God deeply affects his behaviour. To do good is to give evidence of a divine birth; to do evil is to prove that one has never seen God (*cf.* 1 Jn. 3:6). Perhaps in this generalization John has Diotrephes in mind and thus obliquely indicates that he questions whether Diotrephes is a true Christian at all.

12. Just as the thought of Diotrephes led John to write about doing evil, the mention of doing good seems now to remind him of *Demetrius*. A certain Demetrius is mentioned in Acts 19:23ff., a silversmith of Ephesus; but there is no evidence that it is he who is here described. Nor can we say that he is the same as Demas in Paul's letters (Col. 4:14; Phm. 24; 2 Tim. 4:10), although Demas is probably short for Demetrius. According to the *Apostolical Constitutions* John later appointed him Bishop of Philadelphia. We know nothing for certain of this Demetrius beyond what we are told in this one verse. It has been conjectured that John thus commended him because he was the bearer of the letter, a 'travelling assistant of the Apostle' (Findlay), or because he was an object of Diotrephes' malice and Gaius needed to be reassured about him. Either is possible; both are speculative. The former is, however, the more probable as John seems to be commending Demetrius to Gaius as if Gaius did not already know him. What is clear is that Demetrius is given an impressive threefold testimony (*cf.* 1 Jn. 5:8). First, he *is well spoken of by everyone.* The perfect passive *memartyrētai* conveys the idea that the testimony which everybody has borne to Demetrius remains valid. Secondly, this testimony is confirmed *by the truth itself.* This can hardly be a reference to the Son or the Spirit, although each is 'the truth' (Jn. 14:6; 1 Jn. 5:6). It surely means rather that the Christian genuineness of Demetrius did not need human witness; it was self-evident. The truth he professed was embodied in him, so closely did his life conform to it. Then Demetrius had a third witness: *We also speak well of him* (*martyroumen*) with a present and continuing testimony. This again looks like the first person plural of authority, by which John is referring to himself (as in v. 9). The RSV rightly renders it: 'I testify to him too.' This would be enough for Gaius because, even if he did not know any of those who had testified to Demetrius, and even if he had not yet met Demetrius personally to see in him the witness of *the truth itself,* he nevertheless knew and trusted the judgment of John, as John goes on to write: *and you know that our testimony* (*martyria*) *is true* (*cf.* Jn. 21:24).

IV. THE CONCLUSION AND GREETING (13–14)

13–14a. Compare 2 John 12 and commentary there. There are verbal differences between the conclusions of John's second and third letters, such as the tense of the verb *to write* and the reference to *pen and ink* (*kalamos,* the reed used by the ancients for a pen) instead of 'paper and ink'. But the general sense is identical. John has *much to write,* much more than he can include on one sheet of papyrus, but these things he prefers to communicate by word of mouth, for he is planning to visit Gaius *soon*, and then, he says, *we will talk face to face*.

14b. (RSV, 15). *Peace to you*, the Hebrew greeting, invested with new meaning by Jesus after the resurrection (Jn. 20:19, 21, 26), is an appropriate prayer for Gaius if he had to exercise leadership in a church where Diotrephes was stirring up strife. In the second letter, the reference to peace came at the beginning (v. 3), but a similar greeting of peace at the conclusion of a letter occurs in Galatians 6:16; Ephesians 6:23; 2 Thessalonians 3:16 and 1 Peter 5:14. The reciprocal greeting with which the letter ends is from and to *the friends*. This designation of Christians is unique in the New Testament letters. Their relation to each other is normally described in terms of 'brotherhood', not 'friendship'. Nevertheless Jesus called the Twelve his friends (Jn. 15:13–14), and Paul's friends in the city of Sidon are mentioned in Acts 27:3. There does not seem to be any hint here that *friends* are less intimately associated with each other than 'brothers' (*cf.* vv. 3, 5, 10), for the instruction Gaius is given is to *greet the friends there by name*, which the RSV interprets as meaning 'every one of them', and NEB as 'one by one'. Christians should not lose their individual identity and importance in the group. God surely means each local fellowship to be sufficiently small and closely knit for the pastors and the members to know each other personally and be able to greet each other by name. The Good Shepherd calls his own sheep by name (Jn. 10:3); undershepherds and sheep should know each other by name also.